T5-AMY-277

Supreme Court Historical Society

JOURNAL OF
SUPREME COURT HISTORY

2012 VOL. 37 NO. 2

Article Submissions:

The *Journal of Supreme Court History* accepts manuscript submissions on a continual basis throughout the year. Authors are notified within six weeks whether the Board of Editors has accepted their article for publication. Please send submissions to Clare Cushman, Managing Editor, at chcush@aol.com.

GENERAL STATEMENT

The Society, a private non-profit organization, is dedicated to the collection and preservation of the history of the Supreme Court of the United States. Incorporated in the District of Columbia in 1974, it was founded by Chief Justice Warren E. Burger, who served as its first honorary chairman.

The Society accomplishes its mission by conducting educational programs, supporting historical research, publishing books, journals, and electronic materials, and by collecting antiques and artifacts related to the Court's history. These activities and others increase the public's awareness of the Court's contributions to our nation's rich constitutional heritage.

The Society maintains an ongoing educational outreach program designed to expand Americans' understanding of the Supreme Court, the Constitution and the judicial branch. The Society cosponsors Street Law Inc.'s summer institute, which trains secondary school teachers to educate their students about the Court and the Constitution. It also sponsors an annual lecture series at the Supreme Court as well as occasional public lectures around the country. The Society maintains its own educational website and cosponsors Landmarkcases.org, a website that provides curriculum support to teachers about important Supreme Court cases.

In terms of publications, the Society distributes a *Quarterly* newsletter to its members containing short historical pieces on the Court and articles describing the Society's programs and activities. It also publishes the **Journal of Supreme Court History**, a scholarly collection of articles and book reviews, which appears in March, July and November. The Society awards cash prizes to students and established scholars to promote scholarship.

From 1977 to 2006 the Society cosponsored the eight-volume **Documentary History of the Supreme Court of the United States 1789–1800** with a matching grant from the National Historical Publications and Records Commission. The project reconstructed an accurate record of the development of the federal judiciary in the formative decade between 1789 and 1800 because records from this period are often fragmentary, incomplete, or missing.

The Society maintains a publications program that has developed several general interest books: **The Supreme Court Justices: Illustrated Biographies 1789–1995** (1995); **Supreme Court Decisions and Women's Rights: Milestones to Equality** (2010), a guide to gender law cases; **We the Students: Supreme Court Cases for and About High School Students** (2000), a high school textbook written by Jamin B. Raskin; **Black White and *Brown*: The Landmark School Desegregation Case in Retrospect** (2004), a collection of essays to mark the 50th anniversary of the *Brown* case; and **Courtwatchers: Eyewitness Accounts in Supreme Court History** (2011).

The Society is also conducting an active acquisitions program, which has substantially contributed to the completion of the Court's permanent collection of busts and portraits, as well as period furnishings, private papers, and other artifacts and memorabilia relating to the Court's history. These materials are incorporated into exhibitions prepared by the Court Curator's Office for the benefit of the Court's one million annual visitors.

The Society has approximately 6,000 members whose financial support and volunteer participation in the Society's standing and ad hoc committees enables the organization to function. These committees report to an elected Board of Trustees and an Executive Committee, the latter of which is principally responsible for policy decisions and for supervising the Society's permanent staff.

Requests for additional information should be directed to the Society's headquarters at 224 East Capitol Street, N.E., Washington, D.C. 20003, telephone (202) 543-0400, or to the Society's website at www.supremecourthistory.org.

The Society has been determined eligible to receive tax deductible gifts under section 501 (c) (3) of the Internal Revenue Code.

JOURNAL OF

SUPREME COURT HISTORY

2012, vol. 37, no. 2

Introduction

Melvin I. Urofsky

For a long time, scholars as well as interested layfolk have been asking where they can find an index to the *Journal*. While some of the more recent issues have been indexed in various compendia, there has been no easily accessible means of looking up articles and authors that appeared earlier in our history. I must confess that I have often mumbled about the lack of an index when doing my own work. I "know" that someone wrote something about some person or issue, but after nearly twenty years as editor I have no idea when that particular article appeared.

So you can imagine my (scholarly) joy when Joel Fishman, a law librarian and expert indexer, approached us to discuss compiling an index, going back to when we were the Supreme Court Historical Society *Yearbook* in the 1970s. It is a well-done project, and I fully anticipate that people who for whatever reason are trying to find something in the back issues will greet it with the same pleasure I did. The index is also available on the Society's website at http://www. supremecourthistory.org/publications/, where it is fully searchable.

Mark R. Killenbeck of the University of Arkansas Law School provides us some insight on one of the most unusual exchanges of letters between a sitting Supreme Court Justice and the man who appointed him. Thomas Jefferson had never liked John Marshall's leading the Court away from the earlier tradition of seriatim opinions, in which each judge wrote separately on each case, and he fumed even more when the men he and James Madison put on the Court to counter Marshall's influence seemed to meekly fall into line. Although there had been serious discussion about the value of seriatim versus opinions of the Court, this may have been one of the most fascinating exchanges, since it involved a former President and a sitting Justice.

In his essay, John Orth of The University of North Carolina at Chapel Hill, notes that law students tend to fall asleep when the Eleventh Amendment is discussed in federal jurisdiction classes. Well, I do not know if I actually fell asleep (I had a pretty good teacher for that course), but I must admit that the discussion was nowhere near as much fun as John makes it. Moreover, this may be the first time that the

Journal has published a quasi–Science fiction piece with alternate universes.

On many occasions I have noted that the field of constitutional history is a rather close-knit group, and this is even truer of its subset, the history of the Supreme Court. I count both Mark Killenbeck and John Orth as friends as well as colleagues, and I have known Barbara Perry since she was a graduate assistant to another old friend, the great Henry Abrahams. Barbara is a former judicial fellow of the Court, and after a stint at Sweet Briar, has returned to the University of Virginia as a senior fellow at the Miller Center.

We all know that the Constitution provides that the President shall nominate people to the judiciary, and we also know that when vacancies occur, especially on the high court, the President gets a great deal of advice—unwanted as well as wanted—from a lot of people as to whose name should go to the Senate for confirmation. It is not well-known, however, that at least since the early nineteenth century members of the Court have also tendered their views to the Chief Executive on who should be their future colleagues, and how often these suggestions have borne fruit. While not an alternative universe, Barbara's essay will also cause us to rethink some older assumptions.

Finally, and as always, we welcome Grier Stephenson's "Judicial Bookshelf" to inform us about some of the new books that have recently appeared dealing with the Supreme Court and its members. As I have said before, we sometimes tend to take the "Bookshelf" for granted because it is always timely, always perceptive, and always well-written. The fact that we assume so much about it is a testament to just how good a job Grier does.

So, as always, a feast—and this time with some alternate universes thrown in. Enjoy!

No Bed of Roses: William Johnson, Thomas Jefferson and the Supreme Court, 1822–23

MARK R. KILLENBECK

On December 10, 1822, Justice William Johnson sent a remarkable letter to the individual who placed him on the Supreme Court, Thomas Jefferson. Over the course of twenty-one pages, Johnson laid bare his soul, discussing at length his trials and triumphs on the Court and numerous important, often deeply personal issues of the day. It is an extraordinary document, both for what it reveals about its author and for the part it played in an extended exchange between Johnson and Jefferson in a series of letters sent and received between October 27, 1822 and August 11, 1823.

William Johnson has been styled as the "First Dissenter."[1] The label fits the man. But Johnson was more than simply a habitual, albeit appealing, contrarian.[2] He served on the Court from May 7, 1804 until his death on August 4, 1834, a thirty-year period that included virtually all of the key years, and decisions, of the Marshall Court. Johnson was the first of the three individuals Jefferson placed on the Court.[3] He was also arguably the most impor-

tant of them, the one Jefferson hoped would begin a process of changing the Court, from a "subtle corps of sappers and miners constantly working under ground to undermine the foundations of our federated fabric,"[4] to one composed of "Republican[s] . . . of sufficient talents to be useful."[5]

That did not happen. Johnson would, by and large, align himself with John Marshall in a series of decisions that infuriated the man Marshall subsequently derided as "the great Lama of the mountains."[6] Indeed, as I have argued elsewhere,[7] perhaps the most striking thing about Johnson's tenure is not what he wrote, either for the Court or in dissent, but what he did not say as the Court issued a series of opinions Jefferson claimed made "the constitution . . . a mere thing of wax in the hands of the judiciary, which they may twist, and shape in any form they please."[8] Those opinions, and the manner in which they were delivered, played a significant role in the tenor and content of the exchanges between

Jefferson and Johnson, within which the Sage of Monticello waged one last battle for the heart and mind of a man he had never actually met when he elevated him to the nation's highest tribunal.

The December 10th letter has gained a certain degree of notoriety. Numerous authors have quoted Johnson's declaration that his time on the Court "has not been a 'Bed of Roses,'"[9] his claims about his role in changing the manner in which the Court issued its opinions,[10] and, in particular, his biting comments about his fellow Justices: that "Cushing was incompetent, Chase could not be got to think or write—Patterson was a slow man & willingly declined the trouble, & the other two judges [Marshall and Washington] you know are commonly estimated as one judge."[11] But the full text of the December 10th letter has never been printed, a startling omission given its content and importance.[12]

That oversight will presumably be rectified with the eventual publication of the volume in the Jefferson Papers Retirement Series dealing with the years 1822 and 1823.[13] In the interim, it seemed appropriate to provide both a transcript of the letter and a brief discussion of why it merits our attention. There are two principal reasons for this. First, it is important to place those portions of the December 10th letter that have been quoted in the wider contexts offered by its full text and the sequence of letters within which it appeared. Second, the full letter is well worth considering on its own merits, both for what it says about the events and controversies of the period and the lives and views of its author and recipient.

§

William Johnson, Jr. was educated at Princeton and read law under the tutelage of Charles Cotesworth Pinckney in his home city, Charleston, South Carolina.[14] Johnson was by all accounts an intelligent and able individual, "a man of considerable talents and law knowledge."[15] He was also "eccentric and sometimes harsh,"[16] prone to outbursts and with

views and a personality that amply justified John Adams's characterization of him as "a restless, turbulent, hot-headed politician caballing judge."[17] None of this was a matter of public record or knowledge when Justice Alfred Moore resigned in February 1804. That welcome development gave Jefferson the opportunity, as Clare Cushman has perceptively noted, "to shake up the Federalist-dominated Supreme Court by appointing a Democrat-Republic to rein in [John] Marshall."[18] This was a matter of some importance for Jefferson, who complained repeatedly and bitterly about Federalist judges who had "retreated into the judiciary as a stronghold, the tenure of which renders it difficult to dislodge them."[19]

Jefferson has been justifiably praised for the sentiments expressed in his First Inaugural Address, where he stated that "every difference of opinion is not a difference of principle. We have called by different names brethren of the same principle. We are all Republicans, we are all Federalists."[20] But it was quite clear that those conciliatory sentiments did not extend to the man who administered the presidential oath of office, John Marshall, or to the Court over which Marshall now presided. The criticisms began a scant ten days after Jefferson was sworn in, in a letter in which Jefferson expressed both his hope that "the line of party division which has been so strongly drawn" would soon be "obliterated" and his belief that it was unlikely that Federalist party "leaders . . . ever can come over."[21] And while much of the criticism was confined to private letters,[22] Jefferson did wage a very public war against John Adams's "midnight appointments," including that of William Marbury, a contest that provided the occasion for Marshall's first great opinion for the Court in *Marbury v. Madison*.[23] The obvious remedy was for Jefferson to place his own people on the Court, making Alfred Moore's resignation a welcome development.

Jefferson, with the assistance of his Secretary of the Treasury, Albert Gallatin, eventually settled on Johnson as his nominee.

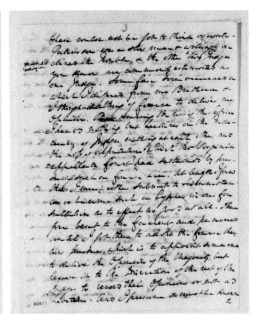

The two pages of the letter containing Johnson's famous words disparaging the Marshall Court Justices are pictured above. The transcriptions may be found at manuscript pages 8 and 9 of the letter at the end of this article.

Johnson seemed a perfect choice, a southerner who was described at the time as "a state judge, an excellent lawyer, prompt, eloquent, of irreproachable character, republican connections, and of good nerves in his political principles. about 35 years old. was speaker some years."[24] The message nominating him was sent to the Senate on March 22, 1804, which gave its "consent" two days later. It was only at that point—as was often the case at the time—that Johnson himself was brought into the process, via a letter from Secretary of State James Madison, who informed him of the President's decision and asked if he would accept a position to which he had already been confirmed.[25]

Jefferson fared better in this respect than John Adams had before him. Adams nominated John Jay on December 18, 1800 as his choice to replace Chief Justice Oliver Ellsworth, who had resigned.[26] Jay was quickly confirmed by the Senate and Adams sent him a letter informing him of that presumably salutary honor. But Jay declined a second engagement as Chief, informing Adams in no

uncertain terms that he had better things to do.[27] Johnson had no such qualms, writing to Madison and telling him that he should convey "my Acknowledgments to the President for this Mark of Attention and Confidence, & to communicate my willingness to accept the Appointment,"[28] asking only that he be given "until the 1st May next" to complete certain local duties and obligations.[29] There were apparently no objections, and Court records have Johnson taking his judicial oath on May 7, 1804.[30]

Johnson did have an impact on the Court, albeit not the one Jefferson envisioned. He wrote the occasional important opinion,[31] and, if his claims can be credited, it was Johnson who induced the Brethren to change their opinion practices from a custom where Marshall alone spoke for the Court to one where all of its members wrote opinions. However, Johnson did little, at least that we can discern, to change the course Marshall was setting. In particular, he was noticeably silent as the Marshall Court issued decision after decision that provoked Jefferson's wrath. Both *M'Culloch v.*

After joining the Court, Justice William Johnson (above) wrote important opinions and dissents and developed a strong voice on the Bench. But he disappointed the President who appointed him, Thomas Jefferson, who hoped he would persuade Chief Justice Marshall and the other Federalist Justices to change course.

Maryland[32] and *Cohens v. Virginia*,[33] for example, were unanimous and were roundly condemned by Jefferson and his states' rights allies as decisions that repudiated "the true principles of the revolution of 1800."[34] Indeed, when Johnson did write, either for the Court or in a separate opinion, he often expressed positions that were at odds with the Jefferson worldview. Notably, the day before *Cohens* was announced, Johnson wrote an opinion for a unanimous Court that arguably expressed an even more expansive view of the implied powers doctrine than the one articulated in *M'Culloch*, declaring: "But what is the fact? There is not in the whole of that admirable instrument, a grant of powers which does not draw after it others, not expressed, but vital to their exercise, not substantive and independent, but auxiliary and subordinate."[35]

This was not the sound Democrat-Republican Justice that Jefferson had hoped for. Johnson was, rather, an integral part of a Court that seemed hell-bent on fashioning a body of work and an approach to constitutional interpretation that violated virtually all of Jefferson's most treasured beliefs. But Johnson was also an unhappy man, dissatisfied with both his work and his salary, to the point where he actively pursued an appointment as Collector of the Port of Charleston, a post he could have had, but one that he ultimately did not accept.[36] Ironically, that process unfolded in the early months of 1819, at precisely the point the Court was considering and deciding *M'Culloch*. And it was presumably that decision Johnson had in mind when he explained his reasons for remaining on the Court:

> The interesting aspect also that the business of the Supreme Court has lately exhibited, its acknowledged importance and weight in the Union, and the responsibility which it has been called on to assume, satisfy me that I ought not to appear to steal away from the discharge of those duties or from my share of that responsibility, in order to fill a station of less general and determinate importance to the Union, and susceptible of being discharged, with perhaps more ability, by so many others.[37]

§

The protracted exchange within which the December 10th letter appeared began in the wake of Johnson's decision in the spring of 1822 to send Jefferson a copy of his two-volume **Sketches of the Life and Correspondence of Nathanael Greene**.[38] Greene, a native of Rhode Island, was an early volunteer in the American revolutionary cause who rose rapidly through the ranks, eventually becoming one of George Washington's most trusted advisors and military commanders. Greene was, by any possible measure, an important figure in the successful conduct of the Revolution. Johnson's biography—a massive work running to more than one thousand pages—was the first systematic account of Greene's

Dissatisfied with both his work and his salary, Johnson actively pursued an appointment as Collector of the Port of Charleston in the early months of 1819, at precisely the point the Court was considering and deciding on *M'Culloch*. A native of Charleston (pictured), Johnson had read law under Charles Cotesworth Pinckney.

life and was written with the support of his family and the benefit of access to Greene's papers. In that respect, it bore an eerie similarity to a project previously undertaken by John Marshall, the first edition of his five-volume biography of George Washington.[39] Both were written by sitting members of the Court who struggled to balance the demands of writing a substantial biography with their judicial responsibilities. Both were "official" lives of their subjects, undertaken with the support of their families. And both authors labored under self-imposed obligations to do justice to, in Johnson's case, "the character of my hero,"[40] and, in Marshall's, the man who "was indeed, 'first in war, first in peace, and first in the hearts of his fellow citizens.'"[41]

Both works were also popular and critical failures. Marshall, for example, declared after reviewing his first volume that he was "mortified beyond measure to find that it has been so carelessly written."[42] Critics agreed, with one observing that "whatever may be the pro-

Justice Johnson sent Jefferson his newly published two-volume biography of Revolutionary War hero Nathaniel Greene (above) in 1822, precipitating a fascinating exchange of letters with the man who had appointed him to the Court. Jefferson seized the opportunity to launch yet another attack on John Marshall, the decisions of the Marshall Court, and the manner in which that Court went about its business.

fessional talents of Chief-Justice Marshall, it is feared that, as a historian, he will add nothing to our literary reputation as a nation."[43] Johnson's **Life of Greene**, in turn, was attacked as a treatment infected by "party feeling, if not personal pique" and lambasted as a stylistic disaster, "below the dignity of the subject . . . tumid and involved, and abound[ing] in figures of speech which will hardly bear the test of criticism."[44]

The allegations regarding the role of "party feeling" were both accurate and telling in the light of what followed. Marshall, for example, used the **Life of Washington** as a vehicle for honoring individuals who "sincerely believed that the real danger which threatened the republic was to be looked for in the undue ascendency of the states."[45] These were, obviously, the Federalists, who were "in favour of enlarging the powers of the federal government, and of enabling it to protect the dignity and character of the nation abroad, and its interests at home."[46] Their opponents, Jefferson's Republicans, "marked out for themselves a more indulgent course."[47] They believed that "it was the great duty of patriotism to restrain the powers of the general government within the narrowest possible limits."[48] And they "resist[ed] every attempt to transfer powers from their own hands into those of congress, powers, which by others were deemed essential to the preservation of the union."[49] These views made it quite clear to Jefferson that the **Life of Washington** was a "party diatribe,"[50] a "five volume libel which represents us as struggling for office, and not at all to prevent our government from being administered into a monarchy."[51]

Johnson, in turn, averred that the task of compiling his **Life of Greene** brought him "to the most perfect conviction, that the distinguishing characteristics of the republican party are more popular and general than to be confined to the maintenance of State, as against United States' authority."[52] He maintained that it was "easy to prove, from a review of historical facts" that the Federalists, while in power, had tried "to exercise power not delegated by the constitution, wherever it afforded a latitude, to the adoption of measures calculated to give a fearful and imposing strength

to the arms of the general government."[53] He qualified these views to one extent, declaring that "State rights, or United States' rights are nothing, except as they contribute to the safety and happiness of the people."[54] But he also made it clear that, if put to the choice between a Federalist Scylla or Republican Charybdis, he would opt for the latter.

It was almost certainly that approach to the Greene biography, and the promise of more to come in the form of a history "of the origin of parties,"[55] that gave Jefferson hope. This was the William Johnson he thought he had elevated to the Court: a man of sound Republican sensibilities, dedicated to the vindication of the "principles of '98," as opposed to the Marshall Court fellow-traveler that his judicial record seemed to offer. And so Jefferson would try, one last time, to enlist Johnson in his cause.

§

We do not know precisely when Johnson's work arrived at Monticello. We do know that, in a letter dated October 27, 1822 Jefferson told Johnson that he had "deferred [his] thanks . . . until I could have time to read it" and could "express the gratification it has afforded me."[56] But the reasons for that praise were telling. Jefferson clearly believed that Greene was an important figure and that committing his story to print was a worthwhile objective.[57] But most of his comments about the **Life of Greene** had little to do with the intrinsic merits of Johnson's work or its nominal subject. Rather, they reflected Jefferson's judgments about the role this "fair history of the Southern war" and its author could play in a continuing quest to rescue the nation from "invidious libel[s] on the views of the Republican party."[58] Even then, these observations were comparatively terse, yielding quickly to the real point of Jefferson's letter: seizing the opportunity to launch yet another attack on John Marshall, the decisions of the Marshall Court, and the manner in which that Court went about its business.

The conflicts between Jefferson and Marshall were deep, long-standing, and both personal and professional. In 1795, for example, Jefferson complained to Madison about Marshall's "lax and lounging manners [which] have made him popular with the bulk of the people in Richmond, and a profound hypocrisy with many thinking men in our country."[59] Jefferson recognized that Marshall had a powerful intellect. But he believed that it, and Marshall's considerable powers of persuasion, were routinely employed to pursue illegitimate ends:

> When conversing with Marshall, I never admit anything. So sure are you to admit any position to be good, no matter how remote from the conclusion he seeks to establish, you are gone. So great is his sophistry, you must never give an affirmative answer, or you will be forced to grant his conclusion. Why, if he were to ask me whether it were daylight or not, I'd reply, "Sir, I do not know, I can't tell."[60]

The ultimate insult came when one of Jefferson's early thoughts about how to neutralize Marshall—"nothing better could be done that to make him a judge"[61]—eventually came true on February 4, 1801. As Chief Justice, Marshall led the Supreme Court out of the shadows and helped it stake its claim to what he believed was its rightful place as a co-equal branch of the federal government. Jefferson was less than pleased and the passage of time had done nothing to lessen the blow. And so, after what can only be characterized as a perfunctory nod to Johnson's **Life of Greene**, Jefferson used the opportunity at hand to attack the manner in which Marshall did business, presumably in the hope that, by forcing each member of the Court to speak, he could isolate and weaken Marshall.

"The subject of my uneasiness," he told Johnson on October 27th, "is the habitual mode of making up and delivering the opinions of the supreme court of the US."[62] Jefferson greatly preferred having each member of the Court express his views, "seriatim," an approach that "showed whether the judges were unanimous or divided, and gave accordingly more or less weight to the judgment as precedent."[63] This, he averred, had been the practice at the Court until "about that time the present C. J. came to the bench."[64] And it was one that made the only possible controls on the Court— "impeachment" and "individual reputation"— meaningful, since a system within which each Justice spoke in every case would force them to "reveal the reasons and authorities which governed their decisions," exposing "the lazy, the modest & the incompetent."[65]

Jefferson concluded the October letter with a general attack on Federalists who now styled themselves as Republicans, an "amalgamation [that] is of name only, not of principle."[66] These individuals had abandoned the lost Federalist cause of "monarchism," substituting in its stead "the point which they think next best, a consolidated government."[67] That was shorthand for both a despised political philosophy and an approach to interpreting the Constitution pursued by a judiciary intent on elevating federal authority over that of the states. Having thus set the stage, Jefferson waited for Johnson's reply.

§

Johnson responded on December 10th. He opened the letter with a discussion of the criticisms lodged against his **Life of Greene**. He had "for some days previous been writhing under the profligate attack made on me in the [*North American Review*] & had just got over the Vexations incident to publishing the notice I thought it incumbent on me to take of it in the City Gazette of the 15 – 20th ult."[68] That review—within which Johnson was accused of writing under the influence of "party feeling" and "personal pique," with his writing style lambasted as "below the dignity of the subject"[69]—while simply one of many, was the one that rankled the most. The "notice"

Johnson mentioned was in turn set out in a series of five letters to the editor of the Charleston *City Gazette and Commercial Daily Advertiser* that carried both his signature and the title "The Reviewer Reviewed."[70]

The allegations about the general tenor of Johnson's work were arguably just. Johnson himself made it quite clear in an Appendix at the end of the second volume that he believed his studies had revealed the "true character" of both the personalities and political parties that had shaped the early years of the nation. The reviewer's critiques of Johnson's writing style were also on point. Florid prose was the norm at the time, but Johnson's **Life of Greene** was an especially difficult read. I cannot, for example, identify where Johnson tells us about a revolutionary war cannon that "vomits death,"[71] not because he did not in fact employ that phrase, but rather because I have not been able to bring myself to read the **Life of Greene** with the care necessary to find it.

Johnson's public responses were detailed and combative. For example, he dealt with the comments on "the character of my style generally" in his fourth "review of the reviewer," declaring, for example, that the phrase "'Vomits death,' used but once ... in the ardour of description" was one "I will not give up for any colder description."[72] Fair enough: to each his own in matters of style and taste, especially since the December 10th letter did not dwell on those matters. Instead, Johnson concentrated on various substantive charges, including claims about the veracity of Richard Henry Lee's memoirs,[73] the relative merits of troops from South Carolina, and, in particular, his claim that Gouverneur Morris had "intimate connections in the Newberg Conspiracy."[74]

Once again, Johnson's public response to these and related criticisms was confrontational and, as such, in character. On the subject of Lee, he debated the issues and events in an exchange of letters in the *City Gazette*, eventually declaring, "I care not what future views may be presented on these subjects. I know that all I have related of the movements of the southern army and its detachments will defy scrutiny."[75] The claims made in the *North American Review*, in turn, were described as "really so extravagant a production, as to prove its own antidote."[76] The "class of readers" who might have read it have "not mind enough to examine the opinions promulgated by those tyrants of the literary world."[77] And the charges levied were "founded in the most palpable misconceptions; misconceptions so conspicuous as to glare in the face of his argument."[78]

Johnson's approach in the December 10th letter retained much of this spirit, characterizing what had been said about the **Life of Greene** as "impudent falsehoods" and "Outrages."[79] But he also made a conscious attempt to associate the charges made against him with Jefferson's own enemies. His comments about Gouverneur Morris, for example, "have unfortunately verified the Observation that 'Party hatred may doze but never dies,'" creating a situation within which "the whole Remains of the Federal party [are] in arms against me."[80] Johnson did not debate the specifics, an approach that stood in stark contrast to the one he took in his public responses. Instead, he used the various examples as a way to set the tone for major themes in the letter: his discussion of sectionalism, the conflicting positions of the two major political parties, and the extent to which these opposing factions claimed to have "had the best interests of the Country at heart."[81]

In each instance, what he said was consistent with his personal views, but it was also couched in terms designed to appeal to Jefferson. So, for example, Johnson contrasted the "Purity of our Intentions & Patriotism of our Efforts" with those of "the Monarchists and Consolidators who called themselves the Federal Party."[82] In a similar vein, he compared the patriotic motives of southern states, which, he claimed, "had asserted the Principles of the Revolution near a Century before they have been supposed to have been given Birth to in Boston,"[83] with "the characteristic Selfishness to the Eastward," states and individuals, that "would grasp in its Embrace Wealth, Fame, Dominion, every thing."[84] In particular, he denounced Massachusetts, speaking ominously of "the adoption of a plan as pregnant of Evil as either of the others—a Separation of the States, as the only Means of restoring [her] Predominance . . . with in the section that she might draw off with her."[85]

Johnson's discussion of these matters was a curious blend of insight, pandering, and self-pity. Jefferson, for example, expressed in his October 27th letter the hope that Johnson would complete a project Johnson mentioned in the **Life of Greene** on "the origin of parties."[86] Johnson was clearly pleased by the request. But, given the reaction to his **Life of Greene**, he asked "what Inducement, my dear Sir, can I have to proceed with that undertaking," citing the "hostility," "poor returns," and other insults that "all conspire to deter me from publishing."[87] He proclaimed his hope that such a work would instead come from Jefferson,[88] or, in the alternative, Madison,[89] even as he expressed the "fear [that] official Delicacy will deprive us of a vast deal of the most essential information."[90] Then, having made the case that others should write this work, he made it clear that, assuming proper "inducements" were forthcoming, he would in fact undertake the supposedly odious task: "I have advanced far in it, & my notes & extracts, by far the most laborious Part of the undertaking would enable me to finish it next Summer."[91]

§

These and related observations set the stage for the heart of the Johnson letter: his discussion of the Supreme Court and his initial response to Jefferson's appeal that he lead the charge toward a return to seriatim opinions. Johnson started that portion of the letter with the declaration that "I really am happy to be favoured with an Excuse for expressing myself freely and confidentially to you."[92] His time on the Supreme Bench "'has not been 'a Bed of Roses' . . . and often, very often, have I wished for someone whom I could consult on the Course proper to be pursued in discharging the Duties which devolved on me there. But unfortunately I have never had a single Individual on the Bench with whom I could confer with unlimited confidence."[93]

This claim—to the extent it was true—was a startling indictment of Johnson, rather than the Court on which he sat. One of the hallmarks of the Marshall Court, at John Marshall's insistence, was the extent to which the members of the Court lived and worked together during the few weeks each year that they were together in Washington. Story, for example, described a climate within which "We live harmoniously and familiarly. We moot questions as they are argued, with freedom, and derive no inconsiderable advantage from the pleasant and animated interchange of legal acumen."[94] His colleagues on the Court "are very interesting men" and "live in the most frank and unaffected intimacy . . . united as one with a mutual esteem which makes even the labors of Jurisprudence light."[95] The boardinghouse arrangement, in turn, helped foster a shared approach in reaching decisions, with the "conferences at our lodgings often com[ing] to a very quick, and, I trust, a very accurate opinion, in a few hours."[96]

Johnson, of course, was an irascible individual and likely uneasy company. That said, narratives about how the Court lived and worked in Washington, and, in particular, about John Marshall's character and outgoing nature, routinely described a situation within which Johnson should have been able to find individuals with whom he could have "conferred and confided." Of course, if Johnson is to be believed, his early years on the Court were dominated by the fall-out from his efforts to end precisely the practice Jefferson complained about so bitterly: the extent to which it was Marshall, and Marshall alone, who spoke for the Court. It seems clear, accordingly, that if Johnson did indeed lack friends on the Court it was almost certainly a matter of his own doing.

Johnson's accounts in the December 10th letter were accordingly a curious mixture of self-pity and self-promotion, mixed with startling revelations about his own ignorance of the manner in which the Court operated when he joined it. For example, he described the "surprise" he experienced when he arrived at the Court, only "to find our Chief Justice in the Supreme Court delivering all the Opinions in cases in which he sat, even in some instances when contrary to his own Judgment & vote."[97] This ran counter to his experiences as a state court judge, where he was "accustomed to delivering seriatim Opinions."[98] Then, in a passage that has been widely quoted, Johnson declared:

> But I remonstrated in vain; the Answer was, he is willing to take the Trouble, & it is a Mark of Respect to him. I soon however found out the real cause. Cushing was incompetent, Chase could not be got to think or write—Patterson was a slow man & willingly declined the trouble, & the other two judges [Marshall and Washington] you know are commonly estimated as one judge.[99]

There were certain grains of truth in these observations. Johnson took his seat on the Court at a point where Samuel Chase likely had little time to devote to his judicial duties, consumed, as he must have been, by his fight against efforts to impeach and convict him. William Cushing was old and in failing health, a reality that had played a role in his being passed over for the vacancy created when Chief Justice Ellsworth had resigned in late 1800. William Paterson, in turn, had been an effective voice on the Court during the 1790s. But he had been seriously injured in an accident while riding the circuit and at the time Johnson joined the Court he was in decline. Bushrod Washington and John Marshall did

Johnson claimed that he induced the Brethren to change their opinion practices, from a custom where Chief Justice Marshall (above) alone spoke for the Court to one where all of its members wrote opinions. But the Justices' workload was increasing dramatically, to the point where it was simply not possible for Marshall to be the sole spokesman.

share a number of common goals, but the allegation that Washington was in effect in Marshall's thrall was overstated, and careful examination of Washington's record reveals an infinitely more complex relationship between him and Marshall than the simplistic one proffered by Johnson.[100]

Johnson may, or may not, have fit comfortably within this group if he had so chosen. He did not help matters, however, by insisting on speaking separately. Once again, in his own words:

> Some case soon occurred in which I differed from my Brethren, & I thought it a thing of course to deliver my Opinion. But during the rest of the Session I heard nothing but lectures on the Indecency of Judges cutting at each other, and the loss of Reputation which the Virginia appellate court had sustained by pursuing such a course etc. At length I found that I

must either submit to circumstances or become such a cypher in our Consultations as to effect no good at all. I therefore bent to the current, and persevered until I got them to adopt the course they now pursue, which is to appoint someone to deliver the Opinion of the Majority, but leave it to the Discretion of the rest of the Judges to record their Opinions or not ad libitum.[101]

The case to which Johnson is referring may have been *Huidekoper's Lessee v. Douglass*,[102] in which Johnson filed his first concurring opinion.[103] Or, more likely, it is *Ex parte Bollman and Ex parte Swartwout*,[104] in which Johnson delivered his first dissent, stating that "[i]n this case, I have the misfortune to dissent from the majority of my brethren,"[105] and ending with the observation that he had experienced "the painful sensation resulting from the necessity of dissenting from the majority of the court. . . ."[106]

Those "painful sensations" did not, however, render Johnson a "cypher" or someone who in any meaningful way "bent to the current." During the next three Terms, for example, he wrote six concurring opinions and six dissents. Nor, for that matter, is it at all clear that Johnson's account was accurate in one important respect: that he was responsible for the Court adopting a new practice. As I have documented elsewhere, the move away from seriatim opinions began even before Marshall arrived on the Court.[107] And the subsequent move away from Marshall being the sole author and voice of Court opinions was almost certainly the product of the reality that the Court's workload was increasing dramatically, to the point where it was simply not possible for Marshall to be the sole spokesman.[108] We do not and cannot know what exact role Johnson played in that process. It is clear, however, that it served his purposes to provide Jefferson with precisely this sort of "insider" account of how the Court went

about its business and of his influence in such matters.

Johnson did not, however, promise to undertake the next step, a full return to seriatim opinions. Instead, he did two things. First, he argued that change was, at least at that point, impossible: "I presume it must be known to you, that to enforce a different Rule now, would be attended with just the same Difficulties as existed when I first came on the Bench. If it would compel incompetent men to quit the Bench I would say enforce it; but I think that it would not, for others would write their opinions merely to command their Votes."[109] He then revealed "the real Evil that exists in the Constitution of that Court. We are too numerous."[110] This prompted Johnson to offer his theory about how the Court should be restructured, by reducing the number of Justices to four and, as a necessary corollary, eliminating the burden of having to ride the circuits.[111]

The proposal was a strange mixture of the illogical and the politically astute. There is, for example, no reason to believe that a four-member Court would necessarily mean that "intrigue" and "cabals" would have been eliminated. Indeed, by making it possible for the Court to be evenly split, Johnson's system provided more rather than fewer incentives to engage in precisely the behavior he complained of. At the same time, Johnson's suggestion that circuit duty be eliminated almost certainly would have had great appeal, at least on the Court, and his recommendation that the salary savings realized by reducing the number of Justices be reallocated had strong political cache.

Two final aspects of the December 10th letter were striking. The first may help explain Johnson's state of mind at the time: his discussion of the problems caused in South Carolina by the Vesey plot, which arose when Denmark Vesey, a slave who had purchased his freedom, was supposedly involved in planning a major slave rebellion. These events, which began in May 1822, eventually resulted in the execution of thirty-seven slaves and the permanent banishment from South Carolina of many more. They also caused a major panic in Charleston, a situation that Johnson's daughter described when she stated that "I would not stay in this city another day . . . my feelings have been so lacerated of late that I can hardly speak or act."[112]

The traditional view of the Vesey plot is that it "was the most elaborate insurrectionary project ever formed by American slaves, and came the nearest to a terrible success. In boldness of conception and thoroughness of organization there has been nothing to compare with it."[113] Recent scholarship strongly suggests that this overstates what happened:

> Unanswered questions about Vesey and his co-conspirators abound. But this much is clear. Vesey and the other condemned black men were victims of an insurrection conspiracy conjured into being in 1822 by the court, its cooperative black witnesses, and its numerous white supporters and kept alive ever since by historians eager to accept the court's judgments while rejecting its morality.[114]

Whatever the truth was, William Johnson was deeply affected by what happened and the revisionist take on what transpired strongly suggests that Johnson's characterization was correct. "This last Summer," he told Jefferson, "has furnished but too much cause for Pain and Anguish. I have lived to see what I really never believed it possible I should see—Courts held with closed Doors and Men dying by the Scores who have never seen the Faces nor heard the Voices of their Accusers."[115] The approach taken by the court trying the accused was, he declared, both "unprecedented & I say, illegal," a judgment shared by South Carolina's governor at the time, Thomas Bennett, Jr., whose message to that effect Johnson feared would not see the light of day.[116]

Johnson took a public stand against the process as it unfolded.[117] He submitted an anonymous letter to the *Charleston Courier*, titled "Melancholy Effect of Popular Excitement,"[118] using the device of recalling a prior slave insurrection as a means of doing exactly what the local court subsequently accused him of: "produc[ing], not only a distrust of our proceedings, but contain[ing] an insinuation that, under the influence of popular excitement, we were capable of committing perjury and murder."[119] The fact that Johnson was the author was widely known and he was bitterly denounced. And his lament to Jefferson to the effect that "if such be the law of this Country, this shall not long be my Country,"[120] proved prophetic, at least in terms of his relationship with South Carolina. For the Vesey episode would become the first in a sequence of quarrels with the citizens of that state that eventually impelled Johnson to "absent himself from the State."[121]

A second notable observation in the latter parts of the letter was his discussion of the current state of political affairs. Johnson, like Jefferson, was concerned about the forthcoming election, seeing no "characters so commanding as to have directed our choice of President for many years to come."[122] James Monroe, the last of the Virginia dynasty, would soon leave office and "Calumnies . . . are already finding their Way into the Papers against some of the Candidates."[123] The Federalists, who had largely receded into the background, were looking "anxiously" to the election "as the occasion that is to bring them again into Notice—perhaps into Power."[124] Various Republicans, in turn, had become "qualified Federalists," posing the risk of "Amalgamation" pursued by "pure Men of both Parties, who were never in Principle, very far remove from each other. Hence, too much leaning to the Bane of our civil Tranquility—the assertion of implied powers."[125]

The idea that the Constitution tolerates implied powers was, of course, anathema to Jefferson, at least in theory. It was a doctrine Jefferson argued against in the very first years of the Republic as he fought the

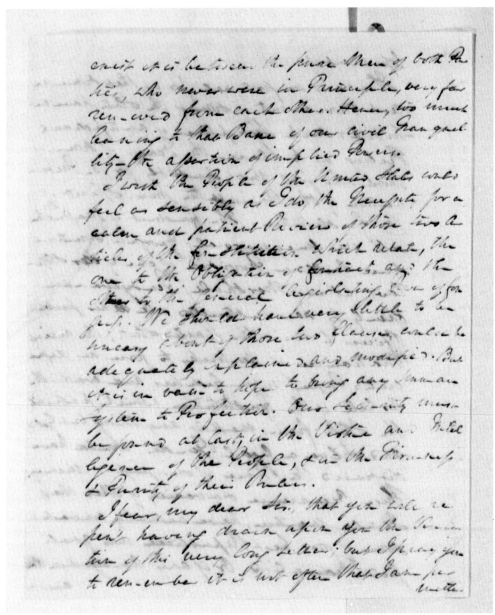

Johnson criticized the notion of implied powers to Jefferson, calling them the "Bane of our civil Tranquility" (see third line of letter reprinted above). But that characterization rang hollow because Johnson had, after all, sat by silently when *M'Culloch* was decided, as he also had during his second year on the Court, when implied powers were first embraced by John Marshall in *United States v. Fisher*. In the next paragraph, Johnson characterized the Contracts Clause and "the general legislating Power of Congress" (almost certainly the Necessary and Proper Clause) as worthy of attention. The transcription may be found at manuscript page 18.

creation of Hamilton's First Bank of the United States.[126] And it was one that Jefferson and his allies complained about at length in the wake of Marshall's opinion for the Court in *M'Culloch*.[127] Johnson seemingly had much to gain in Jefferson's eyes by describing implied powers as the "Bane of our civil Tranquility." But that characterization rang hollow for any number of reasons. Johnson had, after all, sat by silently when *M'Culloch* was decided, as he also had during his second year on the Court, when implied powers were first embraced by John Marshall in *United States v. Fisher*.[128] Five years later, Johnson's first major opinion for the Court, *United States v. Hudson and Goodwin*,[129] included as part of its reasoning the idea that all federal courts must, of necessity, possess and exercise certain implied powers.[130] And, as I have already noted, in *Anderson v. Dunn*,[131] handed down just a year and a half prior to the December 10th letter, Johnson actually expanded the doctrine beyond its arguably mild articulation in *M'Culloch*.

This was entirely understandable, given views Johnson had expressed as a state judge before he joined the Court. In an opinion written in 1801 Johnson had in effect embraced implied powers even before Marshall, declaring that "[t]he national government may pass such laws as may be proper and necessary to avoid all the mischiefs arising from the counterfeiting, and passing, as true, the forged bills of credit of the Bank of the nation."[132] He also recognized what would become the second part of the *M'Culloch* holding, that the realities posed by the exercise of implied powers of necessity limited the authority of the states, observing that "[s]tate governments may not also pass such laws, as they shall deem necessary, to the welfare of their internal concerns, in relation to the same subject."[133] This was, in effect, precisely the sort of judicial smoking gun that would have removed Johnson from consideration in an era, such as the present, where so-called "litmus tests" have become the norm in the confirmation process.

But, as we have seen, Johnson's actual views on important constitutional issues were not grist for the mill when he was nominated. Instead, Gallatin and Jefferson relied on generalized assurances that Johnson was in fact someone with appropriate "republican connections" and "good nerves in his political principles."[134] Those precepts already

included an embrace of implied powers. And they presumably approached judicial review in ways that deferred to Congress when questions arose about the propriety of a given piece of legislation. In *M'Culloch*, for example, Johnson joined an opinion that stated in no uncertain terms that:

> [W]e think the sound construction of the constitution must allow to the national legislature that discretion, with respect to the means by which the powers it confers are to be carried into execution, which will enable that body to perform the high duties assigned to it, in the manner most beneficial to the people.[135]

That power was not unlimited. Congress could not "pass laws for the accomplishment of objects, not entrusted to the government."[136] But judgments about the "degree of ... necessity" were for Congress, not the Court,[137] a holding that prompted Madison to complain about a "broad & pliant rule of construction" that "was anticipated by few if any friends of the Constitution."[138] It was, nevertheless, the rule Johnson favored, grounded in something he espoused in the December 10th letter, a "calm and patient review" of a central constitutional provision, "relat[ing] to ... the general legislating Power of Congress,"[139] the Necessary and Proper Clause. Once again, the sentiments are diametrically opposed to those that had been espoused by Jefferson, who rejected any "tortured" approach to that provision that equated "convenience" with "necessity" and, in doing so, risked "swallow[ing] up all the delegated powers, and reduc[ing] the whole to one power."[140]

What are we to make of Johnson's seeming about-face in the December 10th letter? It is tempting to charge Johnson with hypocrisy, with pandering to one of Jefferson's prejudices in an attempt to curry favor. Or, quite possibly, to see him as someone tweaking the tail of an individual who, as President, had in fact exhibited few discernible qualms about exercising, or at least tolerating, implied powers when they served his purposes.[141] There was, for example, delicious irony in Johnson's repeated references to the Louisiana Purchase in the December 10th letter, which he characterized as a crucial counter to both the "monarchists" and the "separatist" impulses in the New England states."[142] But references to the purchase may also have served as a gentle reminder that Jefferson himself had consciously stepped outside the parameters of his express powers in effecting that transaction.[143]

Ultimately, it seems likely that Johnson's motives were indeed mixed. The December 10th letter was clearly written by a Republican who still opposed many Federalist impulses and a southerner who was proud of his state and his heritage. But it was also, as we shall see, the product of an individual who, while willing to criticize certain aspects of the Court on which he sat, was both unwilling to quit it and proud of the part he had played in fashioning the doctrines it had promulgated.

§

Five letters followed. In the first, dated March 4, 1823, Jefferson paid token acknowledgment to Johnson's travails with his **Life of Greene**, stating that he (and by necessary implication, any reasonable man) did not read the *North American Review*.[144] He then tried to discredit the attacks on Johnson's work, given that "a reviewer can never let a work pass uncensored. He must always make himself wiser than his author."[145] Jefferson then moved on to what were, for him, the real issues and sharpened his attack in ways that were clearly designed to offer Johnson the "inducements" he craved. There was, he stressed, a desperate need for accurate, which is to say, Republican accounts of the founding period and the individuals who fashioned the Constitution and gave it initial life. Johnson's proposed "history of parties" was needed, Jefferson declared, to counter both Marshall's "five volume libel" and the risk posed by the individuals reportedly preparing editions of the life and papers of Alexander Hamilton and John Adams.[146]

Jefferson then reverted to the Court and again urged Johnson to serve as a counterweight to Marshall:

> I cannot lay down my pen without recurring to one of the subjects of my former letter, for in truth there is no danger I apprehend so much as the consolidation of our government by the noiseless, and therefore unalarming, instrumentality of the supreme court. This is the form in which federalism now arrays itself, and consolidation is the present principle of distinction between republicans and the pseudo-republicans but real federalists.[147]

The cure for this was, once again, seriatim opinions, which would prevent Marshall from "cooking up opinions in conclave."[148] The goal was an open decision-making process, within which each member of the Court would speak in every case and, in so doing, be exposed to considered public scrutiny:

> Let him prove by his reasoning that he has read the papers, that he has considered the case, that in the application of the law to it, he uses his own judgment independently and unbiased by party views and personal favor or disfavor. Throw himself in every case on God and his country; both will excuse him for error and value him for honesty.[149]

Johnson replied on April 11, 1823.[150] He agreed that Marshall's **Life of Washington** had received inappropriate attention, renewed his promise to pursue his project on the history of parties, and generally spoke in ways that reinforced the impression that he would indeed become a reliable Republican voice who would "rescue us from the Odium [of] our Federal Opponents."[151] He then declared, in what must have been music to

Jefferson's ears, that "[o]n the Subject of seriatim Opinions in the Supreme Court I have thought much, and have come to the Resolution to adopt your Suggestion on all subjects of general Interest, particularly constitutional questions. On minor subjects it is of little public Importance."[152]

Johnson did not, however, accept Jefferson's implicit argument that the course the Court had charted to date—a journey in which he had been a willing participant—was a mistake: "I cannot I acknowledge but flatter myself that in the main the Country is satisfied with our Decisions."[153] There were, he admitted, "some things . . . from particular Judges which are exceptionable, and I exceedingly regret their publication."[154] But, Johnson insisted, "when the Decisions are examined upon their own Merits independently of the bad or defective Reasons of the Judge who delivers them, I do flatter myself that all in which I ever concurred will stand constitutional scrutiny."[155] And he invited Jefferson to enlighten him regarding which specific instances demonstrated that "the Supreme Court has . . . trespass'd upon their Neighbours Territory, or advanced beyond their own constitutional limits."[156]

Jefferson would have none of it. Responding on June 12, 1823, he did "rejoice in the example you set of seriatim opinions," by which "the sound practice of the primitive court [would] be again restored."[157] But he also said that he would "not undertake" Johnson's request that he specify where "the Supreme Court has advanced beyond its constitutional limits, and trespassed on those of the State authorities," declaring, "I am unable."[158] This reticence was likely a device to spare Johnson's feelings, since these were, after all, decisions in which Johnson had joined. But, having modestly declined to engage in that task Jefferson proceeded to do it anyway, mixing personal reminisces, pointed arguments, and a recommendation that Johnson find what he sought in the published views of various Jefferson allies.[159]

Jefferson offered a comprehensive catalogue of Federalist and Marshall Court sins. In particular, he lambasted the decisions of the Court, beginning with *Marbury* and ending with *Cohens*.[160] The attacks on the Court and its holdings were specific and, in Jefferson's estimation, telling. Careful examination of the Federalist positions—and by logical extension, the doctrines of the Marshall Court—"will betray the genuine monarchism of their principles."[161] Unlike the Federalists, Republicans believed "that wisdom and virtue were not hereditary."[162] And it was quite clear that the Federalist take on the Constitution, in particular Marshall Court doctrines that strengthened the federal hand at the expense of those of the states, were mistaken: "I answer by asking if a single State of the Union would have agreed to the Constitution, had it given all powers to the General Government?"[163]

This extended polemic largely ended the exchange. Jefferson did write Johnson one last time, on July 31, 1823, sending a brief note that fulfilled his promise to give Johnson copies of various published essays that "pulverize every word which had been delivered" by Marshall in *Cohens* and provided the "thoro' examination of the constitutional limits between the General and state jurisdictions which you have asked for."[164] Johnson's equally brief final note was sent on August 11, 1823.[165] By now, all discussions of the Court and its opinion practices were at an end. Johnson simply thanked Jefferson for the materials he sent, promising "early and candid Consideration, the "Result" of which "shall furnish the Subject of a future Communication."[166]

§

There is nothing in the available record indicating that Johnson fulfilled his pledge. I have been unable to find any further letters between the two, either in the Jefferson Papers or in any publication. But we do have the record Johnson created in the opinions he wrote during and after the 1822–23 dialogue. And the tenor and content of those likely explain why there were no further letters.

Johnson wrote almost eighty opinions from February Term 1823 through his death in 1834.[167] None of them were as a member of a Court speaking seriatim, at least in the manner Jefferson proposed. A substantial number of them—twenty-seven— were concurring or dissenting opinions, a reality that was at least nominally consistent with his promise to Jefferson to reclaim his voice and speak his mind. That said, the man that emerged was not the one Jefferson sought. And the content and tone of what he said likely explain why the exchange of views between the two men came to an end.

The first of these opinions may have been the most important. Indeed, it was issued in the first case decided by the Court after Johnson pledged to express his own opinions on constitutional questions, *Gibbons v. Ogden*.[168] Marshall wrote for the Court, articulating a broad definition of the term "commerce," albeit fashioning a holding that arguably gave comfort to state rights advocates when he stressed that "[t]he completely internal commerce of a State . . . may be considered as reserved for the State itself."[169] Johnson issued a separate concurring opinion. In it, he made a public nod toward his private pledge to Jefferson, stating that, "in questions of great importance and great delicacy, I feel my duty to the public best discharged, by an effort to maintain my opinions in my own way."[170] He stressed, however, that "[t]he judgment entered by the Court in this cause, has my entire approbation,"[171] even though he had "views of the subject materially different from those of my brethren."[172]

Marshall's opinion for the Court did not answer directly one important question: what was the exact nature and scope of the federal power to regulate commerce? Was it exclusive, an approach that would have infuriated Jefferson? Or was it concurrent, authorizing federal initiatives in a limited sphere and reserving the bulk of commercial policy and regulation

to the states? Marshall's opinion arguably suggested the latter, even as his reliance on the preemptive effect of the Federal Coasting Licensing Act left room for argument.

Johnson was unwilling to settle for half an answer, a determination influenced by both his core views and recent experiences. Just the previous year, sitting as a circuit judge in his home state, Johnson had been forced to confront the intertwined problems of race relations in the South and the nature and scope of federal power under the Constitution. In the wake of the Vesey controversy, South Carolina passed the Negro Seamen Act, which authorized the seizure of "free Negroes or persons of color" who came into South Carolina on ships docking in its harbors for the duration of the ship's time in the state.[173] Henry Elkison, a British subject, was arrested and jailed. He filed a petition for a writ of habeas corpus, which came before Johnson, acting in his capacity as Circuit Justice.

Johnson refused to free Elkison, recognizing that he had no jurisdiction. Elkison was confined in a state facility, by a state official, and the operative provisions of the Judiciary Act of 1789 only allowed Johnson to consider pleas from individuals "'in custody under or by color of the authority of the United States.'"[174] But, in an exercise of judicial power that bore more than a passing resemblance to Marshall's approach in *Marbury*, Johnson arguably "travells out of his case to proscribe what the law would be in a moot case not before the court."[175] Johnson declared that the operative section of the statute was "utterly incompatib[le] with the power delegated to congress to regulate commerce with foreign nations and our sister states."[176] That power, Johnson maintained, "is a paramount and exclusive right; and this conclusion we arrive at, whether we examine it with reference to the words of the constitution, or the nature of the grant."[177] Moreover, Johnson stressed, the arguments advanced in support of the measure posed risks too great to contemplate:

But to all of this the plea of necessity is urged; and of the existence of that necessity we are told the state alone is to judge. Where is this to land us? Is it not asserting the right of each state to throw off the federal government at its will and pleasure? If it can be done as to any particular article it may be done as to all; and, like the old confederation, the Union becomes a mere rope of sand.[178]

Elkison was decided on August 1, 1823, at the very end of the period during which Jefferson and Johnson were in touch. The opinion and its author were denounced, bitterly, in a series of essays that appeared in the Charleston newspapers.[179] Johnson, adopting a technique pioneered by Marshall in the wake of *M'Culloch*, responded in kind under the pseudonym Philonimus, warning that "if public opinion does not rally to put down such gross attacks, public decency is at an end, and bullies and duellists alone must 'judge the land.'"[180]

A scant six months later, Johnson returned to the issue of the federal commerce power in *Gibbons*. He parted company with Marshall in ways that must have infuriated Jefferson, issuing a concurring opinion that echoed the themes struck in *Elkison*. The states, Johnson stressed, had embraced "selfish principle[s]" during the period after the Revolution.[181] Their insistence on passing "iniquitous laws and impolite measures... was the immediate cause, that led to the forming of a convention."[182] The text that emerged "contain[ed]... positive restrictions imposed by the constitution upon State power."[183] One of those was the Commerce Clause, which, given Johnson's take on the history that informed its drafting and ratification, gave Congress "exclusive grants... of power over commerce."[184]

This embrace of a strong federal presence in national affairs and of the need for exclusive federal powers in certain areas was not in any way diminished by Johnson's dissent, seven-

Increasingly infirm, Jefferson (above) in **1825** continued to complain about "the rapid strides with which the federal branch of our government is advancing towards the usurpation of all the rights reserved to the States, and the consolidation in itself of all powers, foreign and domestic". He and Johnson were no longer corresponding, and Jefferson died the following year.

teen days later, in *Osborn v. President, Directors & Co. of the Bank of the United States*.[185] Johnson refused to accept what he characterized as the majority's conclusion "that the constitution sanctions the vesting of the right of action in this Bank... merely on the ground that a question might *possibly* be raised in it, involving the constitution, or constitutionality of a law, of the United States."[186] But he entertained absolutely no doubts about both the constitutionality of the Bank itself. In particular, he stressed the important role it played in solving problems posed by the irresponsible actions of the states, conduct that required a "specie-paying Bank, with an overwhelming capital, and the whole aid of the government deposits [which] presented the only resource to which the government could resort, to restore that power over the currency of the country, which the framers of the constitution evidently intended to give to Congress alone."[187]

We do not know how Jefferson reacted to either *Gibbons* or *Osborn*. The cases are not mentioned in his major biographies, or, at least that I have found, in his papers. Jefferson did continue to express his strong belief in the wake of *Gibbons*—albeit not in direct response to it—that the constitution divided "the whole field of government . . . into two departments, domestic and foreign" with "the former . . . reserved exclusively to the respective States within their limits."[188] This suggested that he would have been at least thankful for the restraint Marshall showed in *Gibbons*. It also tells us that he was in all likelihood less than pleased with Johnson, who, in fulfilling his pledge to exercise an independent voice, was doing so in ways that were at deep odds with the hopes Jefferson harbored when urging that course.

§

Jefferson did not go "quietly into the night" in the wake of his dialogue with Johnson. He was, by his own admission, nearing the end of his life and increasingly infirm. But he remained vigilant, continuing to complain about "the rapid strides with which the federal branch of our government is advancing towards the usurpation of all the rights reserved to the States, and the consolidation in itself of all powers, foreign and domestic."[189] And, almost certainly with Marshall in mind, he told Madison that "in the selection of our Law Professor" for the nascent University of Virginia "we must be rigorously attentive to his political principles."[190] William Johnson, in turn, continued to fulfill his role as a judicial gadfly, far outstripping his colleagues in the number of concurring and dissenting opinions filed in the period from 1824 through his death in 1834. And he continued to be a vigilant and public critic of constitutional transgressions, taking a defiant public stance against his native state's embrace of nullification during the last years of his life.[191]

Jefferson and Johnson did not confide in one another again. Active exchanges ceased, cut off by a combination of Johnson's judicial apostasies and Jefferson's death on July 4, 1826. The letters exchanged in 1822 and 1823 remain, accordingly, an anomaly, albeit an important one, given the significance of the issues they debated, the perspectives they expressed, and the insights they offer about the individuals who wrote them.

The Letters

The exchanges between Jefferson and Johnson in 1822–23 included eight letters, all of which may be found in the Jefferson Papers at the Library of Congress: four from Johnson to Jefferson, and four from Jefferson to Johnson. Three of these have never appeared in print, including Johnson's December 10, 1822 letter to Jefferson, which is reprinted here. The other two are brief notes: from Johnson to Jefferson, dated June 18, 1822, offering an advance introduction of an individual who proposed to visit Jefferson at Monticello; and from Jefferson to Johnson, dated July 31, 1823, within which Jefferson follows up on his promise to send Johnson copies of various essays that advance the strict Republican position on issues of mutual interest.

The December 10, 1822 letter is twenty-one pages long, written on both sides of ten sheets of paper and one side of an eleventh. The original is in the Jefferson Papers at the Library of Congress, Series 1, Box 163 (September 27, 1822 – May 26, 1823). It can be viewed online at the Jefferson Papers website:

http://memory.loc.gov/cgi-bin/query/ P?mtj:6:./temp/~ammem_wehB::

The following transcript is a "best effort." It owes a great deal to the support and assistance I received from the staff of the Manuscript Division of the Library of Congress, who were unfailingly helpful and courteous during my many visits.

The letter itself is in superb physical condition, a tribute to the quality of the paper used by individuals of Jefferson and Johnson's station. Johnson's handwriting, however, leaves much to be desired, as do his spelling, capitalization, and related practices. I am confident of the general accuracy of the transcript, but less so about the absolute fidelity with which I have deciphered the occasional word. The transcript follows Johnson's practices for spelling, capitalization, and paragraph breaks, with him sometimes indenting the first word and sometimes not. It does not preserve his line-by-line format, opting instead to simply reproduce what Johnson wrote, ignoring only his habit of splitting words into pieces at the end of a line, sometimes using hyphens, and sometime not. It also eliminates Johnson's use of a convention of his time, the placement of a "tip in" at the bottom of most (but not all) pages in the form of a word, syllable, or letters that appear at the top of the next page. Page breaks, themselves, are indicated by numbers in brackets.

[1]

Charleston Decemb 10 th 1822

My dear Sir

Few occurrences could have afforded me more Pleasure than the Receipt of your kind and friendly Letter. I had for some days previous been writhing under the profligate attack made on me in the N∧o American Review, & had just got over the Vexations incident to publishing the notice I thought it incumbent on me to take of it in the City Gazette of the 15 – 20 th ult.

Since that time I have been constantly engaged in Court or in the Studies incident to it, or I should have made an earlier acknowledgment of the Favour I feel conferred upon me, both by the kind Sentiments expressed in your Letter and the Confidence which I feel reposed in me by its Contents. Nor are there wanting other grounds of self-gratulation. I was really apprehensive that Virginia would espouse the cause of Col∧ Lee, and that I should receive from

[2]

my Friends in that quarter a less favourable decision than you have conferred upon me. Nor was I without a Fear that the impudent false-

hood of the No. American Review, in charging me with drawing Comparisons between the troops of Carolina and Virginia – unfavourable to the latter, would be suffered to pass upon the Credit of the Writer. Nothing would have been farther from my Intentions, & I trust there is not a Passage in the Book that can be tortured to such a meaning. But there was still another and a greater ground of Consolation. By convicting Gouveneaur Morris of monarchical Opinions & intimate connections in the Newberg Conspiracy, I have unfortunately verified the Observation "that Party hatred may doze but never dies." The whole Remains of the Federal party are in arms against me & joined to the numerous Connexions & more numerous admirers of Col Lee, they have caused me sensibly to feel, that I never stood in greater need of

[3]

the Countenance of my Friends. Yet I think I have conducted myself in such a Way, that those who identify themselves with Morris's Views or Lee's Fame must acknowledge that it is of their own invoking.

I agree with you most unequivocally in the Opinion that Genl Washington was the only man who could have conducted us through the War of the Revolution. There was a Momentum necessary, which he alone could have given to the mighty operation then going on. I trust I have faithfully persisted in the Acknowledgment of his Preeminence. And yet even here I have not been so fortunate as to avoid giving offence. But you know the characteristic Selfishness to the Eastward; it would grasp in its Embrace Wealth, Fame, Dominion, every thing. I am told I have even given Umbrage by asserting (& proving) that we to the South had asserted the Principles of the Revolution near a Century before they have been supposed to have been given Birth to in Boston. The North American Review of my Work, you will observe, speaks

[4]

of Greene as the most extraordinary Man of the Revolution.

You are pleased to express a Hope that I will give to the Public the Work on the History of Parties to which I alluded in the last Paragraph of my second Volume. But what Inducement, my dear Sir, can I have to proceed with that undertaking? My recent Experience of the Hostility which such a Work must certainly bring upon me, of the poor Return that national or party gratitude would make for the vexations which certainly arise from the making of Enemies; of the feeble Patronage which the American People as yet bestow upon American Productions; of the mortifications inseperable from the carelessness or Ignorance of Printers, and the Villainy & Extortion of Book sellers; all conspire to deter me from publishing, tho I should proceed to complete another Work. I have advanced far in it, & my notes & extracts, by far the most laborious Part of the undertaking would enable me to finish it the next Summer. But I

[5]

acknowledge, when I reflect on the impudent Outrage that I have received in [cf] No A. Review, & see it quietly tolerated by the American People, I am half inclined to think that they have pronounced me inadequate to such an undertaking. I was also informed by Judge Todd at the last Session, that Mr. Madison was engaged on some Work on that Period, which I have flattered myself was upon the same Subject, as someone intimately connected with it. If so, it would be presumptuous in any other to attempt it. He is now, except yourself, the only man living who could do Justice to it. I regret exceedingly that it has not occupied your Hours of Retirement hitherto; for believe me, we have been all looking up to you for the Vindication of the Purity of our Intentions & Patriotism of our Efforts. We were always under the Impression that you would not publish any Work on the subject;

[6]

but while we should piously deprecate the Event that put us in possession of it, you cannot be insensible that we have looked up to you as our common Father, and will believe me when

I assure you that we have hoped for a rich legacy of History from your Pen. I have been informed, and I hope still it may be true, that you have kept a Journal from the earliest Time of your public Career. If so, pray bequeath it to some Friend who will fearlessly do Justice to the Part you have acted, and vindicate us along with you, from the foul Interpretations which have already passed into History against us. It is indeed astonishing that we have so long been indifferent to our Vindications against the insidious Libel you allude to. But having falsified it in the Mind of the American Public, we have never turned our Thoughts to the Opinions of Posterity.

It was that libel, that first suggested to me

[7]

the attempt at a public Vindication and to my shame I acknowlede, that I had given the Volume that contains it so cursory a Reading, that it was not until I came to study it attentively with a view to my Work, that I felt the full force of its Insinuations.

Let who will undertake the Task of vindicating us, the Work must be incomplete without the Aid of yourself and Mr Madison; & even there I fear official Delicacy will deprive us of a vast deal of the most essential Information.

With regard to the Subject of the Supreme Court, I really am happy to be favoured with an Excuse for expressing myself freely and confidentially to you. Be assured that my Situation there has not been "a Bed of Roses". But it partakes in so many respects of the nature of a Cabinet that a Degree of Circumspection is indispensible in lifting the Curtain; and often, very often, have I wished for someone whom I could consult on the Course proper to be pursued in discharging the Duties which devolved upon me there. But unfortunately I have never had a

[8]

single Individual on the Bench with whom I could confer with unlimited confidence.

One thing however I resolved on at a very early Period – to let no private or party feeling run counter to the great Interests of the United States. If an executive, a legislative and judicial Department, are necessary to the well-being of the community, it behooves those who fill those Departments always to have an Eye to the Importance of giving a character to those Departments – of preserving that Respectibility without which they would cease to answer the ends proposed in their Institution. While I was on our State-bench I was accustomed to delivering seriatim Opinions in our appellate Court, and was not a little surprised to find our Chief Justice in the Supreme Court delivering all the Opinions in cases in which he sat, even in some instances when contrary to his own Judgment & vote. But I remonstrated in vain; the Answer was, he is willing to take the Trouble, & it is a Mark of Respect to him. I soon however found out the real cause. Cushing was incompetent,

[9]

Chase could not be got to think or write – Patterson was a slow man & willingly declined the trouble, & the other [x] two judges [Marshall and Washington] you know are commonly estimated as one judge. Some case soon occurred in which I differed from my Brethren, & I thought it a thing of course to deliver my Opinion. But during the rest of the Session I heard nothing but lectures on the Indecency of Judges cutting at each other, and the loss of Reputation which the Virginia appellate court had sustained by pursuing such a course etc. At length I found that I must either submit to circumstances or become such a cypher in our Consultations as to effect no good at all. I therefore bent to the current, and persevered until I got them to adopt the course they now pursue, which is to appoint someone to deliver the Opinion of the Majority, but leave it to the Discretion of the rest of the Judges to record their Opinions or not ad libitum. And I presume it must be known

[10]

to you, that to enforce a different Rule now, would be attended with just the same Difficulties as existed when I first came on the Bench.

If it would compel incompetent men to quit the Bench I would say enforce it; but I think that it would not, for others would write their opinions merely to command their Votes.

And now Sir permit me to unfold to you the real Evil that exists in the Constitution of that Court. We are too numerous. Among seven men you will always find at least one Intriguer, and probably more than ∧ one ∧ who may be acted up on by Intrigue. There will be Cabals; and unfortunately they cannot be enforced. No appellate Court ought to consist of more than four & it is a theoretical Folly to have a greater number. I would alter the present System thus. Let the U.S. be thrown into a Southern, a Western, a Middle, and an Eastern District, & have a Judge ap

[11]

pointed to the Se. Court from each – Give their Circuit Jurisdiction to the District Court, with a direct appeal to the Se. Court – Make us hold two Sessions pr. An. & confine us to the Duties of the Se. Court. Let the Salaries of the three Judges who would be suffered to die or retire, be divided among the District Judges or even a little more, & I think you would have a System cheap, adapted to our growth, & safe. Then the Seriatim opinions might be required with safety. Whoever may be our next President, he may confer a lasting Benefit on the Community by recommending such a System.

But there is a strange habit now growing up – on Congress, of wasting their Time in set speeches & neglecting the great Interests of the Country.

For any of us to recommend the Change, would be to expose ourselves to the Imputation of a Design to curtail our Labours. To me the Consequences would be much the Reverse. My circuit duty is nothing in comparison with a second session at Washington.

[12]

There is no Subject on which I feel myself more at a loss, than that of the present State of Parties. Here we are all in Confusion. The Victory is gained and the Troops are scattered over the Field stripping the Slain. For the spoken opinion there is a portentous Contest impending among ourselves. This is a Crisis in the affairs of the United States. I was in hope that the late War w∧d have elicited characters so commanding as to have directed our choice of a President for many years to come. But it has not done so, & we are left to a Choice among Men who boast of neither Fears nor Triumphs. Men who with all their Merits are not sufficiently removed beyond the Pretentions of those who elect them. I look forward with trembling anticipation, to the Time when a Multitude of competitors shall start up for the high office. It is disgusting to read the Calumnies which are already finding their Way into the Papers against some of the Candidates. But what are these to the Broils and Intrigues

[13]

and Compromises to which these Struggles seem to be drawing?

When the Population of a free State has been once divided into two Parties by an acknowledged line of Demarkation the annihilation of one Party seems necessarily to imply the extinction of the other. Yet it is impossible for things long to continue in that State. New Parties must arise & indeed ought to be desired. The office of good Men is to temper their zeal and direct it to useful Purposes. Along with the Monarchists and Consolidators who called themselves the Federal Party there were always a great many good men who seriously had the best interests of the Country at heart, & who would never have gone into the excesses to which their leaders may have been disposed to carry them. These Men abandoned their Party in Disgust during the late War, & many others did the same from a Desire to claim a

[14]

Participation in the Credit which many Incidents and Consequences of the War gave to the Party that had declared it.

Their leaders then found themselves so decidedly in the Minority, that they appear to have abandoned the Struggle in Despair, & manifested a great Desire to make themselves agreeable to their former Opponents. But, altho' the Leaders on Principle have been cordially received, I agree with you that there has been no amalgamation; & tranquil as the mass of Federalism appears; it exists separately and will show itself on the First Occasion. The next Presidential Election is looked to anxiously as the occasion that is to bring them again into Notice – perhaps into Power. Should they once again be able to give a Tune to the Measures of Government, I cannot anticipate what Course they will pursue. The acquisition of Louisiana in my opinion put down among the thinking ones, all idea of ever establishing a gene

[15]

ral Monarchy; the extent of our Territory and the Scope given to the Propagation of that Class of Men who never can be yoked to the car of Despotism, ought to have satisfied them that such a Project was ridiculous. The same cause also, I am inclined to think, produced an abandonment of the Project of general Consolidation, and I fear caused the adoption of a plan as pregnant of Evil as either of the others – a Separation of the States, as the only Means of restoring the Predominance of Massachusetts with in the section that she might draw off with her.

Hence the unprincipled and ungrateful separation of her Views and Interests during the late War, – capped by the Hartford Convention. Here again Louisiana seems to me to have saved us; for its rich commerce and vast carrying Trade were not to be surrendered – If Great Britain had succeeded in possessing herself of that Country, perhaps it would not have been. The Mississippi manouver succeeded; a measure which besides throwing into the Hands of the white Population of the East the Tillage of our land, the Building of our Houses, and finally all the Wealth of our country, secured the Trade

[16]

of the Missisipi by associating the States North of the Ohio in the interests of the East. It was a cold hearted, selfish, ungenerous effort. Thank Heaven, it was successfully resisted and it is a happy omen that the good sense of the People, appears already to have overcome the impulse that was given to these Passions by a measure so insidiously masked under the best feelings of our nature.

From these considerations I am inclined to think that if the Monarchists and Consolidaters should, through our Desperation again get into Power, their Projects can only be pursued through the medium of a Separation of the States, & that they have already seen it & acted upon it. I feel it my Part to endeavor to pursuade every one, that whatever be the Result of the ensuing Contest, it is the Duty of every good Citizen, freely to resign himself to the public will constitutionally expressed. But I see a curious game going on around me, which I may one Day amaze you with a Deve

[17]

lopement of.

It is very unfortunate for us, that some recent movements of some of the States, have contributed such Symptoms of antifederal Feeling, as to alarm the Fears of some of those who feel most sensibly for the Preservation of the Union in the pure spirit of the Constitution. The conduct of Massachusetts was unequivocal; Georgia, sometime since levelled a provision of one of her stoplaws at our Marshall; Pennsylvania openly by law instructed all her public officers to resist the United States; the recent manouvre of Kentucky to force her depreciated paper upon Creditors, and evade the Article of the Constitution which prohibits the States from making any thing but Gold and Silver a legal Tender, would have disgraced the times of our paper money. These occurrences & a variety of others that I could mention, have actually converted some of our best Republicans into qualified Federalists. Or, if any Amalgamation does

[18]

exist it is between the pure Men of both Parties, who never were in Principle, very far removed from each other. Hence, too much leaning to

that Bane of our civil Tranquility – the assertion of implied Powers.

I wish the People of the United States could feel as sensibly as I do, the Necessity for a calm and patient review of those two Articles of the Constitution which relate, the one to the obligation of contracts, and the other to the general legislating Power of Congress. We should have very little to be uneasy about if those two Clauses could be adequately explained and modified. But it is in vain to hope to bring any human system to Perfection. Our Security may be found at last in the Virtue and Intelligence of the People, & in the Firmness & Purity of their Rulers.

I fear, my dear Sir, that you will repent having drawn upon you the Vexation of this very long letter; but I pray you to remember it is not often that I am per

[19]

mitted to loiter in such company. I have now passed my Half century, and begin to feel lonely among the Men of the present Day. And I am sorry to tell you particularly so in this Place. This last Summer has furnished but too much cause for Pain and Anguish. I have lived to see what I really never believed it possible I should see, – Courts held with closed Doors and Men dying by Scores who have never seen the Faces nor heard the Voices of their Accusers. I see that your Governor has noticed the alarum of Insurrection which prevailed in this Place some months since. But be assured it was nothing in comparison with what it was magnified to. But you know the best way in the World to make Men tractible is to frighten them to Death and to magnify Danger, is to magnify the Influence of those who arrest it. Incalculable are the Evils which have resulted from the exaggerated accounts circulated respecting that affair. Our Republic is reduced to nothing – Stran

[20]

gers are alarmed at coming near us; our Slaves rendered uneasy; the Confidence between us and our Domestics destroyed and all this because of a trifling

Cabal of a few ignorant pennyless unarmed uncombined Fanatics, and which certainly would have blown over without an Explosion had it never come to light. Our Governor has so represented it in his Message No. 2, but the Shame of some & the interests of others will I expect prevent its Publication.

When the Court of Magistrates & Freeholders who tried the Slaves implicated were pursuing that course of sitting in conclave & convicting men upon the secret ex parte Examination of Slaves without oath, whose names were not I believe revealed even to the owners ∧ of the accused∧, the Governor, whose feelings revolted at this unprecedented & I say, illegal mode of trial, consulted the Attorney General (the Gentleman lately elected Senator) on the legality of these Proceedings, and you will be astonished to hear

[21]

that he gave a direct Opinion in Favour of it. If such be the law of the Country, this shall not long be my Country. But I will first endeavour to correct the Evil.

And now my dear Sir, permit me to close this unmerciful letter, by rendering you my sincere Thanks, for the very friendly Sentiments with which you have honored me. And as there is no one existing whose good Opinion I value above yours, so no one can more sincerely subscribe himself.

Yours with every Sentiment of Veneration & Friendship

Will∧m∧ Johnson

ENDNOTES

[1] *See, e.g.*, Donald G. Morgan, **Justice William Johnson, The First Dissenter: The Career and Constitutional Philosophy of a Jeffersonian Judge** (1954) [Morgan, **Johnson**]; Donald G. Morgan, "The Origin of Supreme Court Dissent," 10 *Wm. & Mary Q.* 353 (3rd Series, 1953).

[2] Johnson's personality and accomplishments were perhaps best captured in these pages by Professor Van Burkleo when she stated that "[f]or those of us who gravitate toward rebels and upstarts, Supreme Court Justice William Johnson has uncommon appeal, if only because he was the first member of the federal Bench to kick up his heals in a sustained, effective, and deliberate way." Sandra F. VanBurkleo, "In Defense of 'Public Reason': Supreme Court Justice William Johnson," 32 *J. S. Ct. Hist.* 1, 1 (2007).

[3] The second and third were, respectively, Henry Brockholst Livingston, who sat on the Court from January 20, 1807 through March 18, 1823, and Thomas Todd, a member of the Court from May 4, 1807 through February 7, 1826. See Members of the Supreme Court of the United States, at http://www.supremecourt.gov/about/members_text.aspx.

[4] Letter from Thomas Jefferson to Thomas Ritchie (Dec. 25, 1820), in XII **The Works of Thomas Jefferson**, 175, 177 (Paul Leicester Ford ed., 1905) [Jefferson, **Works**].

[5] Letter from Albert Gallatin to Thomas Jefferson (Feb. 15, 1804), in 1 **The Writings of Albert Gallatin** 177, 178 (Henry Adams ed., 1879).

[6] Letter from John Marshall to Joseph Story (Sept. 18, 1821), in IX **The Papers of John Marshall**, at 183, 183 (Charles F. Hobson ed., 1998) [Marshall, **Papers**].

[7] Mark R. Killenbeck, "William Johnson, The Dog That Did Not Bark?", 62 *Vand. L. Rev.* 407 (2009) [Killenbeck, "Dog"].

[8] Letter from Thomas Jefferson to Spenser Roane (Sept. 16, 1819), in XII Jefferson, **Works**, at 135, 137. The focus here was on *M'Culloch v. Maryland*, 17 U.S. (4 Wheat.) 316 (1819), which, like so many of the great "nationalist" Marshall opinions, was unanimous.

[9] *See, e.g.*, Morgan, **Johnson**, at 181.

[10] *See, e.g.*, G. Edward White, **The Marshall Court and Cultural Change, 1815–35**, at 186 n. 126 (1988) [White, **Marshall Court**].

[11] *See* Clare Cushman, **Courtwatchers: Eyewitness Accounts in Supreme Court History** 26 (2011) [Cushman, **Courtwatchers**].

[12] Five of the letters in the sequence have appeared in print. Each is quoted, and the citations provided, in this article. The second letter that has not been published, from Jefferson to Johnson on July 31, 1823, is a one-page note whose brevity and content make the failure to print it understandable.

[13] That project is moving faster than parallel efforts to publish definitive editions of Jefferson's papers through his years as President, an undertaking that began in 1950 and now has thirty-six volumes in print that take us through March 3, 1802. Volume 8 in the Retirement Series, which spans the period from October 1, 1814 through August 31, 1815 was published in late January, 2012, which at the current rate of approximately one volume per year means it will be some time before the editors get the December 10, 1822 letter in print.

[14] This brief summary of Johnson's upbringing and early career is taken from various sources, in particular Morgan, **Johnson**, at 3–22. For a suitably brief account, see Killenbeck, "Dog," at 409–10.

[15]6 **Memoirs of John Quincy Adams, Comprising Portions of His Diary from 1795 to 1848** (Mar. 27, 1820), at 43 (Charles Francis Adams ed., 1875).

[16]*Id.*

[17]*Id.*

[18]Cushman, **Courtwatchers**, at 26.

[19]Letter from Thomas Jefferson to Joel Barlow (Mar. 14, 1801), in X **The Writings of Thomas Jefferson** 222, 223 (Andrew A. Lipscomb & Albert Ellery Bergh eds., 1903) [Jefferson, **Writings**].

[20]Thomas Jefferson, First Inaugural Address (Mar. 4, 1801), in 1 **A Compilation of the Messages and Papers of the Presidents** 309, 310 (James D. Richardson ed., 1897). Marshall actually spoke favorably of the "inauguration speech," describing it as "in the general well judged & conciliatory. It is in direct terms giving the lie to the violent party declamation which has elected him." Letter from John Marshall to Charles Cotesworth Pinckney (Mar. 4, 1801), in VI Marshall, **Papers**, at 89, 89.

[21]Letter from Jefferson to Barlow (Mar. 14, 1801), X Jefferson, **Writings**, at 223.

[22]*See, e.g.*, Letter from Thomas Jefferson to John Dickinson (Dec. 19, 1801), in *id.* at 301, 302 ("the remains of federalism are to be preserved . . . and from that battery all the works of republicanism are to be beaten down and erased. By a fraudulent use of the Constitution, which has made the judges irremovable, they have multiplied useless judges merely to strengthen their phalanx.").

[23]5 U.S. (1 Cranch) 137 (1803). Complaints about Marbury are a recurring theme in Jefferson's correspondence. *See, e.g.*, Letter from Thomas Jefferson to George Hay (June 2, 1807), in 11 Jefferson **Writings**, at 213, 213, & 215 ("in the outset, [having] disclaimed all cognizance of the case" Marshall "then went on to say what would have been their opinion," a "gratuitous" exercise that constituted "an extrajudicial opinion and, as such, of no authority"). For an argument that in the short term Marshall won the battle, but lost the war, see Bruce Ackerman, **The Failure of the Founding Fathers: Jefferson, Marshall, and the Rise of Presidential Democracy** (2005).

[24]Memorandum from Thomas Sumter and Wade Hampton, "Characters of the lawyers of S.C. (Feb. 17, 1804)," in Gaillard Hunt, "Office-Seeking during Jefferson's Administration," 3 *Am. Hist. Rev.* 270, 282 (1898) [Sumter & Hampton, "Characters"].

[25]7 **The Papers of James Madison: Secretary of State Series** 79 n. 1 (David B. Mattern et al., eds., 2005) (referencing Madison's letter of Mar. 31, 1804 and noting that it "has not been found") [Madison, **Sec'y State**].

[26]*See* "John Jay: Appointment as Chief Justice in 1800," in 1 **The Documentary History of the Supreme Court of the United States, 1789–1800, Part 1: Appointments and Proceedings**, at 144–47 (Maeva Marcus et al., eds., 1985).

[27]Letter from John Jay to John Adams (Jan. 2, 1801), *id.* at 146–47. This set in motion the chain of events that led to Marshall's appointment, a protracted process within which Adams turned to Marshall only after other attempts to fill the seat came to naught. For the full, and not often told, story, see Kathryn Turner, "The Appointment of Chief Justice Marshall," 17 *Wm. & Mary Q.* 143 (1960).

[28]Letter from William Johnson to James Madison (Apr. 18, 1804), in 7 Madison, **Sec'y State**, at 78.

[29]*Id.*

[30]*See* Members of the Supreme Court of the United States, at http://www.supremecourt.gov/about/members_text.aspx.

[31]*See, e.g., United States v. Hudson and Goodwin*, 11 U.S. (7 Cranch) 32 (1810) (holding that federal courts cannot exercise a common law jurisdiction in criminal cases). The best brief treatment of Johnson's views is Herbert A. Johnson, "The Constitutional Thought of William Johnson," 89 *S.C. Hist. Mag.* 132 (1988).

[32]17 U.S. (4 Wheat.) 316 (1819).

[33]19 U.S. (6 Wheat.) 264 (1821).

[34]Letter from Thomas Jefferson to Spenser Roane (Sept. 6, 1819), XII Jefferson, **Works**, at 136.

[35]*Anderson v. Dunn*, 19 U.S. (6 Wheat.) 204, 225–26 (1821) (holding that the House of Representatives had the power to "punish for contempts" even though "there is no power given by the constitution to either House" to do so).

[36]*See* Morgan, **Johnson**, at 107–09. Johnson's name was actually submitted for the post before he changed his mind. Another South Carolinian, Langdon Cheves, was in line for the vacancy on the Court that would have been created if Johnson had stepped down. Cheves instead became president of the Second Bank of the United States. *See* Archie Vernon Huff, Jr., **Langdon Cheves of South Carolina** 104–06 (1977).

[37]Letter from William Johnson to William H. Crawford (Mar. 31, 1819), *quoted in* Morgan, **Johnson**, at 109.

[38]William Johnson, **Sketches of the Life and Correspondence of Nathanael Green, Major General of the Armies of the United States, In the War of the Revolution: Compiled Chiefly from Original Materials** (1822) [Johnson, **Life of Greene**]. It was printed in Charleston, S.C., by A. E. Miller at Johnson's expense.

[39]John Marshall, **The Life of George Washington, Commander in Chief of the American Forces** (1804–07) [Marshall, **Life of Washington**]. This first edition was poorly done and roundly condemned. Much to Marshall's relief, a second edition, "revised and corrected by the author," was published in 1832. The text of that edition was reprinted in 1926 by "The Citizen's Guild of Washington's Boyhood Home, Fredericksburg, Va.," and this is the version I cite in this article.

[40]Johnson, I **Life of Greene**, at viii.

[41] Marshall, I **Life of Washington**, at xi. Marshall is here quoting, albeit slightly inaccurately, Henry Lee's eulogy ("First in war, first in peace, and first in the hearts of his countrymen.").

[42] Letter from John Marshall to Caleb Wayne (Aug. 10, 1804), in 6 Marshall, **Papers**, at 320, 321.

[43] *New York American Citizen*, Aug. 15, 1804, *quoted in* Editorial Note, "The Life of George Washington," in VI Marshall, **Papers**, at 219, 223. The reasons for writing the biography, the process, and its reception are discussed in Albert J. Beveridge, III **The Life of John Marshall** 222–73 (1919), and Editorial Note, *supra*, at 219–30. Marshall remained haunted by the first edition's defects until the opportunity to correct them presented itself. *See, e.g.*, Letter from John Marshall to Bushrod Washington (Dec. 27, 1821), in IX Marshall, **Papers**, at 195, 195 ("it is one of the most desirable objects I have in this life to publish a corrected edition of that work").

[44] "Review," 15 *No. Am. Rev.* 416, 429 (1822). This negative review was simply one of many, but was also, as the December 10th letter makes clear, the one that most incensed Johnson. Johnson's biographer concedes certain of the criticisms, but maintained that "this voluminous work . . . sparkles with the observations of an incisive intellect on a vast array of subjects." Morgan, **Johnson**, at 150.

[45] Marshall, IV **Life of Washington**, at 395.

[46] *Id.* at 194.

[47] *Id.*

[48] *Id.* at 395.

[49] *Id.* at 194.

[50] Letter from Thomas Jefferson to John Adams (Aug. 10, 1815), in XI Jefferson, **Works**, at 484, 485.

[51] Letter from Thomas Jefferson to William Johnson (Mar. 4, 1823), in *id*. at 277, 278.

[52] Johnson, II **Life of Greene**, at 476.

[53] *Id.* at 475.

[54] *Id.* at 475–76.

[55] *Id.* at 476

[56] Letter from Thomas Jefferson to William Johnson, Oct. 27, 1822, in XII Jefferson, **Works**, at 246, 246.

[57] *See, e.g. id.* ("Greene was a truly great man"); *id.* at 247 "("Greene was second to no one in enterprise, in resource, in sound judgment, promptitude of decision, and every other military talent").

[58] *Id.* at 246, 247.

[59] Letter from Thomas Jefferson to James Madison (Nov. 26, 1795), in 16 **The Papers of James Madison** 134, 134 (J. C. A. Stagg et al. eds., 1989) [Madison, **Papers**].

[60] Thomas Jefferson to Joseph Story, *quoted in* 1 **Diary and Letters of Rutherford Birchard Hayes, Nineteenth President of the United States** (Sept. 20, 1843), at 116 (Charles Richard Williams ed., 1922).

[61] Letter from Thomas Jefferson to James Madison (June 29, 1792), in 14 Madison, **Papers**, at 333, 333.

[62] Letter from Thomas Jefferson to William Johnson (Oct. 27, 1822), in XII Jefferson, **Works**, at 247.

[63] *Id.* at 248.

[64] *Id.* at 249. Jefferson was wrong. *See* Killenbeck, "Dog," at 414–17 (briefly tracing the history and showing that the move from a Court speaking seriatim to the practice of a single opinion for the Court began under Chief Justice Ellsworth).

[65] Jefferson to Johnson (Oct. 27, 1822), XII Jefferson, **Works**, at 250.

[66] *Id.* at 251.

[67] *Id.*

[68] Letter from William Johnson to Thomas Jefferson (Dec. 10, 1822), *infra* at 1 [December 10th Letter]. Individual page cites for this letter are to the manuscript page, as transcribed in this article.

[69] "Review," 15 *No. Am. Rev.* at 429.

[70] These appeared from Thursday, November 14 through Tuesday, November 19, 1822

[71] Johnson, **Life of Greene**, *quoted in* 15 *No. Am. Rev.*, at 429.

[72] William Johnson, IV "The Reviewer Reviewed," *Charleston City Gazette and Commercial Daily Advertiser*, Nov. 18, 1822, at 1 [*City Gazette*].

[73] December 10th Letter, at 1–2 (noting claims lodged by the "numerous admirers of Col Lee" and "Lee's Fame"). *See also* Letter from Thomas Jefferson to William Johnson (Oct. 27, 1822), in XII Jefferson, **Works**, at 246 ("I am glad too to see the Romance of Lee removed from the shelf of History to that of Fable.").

[74] December 10th Letter at 2. For a discussion of the Newburgh Conspiracy, which arose when the Continental Congress failed to honor promises of pay and pensions made to the Revolutionary army, see Richard H. Kohn, "The Inside History of the Newburgh Conspiracy: America and the Coup d'Etat," 27 *Wm. & Mary Q.* (3rd Series) 187 (1970). Vindicating Johnson, Kohn states that "Gouverneur Morris's role is more hidden" but that his letters "imply an active role." *Id.* at 193 n. 19.

[75] William Johnson, "For the City Gazette," *City Gazette*, June 5, 1822, at 2.

[76] Johnson, I "The Reviewer Reviewed," *City Gazette*, Nov. 14, 1822, at 1.

[77] *Id.*

[78] *Id.*

[79] December 10th Letter, at 2, 5.

[80] *Id.* at 2.

[81] *Id.* at 13.

[82] *Id.* at 5 and 13.

[83] *Id.*

[84] *Id.* at 3.

[85] *Id.* at 15. Johnson "documents" this claim by noting "the unprincipled and ungrateful separation of her Views and Interests during the late War," the War of 1812, "capped by the Hartford Convention." *Id.*

[86] II Johnson, **Life of Greene**, at 476. *See* Jefferson to Johnson (Oct. 27, 1822), XII Jefferson, **Works**, at 247 ("I look forward with anxiety to that you promise in the last paragraph of your book").

[87] December 10th Letter, at 4.

[88] *Id.* at 6 ("you cannot be insensible that we have looked up to you as our common Father, and will believe me when I assure you that we have hoped for a rich legacy of History from your Pen").

[89] *Id.* at 5 (noting that Justice Thomas Todd had informed him that Madison "was engaged on some Work on that Period" and "if so, it would be presumptuous in any other to attempt it").

[90] *Id.* at 7.

[91] *Id.* at 4–5.

[92] *Id.* at 7.

[93] *Id.* at 7–8.

[94] Letter from Joseph Story to Nathaniel Williams (Feb. 16, 1812), in 1 **Life and Letters of Joseph Story** 213, 214 (William W. Story ed., 1851).

[95] Letter from Joseph Story to Samuel P. P. Fay (Feb. 24, 1812), in 1 *id.*, at 215, 215.

[96] *Id.* at 215–16. For a more detailed discussion of the boarding house tradition under Marshall, see Cushman, **Courtwatchers**, at 16–18 & 28–29; G. Edward White, "Imagining the Marshall Court," 1986 *Yearbook of the Supreme Court Historical Society* 77.

[97] December 10th Letter, at 8. As I documented in Killenbeck, "Dog" at 416, Johnson should not have been in any way "surprised" by a practice that began prior to Marshall's arrival on the Court and was the norm by the time Johnson took his seat.

[98] December 10th Letter, at 8.

[99] *Id.* at 8–9.

[100] For a defense of Justice Washington that shows that the "one judge" claim is incorrect, see Herbert A. Johnson, "Bushrod Washington," 62 *Vand. L. Rev.* 447 (2009).

[101] December 10th Letter, at 9.

[102] 7 U.S. (2 Cranch) 1 (1805). Marshall spoke for the Court, which sided with a group of speculators and overruled the Pennsylvania Supreme Court's interpretation of the operative state statute. For a discussion of the case and its significance, see R. Kent Newmyer, **John Marshall and the Heroic Age of the Supreme Court** 212–22 (2001).

[103] *Huidekoper's Lessee*, 7 U.S. (2 Cranch) at 72 (Johnson, J., concurring) ("there was a question suggested and commented on in the argument which has not been noticed by the court, but which appears to me to merit some consideration"). This was actually one of two separate opinions filed that Term. *See United States v. Fisher*, 6 U.S. (2 Cranch) 358, 397 (1805) (statement of Washington, J.) (implicitly dissenting when he "declar[es] the reasons which induced the circuit court . . . to pronounce the opinion which is to be re-examined here").

[104] 8 U.S. (4 Cranch) 75 (1807). This grew out of the Burr Conspiracy, with Marshall holding for the Court that it had the power to issue the writs of habeas corpus at issue.

[105] *Id.* at 101.

[106] *Id.* at 107.

[107] Killenbeck, "Dog," at 415–17.

[108] *Id.* at 421.

[109] December 10th Letter, at 9–10.

[110] *Id.* at 10.

[111] *Id.* at 10–11.

[112] Letter from Ana Hayes Johnson to Elizabeth E. W. Haywood (July 27, 1822), *quoted in* Richard C. Wade, "The Vesey Plot: A Reconsideration," 30 *J. So. Hist.* 143, 145–46 (1964).

[113] Thomas Wentworth Higginson, "Denmark Vesey," *Atlantic Monthly*, Vol. 7, No. 44, at 728 (June, 1861).

[114] *See, e.g.,* Michael P. Johnson, "Denmark Vesey and His Co-Conspirators," 58 **Wm. & Mary Q.** (3rd Series) 915, 971 (2001) [M. Johnson, "Vesey"].

[115] December 10th Letter, at 19.

[116] *Id.* at 20 (noting the governor's "Message No. 2"). Bennett was Johnson's brother-in-law and close friend. It appears that this report was in fact given to the South Carolina legislature in the fall of 1822. M. Johnson, "Vesey," at 938.

[117] *See generally* Timothy S. Huebner, "Divided Loyalties: Justice William Johnson and the Rise of Disunion in South Carolina, 1822–1834," 1995 *J. S. Ct. Hist.* 19 [Huebner, "Divided Loyalties"].

[118] *Charleston Courier*, June 21, 1821, at 1.

[119] Letter from Members of the Court of Magistrates and Freeholders, Charleston, S.C. to William Johnson, *quoted in* William Johnson, **Public of Charleston** 8–9 (1822). Johnson prepared this sixteen-page pamphlet and had it printed and distributed in the vain hope that it would help restore his reputation and good name.

[120] December 10th Letter, at 21.

[121] Morgan, **Johnson**, at 277 n. 76 (quoting John Belton O'Neall, I **Biographical Sketches of the Bench and Bar of South Carolina** 78 (1859)). The second and third major disputes involved Johnson's decision declaring the 1823 South Carolina Negro Seaman Act unconstitutional and the Nullification controversy.

[122] December 10th Letter, at 12.

[123] *Id.*

[124] *Id.* at 14.

[125] *Id.* at 17–18.

[126] For a discussion of those events, and in particular Jefferson's arguments against implied powers, see Mark R. Killenbeck, "Pursuing the Great Experiment: Reserved

Powers in a Post-ratification, Compound Republic," 1999 *S. Ct. Rev.* 81, 117–24 [Killenbeck, "Pursuing"].

[127] For a discussion of the reaction to *M'Culloch*, see Mark R. Killenbeck, ***M'Culloch v. Maryland*: Securing a Nation** 141–58 (2006).

[128] 6 U.S. (2 Cranch) 358 (1805).

[129] 11 U.S. (7 Cranch) 32 (1810).

[130] *Id.* at 34.

[131] 19 U.S. (6 Wheat.) 204 (1821).

[132] *State v. Pitman*, 3 S.C.L. (1 Brev.) 32, 34 (1801).

[133] *Id.*

[134] Sumter & Hampton, "Characters," at 282. As I have noted, *see* Killenbeck, "Dog," at 430 n. 143, all of this arguably made Johnson the first true "stealth nominee" to the Court. This assumes, of course, that the very notion that there is or could be a "stealth nominee" is in any way a credible or useful construct. For reasons I hope to some day have the time to explain, I reject both the construct and its application to its most famous victim, Justice David Souter.

[135] *M'Culloch*, 27 U.S. (4 Wheat.) at 421.

[136] *Id.* at 423.

[137] *Id.*

[138] Letter from James Madison to Spencer Roane (Sept. 2, 1819), in 8 **The Writings of James Madison**, 447, 448 (Gaillard Hunt ed., 1908). I discuss these matters at greater length in Mark R. Killenbeck, "Madison, *M'Culloch*, and Matters of Judicial Cognizance: Some Thoughts on the Nature and Scope of Judicial Review, 55 *Ark. L. Rev.* 901 (2003).

[139] December 10th Letter, at 18.

[140] Thomas Jefferson, "Opinion against the Constitutionality of a National Bank" (Feb. 15, 1791), in III Jefferson, **Writings**, at 145, 149–52.

[141] For example, Jefferson argued that a constitutional amendment was required before the federal government could undertake internal improvement projects, but also approved the construction of the first major such endeavor, the Cumberland Road. *See* Killenbeck, "Pursuing," at 127–31.

[142] December 10th Letter, at 14–15 ("The acquisition of Louisiana in my opinion put down among the thinking ones, all idea of ever establishing a general Monarchy"); *id.* at 15 ("Here again Louisiana seems to me to have saved us").

[143] Jefferson privately conceded that the purchase posed constitutional problems. See Letter from Thomas Jefferson to John Breckinridge (Aug. 12, 1803), in 10 Jefferson, **Writings**, at 5, 7 ("The Constitution has made no provision for our holding foreign territory, still less for incorporating foreign nations into our Union."). He also asked that these doubts be concealed. *See* Letter from Thomas Jefferson to John Breckinridge (Aug. 18, 1803), in *id.* at 7, 8 ("A letter received yesterday shews that nothing must be said on that subject which may give a pretext for retracting but that we

should do sub silentio what shall be found necessary."). The same strategy and rationale were expressed in letters that same day to Thomas Paine and James Madison. *See id.* at 8.

[144] Letter from Thomas Jefferson to William Johnson (Mar. 4, 1823), in XII Jefferson, **Works**, at 277.

[145] *Id.*

[146] *Id.* at 277–78.

[147] *Id.* at 279.

[148] *Id.* at 280.

[149] *Id.*

[150] Letter from William Johnson to Thomas Jefferson (April 11, 1823), in 1 *S.C. Hist. & Gen. Mag.* 206 (1900).

[151] *Id.*

[152] *Id.* at 209.

[153] *Id.* at 210.

[154] *Id.*

[155] *Id.*

[156] *Id.* at 209.

[157] Letter from Thomas Jefferson to William Johnson (June 12, 1823), in XV Jefferson, **Writings**, at 439, 451. This letter also appears in XII Jefferson, **Works**, at 252–59, albeit as an extended footnote.

[158] XV Jefferson, **Writings**, at 444.

[159] *Id.* at 444–46 (commending the essays of Spencer Roane and others published in the Richmond *Enquirer*).

[160] *See id.* at 447–48 (giving his history of *Marbury* and condemning the bulk of the opinion as "being merely an obiter dissertation of the Chief Justice"); *id.* at 444–46 (discussing *Cohens* and its violations of "the constitutional limits between the General and State jurisdictions").

[161] *Id.* at 440.

[162] *Id.* at 441.

[163] *Id.* at 444.

[164] *Id.* at 445, 445–46. The promised essays were by Spencer Roane, writing as Algernon Sidney in the Richmond *Enquirer*, plus those of two other pseudonymous authors in the same paper, Fletcher of Salton and Somers. Jefferson did not have those essays in hand when he wrote the June 12th letter. He sent them with the July 31st note, which has not been reprinted, but is available in the Jefferson Papers at the Library of Congress.

[165] Letter from William Johnson to Thomas Jefferson (Aug. 11, 1823), in 1 *S.C. Hist. & Gen. Mag.*, at 211–12.

[166] *Id.* at 211.

[167] *See* Morgan, **Johnson**, at 306–07.

[168] 22 U.S. (9 Wheat.) 1 (1824). *Gibbons* was announced on March 2, 1824 and was the first case decided in February Term, 1824.

[169] *Id.* at 195. White characterizes the result in *Gibbons* as an expression of "concurrent power theory," as opposed to "compact theory" and, as such, "the principal basis on which state sovereignty was to be resurrected." White, **Marshall Court**, at 575.

[170] *Gibbons*, 22 U.S. (9 Wheat.) at 223.

[171] *Id.* at 222 (Johnson, J., concurring).

[172] *Id.* at 222–23.

[173] Morgan, **Johnson**, at 192.

[174] *Elkison v. Deliesseline*, 8 Fed. Cas. 493, 496–97 (C.C.S.C. 1823) (No. 4366).

[175] Letter from Thomas Jefferson to William Johnson (June 12, 1823), in XV Jefferson, **Writings**, at 447.

[176] *Elkison*, 8 Fed. Cas. at 495.

[177] *Id.*

[178] *Id.* at 496.

[179] The Vesey incident and *Elkison* also factored into Johnson's final letter to Jefferson, within which he noted that "I have received a Warning to quit this city. I fear nothing so much as the Effects of the persecuting Spirit that is abroad in this Place." Letter from William Johnson to Thomas Jefferson (Aug. 11, 1823), in 1 *S.C. Hist. & Gen. Mag.*, at 212.

[180] Philonimus, "Review of the Numbers of Caroliniensis—No. 4," *Charleston Mercury*, Sept. 5, 1823, at 2.

[181] *Gibbons*, 22 U.S. (9 Wheat.) at 224 (Johnson, J., concurring).

[182] *Id.*

[183] *Id.* at 236.

[184] *Id.* at 236.

[185] 22 U.S. (9 Wheat.) 738 (1824).

[186] *Id.* at 874 (Johnson, J., dissenting).

[187] *Id.* at 873.

[188] Letter from Thomas Jefferson to Edward Livingston (April 4, 1824), in XII Jefferson, **Works**, at 348, 349.

[189] Letter from Thomas Jefferson to William B. Giles (Dec. 26, 1825), in *id.*, at 424, 424.

[190] Letter from Thomas Jefferson to James Madison (Feb. 17, 1826), in *id.* at 455, 456.

[191] *See* Huebner, "Divided Loyalties," at 26–28.

The Judicial Amendment

The Judicial power of the United States shall not be construed to extend to any suit in law or equity, commenced or prosecuted against one of the United States by Citizens of another State, or by Citizens or Subjects of any Foreign State.

—*Eleventh Amendment*

The Eleventh Amendment is one of a cluster of amendments adopted during the first two decades after the ratification of the United States Constitution while most members of the founding generation were still alive and active in national affairs. With these amendments, the Founders completed—if not perfected—the work begun at Philadelphia in the sweltering summer of 1787. The constitutional settlement thus arrived at endured without change for sixty years until (in the aftermath of bloody conflict) a new set of amendments—Thirteen, Fourteen, and Fifteen—rebalanced the federal union.

The first ten amendments, collectively known as the Bill of Rights, were ratified in 1791 in satisfaction of an undertaking that a declaration of rights comparable to those already in many state constitutions would be added to the federal document. In 1804, the Twelfth Amendment rejiggered the original mechanism for selecting the President and Vice-President, which had proved unsatisfactory in the prior election. In between, the Eleventh Amendment addressed the jurisdiction of the federal courts.

Despite more than 200 years of sporadic litigation, the exact significance of the Eleventh Amendment remains unclear—and is still contentious. So contentious, in fact, that a significant minority of Supreme Court Justices in the last years of the twentieth century, two centuries after the Amendment's ratification, took the unusual step of announcing that they did not accept that the constitutional questions raised by the Amendment had been finally settled and that they would continue to dissent in similar cases in the future.[1]

In a couple of regards, this serious and continuing disagreement among the nation's top judges is surprising. The Eleventh Amendment, one sentence consisting of a mere forty-three words, is among the briefest additions to the Constitution, and its grammar and language are simple and straightforward. Unlike those phrases in the Bill of Rights that cry out for judicial explication—such as "free exercise of religion" in the First Amendment and "probable cause" in the Fourth—or those pregnant but ambiguous phrases that seem to invite judicial creativity—such as "due process of law" in the Fifth Amendment and "cruel and unusual punishment" in the Eighth—the words of the Eleventh Amendment are clear and easily understood. The text is composed of nouns of common legal usage: power, suit, law, equity, citizen, state, foreign state.

And, unlike the curious lacuna in the Twelfth Amendment, which provides that after the certificates of the electors are opened by the president of the Senate (a.k.a. the Vice-President of the United States) in the presence of both houses of Congress, "the votes shall then be counted"—without saying who shall do the counting—the Eleventh Amendment is, on its face, apparently clear and self-explanatory. In addition, the subject matter of the Amendment, jurisdiction, is technical, seemingly of interest only to lawyers, and lacking the high emotional valence of the rights spelled out in the first ten amendments. Even law students have been known to yawn over their federal jurisdiction books.

Yet the Eleventh Amendment, as the lawyers know, trenches on the power of federal courts to protect those highly valued rights and actually affects the very essence of the constitutional settlement worked out with so much difficulty in Philadelphia just a few years earlier. The federal government may be a government of delegated powers, but those powers impact the people directly through the judges, both state and federal, who are bound by the Constitution, laws, and treaties of the United States, "any Thing in the Constitution or Laws of any State to the Contrary notwithstanding."[2] This is, perhaps, the single most important difference between the Constitution and the Articles of Confederation, which operated through the states. The seemingly perennial disagreement among the judges over the reach of the Eleventh Amendment may not, after all, be so hard to understand.

Before I attempt to say something new about the Eleventh Amendment—assuming anyone can say anything new, given the volume of literature on the subject including a now twenty-odd-year old book of my own[3]— let me list what we know about the Amendment:

- It was adopted in 1798—or was it 1795?
- It applies to suits filed after its effective date (whenever that was)—or also to suits that were pending at the time?
- It applies to suits brought by citizens of one state against another state—or also to suits brought by citizens against their own state?
- It applies to suits against states brought by citizens or subjects of foreign states— or also to suits against states brought by foreign sovereigns?
- It applies to suits involving claims against states within the diversity jurisdiction of the federal courts—or also to suits raising federal questions?
- It applies to suits in law or equity—or also to suits in the admiralty and maritime jurisdiction?
- It applies to suits in federal courts—or also to adjudications by federal administrative agencies?
- It deprives the federal courts of jurisdiction—or allows a state to waive the jurisdictional bar and in effect confer jurisdiction on the courts?
- And, most important of all, it amends, that is, changes the original understanding concerning the judicial power of the United States—or restores that understanding?

The answer to all the interrogatories, by the way, is "Yes."

So . . . , what else do we know about the Eleventh Amendment?

- It applies to suits against states—or also to suits against state officers?

- It applies to suits against states brought by citizens of another state—or also to suits against states brought by another state?
- It applies to suits against states brought by foreign citizens or subjects—or also to suits against states brought by the United States?
- It applies to suits against states—or also to suits against municipal subdivisions of states?

The answer to these questions is "Not necessarily."

Now that we have that cleared up..., let's consider some other questions about the Eleventh Amendment. The difficulty concerning the date of adoption stems from the fact that President John Adams proclaimed the ratification of the Amendment on January 8, 1798,[4] and for most of the Amendment's long history that has been the date given for its effectiveness. But the Amendment had actually attained the necessary number of state ratifications by February 7, 1795,[5] and later—much later, on June 5, 1939, to be exact—the Supreme Court ruled that Congress is the sole judge of the completion of the ratification process, so by implication the president has no role to play in amending the Constitution. (That is, if I am reading the somewhat confusing decision in *Coleman v. Miller*[6] correctly.) In consequence, the earlier date for the ratification of the Eleventh Amendment has begun making its way into many, but not all, copies of the Constitution[7]—on the theory that since 1939 we know how to determine the effective date of amendments, even those adopted more than a century earlier. Once a constitutional question has at last been answered, the answer has always been the correct one, whether prior generations (including the founding generation) knew it or not. The later decision speaks, in the old language of the law, *nunc pro tunc* (now for then).

That President Adams might have wanted to be officially involved in the ratification

In *Chisholm v. Georgia,* the Supreme Court ruled that citizens of one state (South Carolina, in the suit) may indeed sue citizens of another state (Georgia) in a federal court, as provided by Article II, Section 2. Above is an announcement of the Court's decision in the March 13, 1793 *Columbia Centinel*, published in Boston. The decision eventually led to the Eleventh Amendment, which repealed this section of the Constitution in 1798.

process is not at all unlikely. As a Federalist, whatever Adams thought of an amendment affecting federal judicial power, he certainly could not have been, as President, indifferent to an amendment that concerned suits brought by citizens or subjects of foreign states. This directly affected America's relations with foreign powers and could conceivably develop into a *casus belli*. Sending warships to protect foreign creditors would become rather common in later years.[8] Although no other amendment since has posed the same direct threat to foreign affairs, a President must remain ever vigilant to constitutional changes that could cause international complications, but the chief executive officer of the United States must do so from the sidelines.

So far, I have managed to speak about the Eleventh Amendment without once mentioning the thing that usually comes first in such discussions: the *cause célèbre, Chisholm v. Georgia* (1793).[9] In that case, a Supreme Court, headed by Chief Justice John Jay and composed of Justices who had helped draft the Constitution at Philadelphia or who had supported the unamended text at their state ratifying conventions (or both), held that Article III conferred original jurisdiction on the Court over a suit to collect a debt against a state brought by a citizen of another state.[10] To reverse this result, the Eleventh Amendment was promptly proposed by Congress and quickly ratified by the requisite number of states.

At the risk of appearing to trivialize an important constitutional issue, I would like to take a few minutes to explore not what was, but what might have been—to conduct, in other words, a few "thought experiments"; or, to put it more dramatically, to pay a brief visit to what fans of science fiction know as "alternate worlds." Sometimes we understand a little better where we are if we pause to peer down the road not taken.

What if Chisholm had come out the other way? What if, in other words, as in that even greater *cause célèbre, Marbury v. Madison*[11] a decade later, the Court had dismissed the

suit for want of jurisdiction? There would then have been no Eleventh Amendment, and later judges would have been spared much constitutional soul-searching.[12] But to explore this particular alternate universe—*the one in which the Eleventh Amendment had never been adopted*—we must consider exactly *how Chisholm* could have come out the other way. It could have been, of course, because the Justices decided that Article III did not extend the judicial power of the United States to such a case. And that would have been that.

Or, the Court could have dismissed *Chisholm* for want of jurisdiction on statutory rather than constitutional grounds. This was the result preferred by Justice James Iredell of North Carolina, the lone dissenter in *Chisholm*, who spent most of his long dissenting opinion arguing that the Judiciary Act of 1787 did not provide for process against a state and therefore did not implement the full extent of Article III jurisdiction, whatever that was. Aware from his own experience of the widespread fear of federal power—as a delegate to the North Carolina ratifying convention in 1788, he had labored in vain to prevent his state from rejecting the Constitution for just that reason[13]—Iredell foresaw the reaction the majority's decision in *Chisholm* would produce. Just as, ten years later, Chief Justice John Marshall would use a strained construction of the same Judiciary Act to avert the crisis that would have resulted from a decision in favor of Marbury et al., so Iredell tried to convince his Brethren that they could side-step the issue in *Chisholm*. They could defer to Congress to decide if the time was ripe to extend federal jurisdiction over suits against a state brought by citizens of another state. When and if necessary, the Court could confront the constitutional question, although Iredell hesitantly ventured his "extra-judicial" opinion against constitutionality in two sentences at the end of his twenty-one-page dissent.[14]

If *Chisholm* had come out the other way, how would American constitutional history have been different? *What, in other words,*

Without the humiliation of the reversal of *Chisholm* by the Eleventh Amendment, John Jay (above) likely would have accepted President John Adams reappointment as Chief Justice in 1801 and John Marshall would not have been appointed. (Jay had already been confirmed by the Senate without his knowledge.)

if the Eleventh Amendment had never been adopted? The answer, assuming I knew what it was, would fill many more than a few pages. But one thing does seem fairly certain: John Marshall would never have become Chief Justice—with momentous consequences for the history of the Republic. Without the humiliation of the reversal of *Chisholm* by the Eleventh Amendment, John Jay likely would have accepted President John Adams's reappointment as Chief Justice in 1801. (Jay had already been confirmed by the Senate without his knowledge.) In fact, Jay refused the honor of being the once-and-future Chief Justice because, as he explained to the President, he was "perfectly convinced that under a system so defective [the Court] would not obtain the energy, weight, and dignity which was essential to its affording due support to the national government; nor acquire the public confidence and respect which, as the last resort of the justice of the nation, it should possess."[15]

To follow this alternate time-path just a little farther: Had Jay accepted reappointment and served until near the end of his long life, and had his final illness caused him to resign just a few months short of his death on May 17, 1829, his successor would have been chosen by John Quincy Adams, not by Andrew Jackson, and Roger B. Taney would never have become Chief Justice!

Paying a visit to another alternate universe, I would like to wander down a different time-trail. *What if the federal government had adopted the practice that became nearly universal with state constitutions of integrating amendments in the constitutional text, rather than appending them at the end?* Integration in the text, by the way, is exactly what James Madison expected would be the case with the Bill of Rights.[16] A dozen years ago, Edward Hartnett in an article in *Constitutional Commentary* showed us what such a constitution might have looked like.[17] In this case, of course, there would have been no amendments at all, at least, not in the sense of distinct and permanently labeled "Amendments."

Justice James Iredell tried to convince his Brethren that they could side step the issue in *Chisholm*, but he ended up dissenting in the landmark case.

How integration could have worked with the Eleventh Amendment can be readily illustrated by the Twelfth Amendment, which rewrote Article II, Section 1, Clause 3, by requiring that electors vote separately for President and Vice-President. After 1804, copies of the Constitution could simply have substituted the words of the Twelfth Amendment for the superseded language, which would have remained of interest to no one but legal historians. (No disrespect intended!)

The reason, by the way, that the Twelfth Amendment left unanswered the question of who counted the votes of the electors—which could have been important in the constitutional crisis caused by the presidential election of 1876—is because that was not the problem that precipitated the Amendment. Acting like the good common law lawyers that they were, the drafters solved the problem they had, not all imaginable problems—just what they had done with the Eleventh Amendment a few years earlier.

Where, in this alternate universe, would the Eleventh Amendment have been inserted in the Constitution? Article III, which begins with the words "the judicial power of the United States," the very same words that begin the Eleventh Amendment, seems to be the logical place. But one of the (many) problems posed by the Amendment is that its wording does not, after that opening phrase, track the language of the Judicial Article the way the Twelfth Amendment tracks the language of the original constitutional text. Article III, Section 2 provides (eliding extraneous matter): "The judicial Power shall extend . . . to Controversies . . . between a State and citizens of another State . . . and between a State . . . and foreign . . . Citizens or Subjects." I suppose the Eleventh Amendment, lightly edited in the interest of style, could have been simply tacked onto the end of that sentence: *" . . . but shall not extend to any suit in law or equity, commenced or prosecuted against a State by citizens of another State, or by citizens or subjects*

of any foreign State." In other words, federal judicial power *does* extend to controversies in which the State appears as party plaintiff, but not to those in which it appears as party defendant.[18] (You might have noticed that I dropped the word "construed"—*shall not be construed to extend*—as inconsistent with the phrasing of the rest of Article III, though that could be significant.)

This, of course, is to omit the accumulated judicial glosses that I referred to earlier when I listed what we seem to know about the Eleventh Amendment. To accommodate those would take a lot more words—and drafting skills that probably exceed mine. Of particular difficulty, it seems to me, would be what to do about the power of a state to waive the lack of jurisdiction, if it chose, and allow itself to be sued—in effect, conferring jurisdiction on the Court in excess of the constitutional grant?—something even the combined strength of Congress and the President cannot do, at least according to *Marbury v. Madison.* How much difference the integration of the Amendment into the constitutional text would have made would, of course, depend on exactly what it said, and where it was. But whatever the exact text and context, it would have presented a somewhat different problem for constitutional analysis than leaving it freestanding after the Bill of Rights.

Switching to yet another time-path, I would like to consider one more might-have-been. *What if the Constitution had provided for appeal from decisions of the Supreme Court to the Congress, perhaps specifically to the Senate?* There was, of course, the English example of appeal to the House of Lords, only last year formally abolished.[19] And in New York until 1846 appeal lay from the state Supreme Court to the Court for the Correction of Errors, composed of the entire New York Senate, augmented by the state's Chancellor and the justices of the state Supreme Court.[20] (It was the abolition of this court and its replacement by the New York Court of Appeals,[21] by the way, that created the present anomaly—to the confusion of many law students—whereby the New York Supreme Court is not the court of last resort in that state.)

Had *Chisholm* been appealed to the U.S. Senate, it seems obvious that that court would have reversed it, but this would have precipitated not an additional sentence in the text of the Constitution, but a judicial precedent. The decision in *Chisholm* would perforce have covered the specific facts of that case—a suit against one of the United States brought by citizens of another state—and might well have included (in dicta) the closely similar case of a suit against a state brought by citizens or subjects of any foreign state. More than that was, at the time, unnecessary.

Without in the least diminishing the significance of constitutional precedent as opposed to constitutional provision, case law *is* different. I am not thinking here about the fact that cases, even great constitutional cases, can be overturned more easily than constitutions can be amended, although that is obviously so.[22] What does interest me is speculation about what the lower federal courts—in this alternate universe including even the U.S. Supreme Court—would have done in future cases with what might have been called "the rule in *Chisholm*," and what the Senators over the years would have done in other similar cases. The record in England and New York, by the way, suggests that only a small percentage of cases would ever have reached the Senate, so the law would have been developed, mostly, by the familiar federal courts.

The precedent set by this hypothetical Senatorial decision in *Chisholm* would, of course, have had to develop within the constraints imposed by the divided sovereignty of the federal union: enough federal judicial power to maintain the supremacy of the federal government in those areas wherein it is sovereign, but not so much that it infringed the retained sovereignty of the states. Of course, if Civil War and Reconstruction Amendments later formed part of this alternate universe, the balance would have had to have been periodically adjusted.

One can rather easily imagine a time-path along which federal courts, headed in this imaginary world by the Senate, confronted (in one order or another) suits against a state by its own citizens, suits against a state by foreign sovereigns, suits against a state in the admiralty and maritime jurisdiction, and suits against a state by federal administrative agencies—in each case deciding against jurisdiction because of "*Chisholm* immunity." Likewise, one can imagine suits against state officers, suits against a state brought by

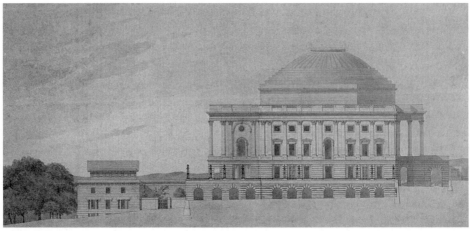

The author posits that had *Chisholm* been appealed to the U.S. Senate, it would have reversed it, and that this would have precipitated not an additional sentence in the text of the Constitution but a judicial precedent.

another state, suits against a state brought by the United States, and suits against municipal subdivisions of a state—in some of which, at least, exceptions were found to that same immunity. Oddly enough, on this imaginary time-path federal jurisdiction would have come to look very much like it does in the real here-and-now: state sovereign immunity respected insofar as that is consistent with the necessary federal supremacy. Or, as the real U.S. Supreme Court put it in a real case, exceptions to Eleventh Amendment immunity are permitted insofar as "necessary to permit federal courts to vindicate federal rights and hold state officials responsible to 'the supreme authority of the United States.'"[23] Quite possibly, in other words, the end of all our exploring of alternate worlds would be to arrive where we started—and know the place for the first time.

The curious history—the real history—of the Eleventh Amendment can perhaps be best understood by recognizing that it is unique among the twenty-seven amendments. Unlike amendments that enumerate civil rights—such as the Bill of Rights and the Fourteenth Amendment—or amendments that make what might be called mechanical changes to the original set-up—such as the Twelfth Amendment (concerning presidential election) and the Seventeenth (concerning the election of Senators)—the Eleventh Amendment is not concerned with adding to or altering the text, but rather with changing how the text is to be "construed"—an odd word, as I mentioned earlier, to find in a constitution or statute; more common in judicial opinions.

At the end of the eighteenth century, written constitutions were new on the face of the earth, and constitutional amendments were perforce even newer. (Some of the earliest state constitutions did not even allow for the possibility.) When a decision of the Supreme Court appeared mistaken, it was natural to correct it by appeal to higher authority. Without a Senatorial Court for the Correction of Errors, correction could come only through the amendment process spelled out in Article V. In a union composed of a small number of seaboard states, recently independent and not yet riven by sectional strife, it was a quick and simple process, taking only a matter of months—less than it takes today to get to an appellate court. All that was needed, as with a judicial appeal, was to reverse the result and state the holding. If further corrections were required, they would come the common law way, case by case.

The explication of a text is unlike the evolution of a precedent. Textual exegesis means defining terms and concepts, deciding what is covered and what is not—"in or out," so to speak. It is not supposed to add anything to the text, only to discover what has always been there, at least potentially. This, of course, is not without difficulty, and sometimes it does seem to go beyond bounds. The farther reaches of "due process," the substantive applications, perhaps come closest. And, at one time, the "penumbral theory," used to support a constitutional right of privacy, seemed to risk breaking free of the text altogether, until it was reined in, and the right of privacy domesticated in the Due Process Clause.[24]

More like an appellate decision than a constitutional text, the Eleventh Amendment spurred the growth of a body of law that resembles the development of a precedent, albeit one of an extraordinary sort, more than a case of tortured textual analysis, what the Court (the real Court) called "ahistorical literalism."[25] The Eleventh Amendment, in other words, is the "judicial amendment" in more ways than one—an amendment to the Judicial Article but also a judicial decision in the form of a constitutional amendment.

ENDNOTES

[1] See, e.g., *College Sav. Bank v. Florida Prepaid Postsecondary Educ. Expense Bd.*, 527 U.S. 666, 699 (1999) (Breyer, J., dissenting, joined by Stevens, Souter, & Ginsburg, JJ.) ("[A]lthough I accept this Court's pre-*Seminole Tribe* sovereign immunity decisions, I am not yet ready to adhere to the proposition of law set forth in *Seminole Tribe*."). The reference is to *Seminole Tribe v. Florida*, 517 U.S. 44 (1996) (holding that congressional power under

the Commerce Clause does not extend to abrogation of state sovereign immunity as recognized by the Eleventh Amendment).

[2] U.S. Const. art. VI.

[3] John V. Orth, **The Judicial Power of the United States: The Eleventh Amendment in American History** (1987). Authority for the following items marked by bullet points may be found in that book.

[4] 1 **Messages and Papers of the Presidents, 1789–1897,** at 260 (James D. Richardson ed., 1896).

[5] Clyde E. Jacobs, **The Eleventh Amendment and Sovereign Immunity** 66–67 (1972).

[6] 307 U.S. 433 (1939).

[7] Two annotated editions of the Constitution, both published in 2009, illustrate the point. Seth Lipsky, **The Citizen's Constitution: An Annotated Guide** 245 (2009) (Eleventh Amendment ratified 1798); Jack N. Rakove, **The Annotated U.S. Constitution & Declaration of Independence** 245 (2009) (Eleventh Amendment ratified 1795).

[8] As Chief Justice Morrison R. Waite later observed: "[I]f a sovereign assumes the responsibility of presenting the claim of one of his subjects against another sovereign, the prosecution will be 'as one nation proceeds against another, not by suit in the courts, as of right, but by diplomatic negotiation, or, if need be, by war.'" *New Hampshire v. Louisiana,* 108 U.S. 76, 90 (1883) (quoting *United States v. Dickelman,* 92 U.S. 520, 524 (1875)).

[9] 2 U.S. (2 Dall.) 419 (1793).

[10] "The judicial Power shall extend...to Controversies...between a State and Citizens of another State.... In all Cases...in which a State shall be Party, the supreme Court shall have original Jurisdiction." U.S. Const. Art. III, § 2.

[11] 5 U.S. (1 Cranch) 137 (1803).

[12] Actually, as my wife pointed out to me on the way to delivering this lecture at the Supreme Court, there still would have been an Eleventh Amendment; it just would have been a different amendment, the one we now know as the Twelfth Amendment!

[13] *See* Willis P. Whichard, **Justice James Iredell** 53–75 (2000). See also Walter F. Pratt, Jr. "Law and the Experience of Politics in Late Eighteenth-Century North Carolina: North Carolina Considers the Constitution," 22 *Wake Forest L. Rev.* 577 (1987).

[14] 2 U.S. (2 Dall.) at 449–50. *See also* John V. Orth, "The Truth About Justice Iredell's Dissent in *Chisholm v. Georgia,*" 73 *N.C. L. Rev.* 255 (1994).

[15] Letter from John Jay to John Adams (Jan. 2, 1801), quoted in Albert J. Beveridge, 3 **The Life of John Marshall** 55 (1919). Marshall knew he was the default choice. As he recalled years later, "When I waited on the President with Mr. Jay's letter declining the appointment he said thoughtfully, 'Who shall I nominate now? I replied that I could not tell.... After a moment's hesitation he said, 'I believe I must nominate you.'" Quoted in Jean Edward Smith, **John Marshall, Definer of a Nation** 14 (1996).

[16] *See* James R. Stoner, **Common Law and Liberal Theory** 221 (1992). See Madison's presentation of his amendments to Congress in 1 *Annals of Cong.* at col. 457 (Joseph Gales ed. 1789). In contemporary state constitutions, by the way, the declarations, or bills, of rights come at the beginning, not at the end. See, e.g., N.C. Const. of 1776, discussed in John V. Orth, **The North Carolina State Constitution: A Reference Guide** 2–7 (1993).

[17] Edward Hartnett, "A 'Uniform and Entire' Constitution; Or, What if Madison Had Won?" 15 *Const. Com.* 251 (1998).

[18] What would have happened with an appeal by writ of error in which the state, originally the plaintiff, now appeared as the nominal defendant, must remain subject to speculation. *See, e.g., Cohens v. Virginia,* 19 U.S. (6 Wheat.) 264 (1821).

[19] For a valedictory review of the modern history of the House of Lords as a judicial institution, see **The Judicial House of Lords, 1876–2009** (2009) (Louis Blom-Cooper, Brice Dickson, and Gavin Drewry eds.).

[20] N.Y. Const. of 1777, § 32; N.Y. Const. of 1821, art. V, § 1.

[21] N.Y. Const. of 1846, art. VI, § 2.

[22] *See,* e.g., Edward H. Levi, **An Introduction to Legal Reasoning** 57–102 (1949).

[23] *Pennhurst State School & Hospital v. Halderman,* 465 U.S. 89, 105 (1984) (quoting *Ex parte Young,* 209 U.S. 123, 160 (1908)).

[24] *See generally* John V. Orth, **Due Process of Law: A Brief History** 73–84 (2003).

[25] *Alden v. Maine,* 527 U.S. 706, 730 (1999).

Ambition Counteracting Ambition: Separation of Powers in Supreme Court Appointments

BARBARA A. PERRY

A 2005 American Bar Association–Harris Poll discovered that more than one-fifth of Americans surveyed thought the three branches of government were "Democrat," "Republican," and "Independent."[1] How unfortunate that many Americans have so little understanding of this crucial element in our nation's constitutional structure. Professor M.J.C. Vile, the noted British political theorist and author of a seminal book on the separation of powers, observed that the principle of dividing government authority along functional lines (legislative, executive, and judicial) attempted to vitiate the paradox that "[f]reedom ordains rules, [yet] [g]overnment is lost liberty."[2] "It is essential," Vile wrote, "for the establishment and maintenance of political liberty that the government be divided into three branches.... Each branch of the government must be confined to the exercise of its own function and not be allowed to encroach upon the functions of other branches.... In this way each of the branches will be a check

to the others and no single group of people will be able to control the machinery of the State."[3]

No political scientist could begin a separation of powers discussion without referring initially to James Madison's oft-quoted *Federalist Paper #51*, where he described the need for what he called "the necessary partition of power among the several departments" (his word for the branches of government). "By so contriving the interior structure of the government ...," Madison argued, "its several constituent parts may, by their mutual relations, be the means of keeping each other in their proper places."[4] The Father of the Constitution explained that the "separate and distinct exercise of the different powers of government" is "essential to the preservation of liberty...."[5] Thus, "each department should have a will of its own," and "the members of each should have as little agency as possible in the appointment of the members of the others." In theory, Madison suggested, all appointments should flow through "the people" and not overlap. Yet,

At the 1787 Philadelphia Convention, Ben Franklin explained the effectiveness of the Scottish method for selecting judges. Once a lawyer became a judge, his practice was divvied up among the rest of the bar, thus ensuring that his fellow bar members would always select the most qualified candidate with the most robust practice.

he recognized that, in practice, some selection procedures would have to deviate from this principle, especially for the judiciary: "first, because peculiar qualifications being essential in the members, the primary consideration ought to be to select that mode of choice which best secures these qualifications; second, because the permanent tenure by which the appointments are held in that department must soon destroy all sense of dependence on authority conferring them."[6]

At the 1787 Philadelphia Convention, the Constitution's Framers spent more time discussing the *process* of judicial selection than the *criteria* for choosing federal judges. According to Madison's Convention *Notes*, the delegates initially considered appointment of federal judges by the national legislature. James Wilson, Pennsylvania's brilliant representative and future member of the Court, opposed the proposal, arguing that "[i]ntrigue, partiality, and concealment" resulted from judicial appointments by legislatures. Moreover, the primary reason for creating a sin-

gle executive, Wilson reminded his colleagues, was so that *one* official would be "responsible" for nominations. John Rutledge of South Carolina, who chaired the Convention's Committee on Detail, countered that granting "so great a power to any single person," would cause "the people . . . [to] think we are leaning toward monarchy."[7] Rutledge would receive two appointments from President George Washington to serve on the U.S. Supreme Court. He resigned his Associate Justice seat before the Court ever convened to accept appointment as the chief justice of the South Carolina Supreme Court. Congress failed to confirm his recess appointment to Chief Justice in 1795, after he had already served five months in the center seat.[8]

Madison, too, opposed legislative selection of judges. "Beside the danger of intrigue and partiality," the Father of the Constitution allowed, "many of the [legislature's] members were not judges of the requisite qualifications."[9] Yet he did not want the executive to have the sole appointment power. According to his notes on the Convention, Madison "rather inclined to give the [the power of judicial appointment] to the Senate because its members would be "sufficiently stable and independent to follow their deliberate judgments."[10] Even a Founding Father cannot be right all of the time.

At this point in the early stages of the Convention, on June 5th, the first discussion of how to choose the "National Judiciary" occurred. Benjamin Franklin, as he often did, offered an "entertaining" anecdote to break the tension. Franklin described the Scottish method of allowing lawyers to select members of their own profession to sit on the bench. The possibility of dividing the newly selected judge's practice among themselves always motivated the Scottish attorneys to nominate the most qualified members of the bar who obviously would then have the most lucrative legal practice to divvy up among themselves.[11]

Mid-way through the Convention, Massachusetts delegate Nathaniel Ghorum suggested that federal judges be "appointed by the Executive with the advice and consent of the [Senate]."[12] Madison proposed a variation on Ghorum's idea: the executive appointment of jurists with "the concurrence of 1/3 at least" of the legislature's upper house. "This would unite," Madison declared, "the advantage of responsibility in the Executive with the security afforded in the 2d branch against any incautious or corrupt nomination by the Executive."[13] Thus, in judicial appointments, the Convention began moving toward a variation on the theme of separation of powers that included another crucial component of American constitutionalism, namely, checks and balances. The branches would not be purely separate; they would interact in a contrapuntal mode. As Madison would write to promote the new Constitution's ratification, again in *Federalist Paper #51*, "The great security against a gradual concentration of the several powers in the same department consists in giving to those who administer each department the necessary constitutional means and personal motives to resist encroachment of the others." Or, as he famously expressed it, "Ambition must be made to counteract ambition. The interest of the man must be connected with the constitutional rights of the place."[14]

In the waning days of the Philadelphia Convention, on Sept. 7, 1787, the delegates settled upon a Madisonian compromise for selecting "Judges of the Supreme Court" through presidential *nomination*, with *appointment* contingent upon the Senate's prerogative to advise and consent.[15] Though Madison had made reference to "requisite qualifications" for judges at the Convention, neither he nor his fellow delegates were more specific in their Philadelphia discussions and most certainly not in the document they produced. The U.S. Constitution is wholly silent on criteria for selecting members of the Supreme Court.

Once more, the *Federalist Papers* (this time Alexander Hamilton's #78) provide some elaboration on the Founders' thoughts regarding judicial selection. Hamilton penned several comments on the importance of merit in the selection process and the necessity of choosing "men who are best qualified" for their respective offices. Yet he was hardly more specific than the document he was expounding. Integrity and knowledge of the laws, acquired through "long and laborious study" were his only expressed elements of the general criterion of merit.[16]

In 2009 the Supreme Court Historical Society asked me to speak on the Court's role in appointments to its Bench. "Has it been a by-stander or an active participant?" the Society queried. For a moment, my professional life flashed before my eyes, in a sort of near career-death experience. I had been invited to give a talk at the Supreme Court, with the Chief Justice in the audience, and I had been given a trick question. The Founders had *not* assigned a role for the Court in the appointment of its own members.

Yet, as I pondered the question, and reflected on the history of Supreme Court nominations, I recalled instances when members of the high tribunal *have* played a part in the drama that often surrounds the selection of those individuals who occupy its Bench. The most direct impact that sitting Justices have had on nominations has occurred when they suggested nominees to the President and/or supported candidates for the Court once chosen by the President. (The Society requests that its speakers cover Court history up to the nomination of the most senior sitting Justice. In 2009–10, Justice John Paul Stevens was the Court's most senior member, having taken his seat in 1975. Thus, my examination of this intriguing topic ends at that year.)

Sitting Justices Supporting Judicial Nominees (1853–1974)

Nineteenth Century
It appears that 1853, during President Franklin Pierce's administration, marks the first instance of the Court successfully

recommending a nominee to the President. As Henry Abraham, the dean of Supreme Court appointment scholars, has observed, "In what probably still stands as a unique action, the entire incumbent membership of the Court wrote to Pierce in behalf of [John A.] Campbell and deputized Associate Justices [John] Catron and [Benjamin] Curtis to deliver the supportive letters to the president personally."[17] The Justices' campaign for Campbell was highly successful. The President considered no other candidates, and the Senate approved his nomination with alacrity. Although personally opposed to secession, Campbell, an Alabaman, resigned from the Court in 1861 and became assistant secretary of war for the Confederacy.[18]

President Lincoln typically kept his own counsel when filling Supreme Court vacancies, but his first appointment, John McLean, came highly recommended by retiring Justice, Noah Swayne, a close friend of McLean. Incumbent Justice Stephen J. Field nudged Lincoln, via a telegram, to name Salmon P. Chase as Chief Justice when Roger B. Taney died in 1864.[19]

During President Ulysses S. Grant's administration, two members of the Supreme Court made recommendations to him for filling a pair of vacancies on the high tribunal in 1870. Justice Robert Grier had finally retired at the urging of his colleagues, when age-related illnesses made his service no longer feasible. Though a Democrat, he recommended Republican Joseph P. Bradley, who had the support of Justice Swayne, as well. Grier also supported William Strong's selection to the Court by President Grant in his second 1870 appointment.[20]

Hayes's presidency illustrated another instance of a Supreme Court nomination suggested by an incumbent member of the Bench. When Justice Strong departed the Court in 1880, after a decade of service, Chief Justice Morrison R. Waite recommended William Woods. Though a one-term President, Hayes had an additional opportunity to nominate a Justice, only two months before leaving office in 1881. Stanley Matthews, Hayes's classmate at Kenyon College, had also been supported by his close friend, retiring Justice Swayne, whose seat Matthews would fill. The Democratic Senate refused to take up a vote on the lame-duck Republican President's nominee, but his successor, the ill-fated James Garfield, would renominate Matthews and see a narrowly split Senate confirm him by one vote. After Garfield's assassination, his successor, Chester Arthur, met with members of the Court (particularly Samuel F. Miller and John

Though a Democrat, Justice Robert Grier (left) recommended to President Ulysses S. Grant (center) that he appoint Republican Joseph P. Bradley (right) to replace him on the Bench. Grier also supported Republican William Strong's selection to the Court by Grant in his second 1870 appointment.

Chief Justice Taft (left) lobbied President Warren Harding (middle) to appoint both George Sutherland and Pierce Butler to the Supreme Court. He thought that Butler's many years as a railroad lawyer suggested that the Minnesota Catholic would be a logical and reliable counter to Justice Brandeis' and Justice Holmes' perceived radicalism. Taft and Harding were photographed in 1922 at the dedication of the Lincoln Memorial; Robert Todd Lincoln is at right.

Marshall Harlan), who supported Horace Gray to be their new colleague on the Bench.[21] In addition, Justice Harlan recommended Melville W. Fuller to President Grover Cleveland to replace Chief Justice Waite after his death in 1888. Fuller had actually recommended an Illinois attorney, John Scholfield, for the post, but he declined Cleveland's offer. The Chief Justiceship went to Fuller, a corporate lawyer, whom the press labeled "the most obscure man ever nominated" for that exalted position.[22]

When Justice Matthews died in 1889, President Benjamin Harrison took nine months to compile a long list of possible nominees and then narrowed it to two: David J. Brewer and Henry Billings Brown. Two conservative friends from the Midwest, they possessed similar credentials—degrees from Yale,

as well as service on state and federal courts. Brewer and Brown deferred to each other, but President Harrison selected Brewer first, having heard about his graciousness regarding the Court's vacancy. A short time later, Justice Miller suffered a stroke, and Harrison had the opportunity to name the runner up, Brown, to the High Court. Brown would later return the support given to him by 6th U.S. Circuit Judge Howell Jackson by recommending Jackson to fill the 1893 vacancy created by Justice Lucius Q. C. Lamar's death. Apparently, Jackson's friendship with Benjamin Harrison from their days in the U.S. Senate overcame their partisan differences. Nor did the Senate's Republican majority delay Jackson's confirmation, despite the lame-duck status of his appointing President.[23]

Twentieth Century

After a bruising confirmation battle, Justice Louis D. Brandeis was only on the Court a few months when he became one of several high-ranking supporters of John Hessin Clarke's nomination. President Woodrow Wilson named Clarke to the seat vacated by Justice Charles Evans Hughes to run, albeit unsuccessfully, for the presidency in 1916.[24]

Not surprisingly, Chief Justice William Howard Taft, the only individual to lead both the executive and judicial branches (eight years apart), is among the top two recommenders of nominees to the President. His chief rival (pun intended) in this contest is Chief Justice Warren Burger. Although most scholars rate Taft as merely an "average" President from his one-term tenure (1909–1913), he is often accorded "near great" status for his Chief Justiceship (1921–1930). His vision and leadership in planning a stunning home for his beloved Court are unparalleled, though, sadly, he did not live to see its completion. As President, he was an unhappy chief executive, having been persuaded to run by his mentor, Theodore Roosevelt, who then launched a third-party candidacy against him in 1912, precipitating Taft's defeat in his bid for a second term, and allowing Democrat Woodrow Wilson to win the presidency. As the Court's sole former President to have served on the Bench, Taft is the only person to have engineered his own future appointment from the White House. Several biographers suggest that President Taft promoted Justice Edward Douglass White to the Chief's position, rather than his younger colleague, Justice Hughes, because the latter was only forty-eight years of age and would probably serve long enough to preclude a future President from appointing Taft as Chief Justice.[25] White, fifty-five years old at the time of his promotion, served until 1921, when President Warren Harding fulfilled Taft's highest aspiration in becoming Chief Justice of the United States Supreme Court.

Once he ascended to, what he considered, Heaven on Earth, Chief Justice Taft began actively participating in every presidential decision to fill vacancies on his Court. He wrote to George Sutherland, "I look forward to having you on the bench with me. I know, as you do, that the president intends to put you there."[26] President Harding was happy, indeed, in 1922 to place on the Supreme Court his brilliant friend from their days in the U.S. Senate. Harding's next choice for the Court, Pierce Butler, was actually his second pick. The President first approached renowned litigator John W. Davis, whom he considered to have "sound views," despite his Democratic party affiliation. Davis declined, so Taft turned to Butler, whose many years as a railroad lawyer suggested that the Minnesota Catholic would be a logical and reliable counter to Justice Louis D. Brandeis' perceived radicalism. Taft referred to Brandeis and his fellow Justice, Oliver Wendell Holmes, Jr., as a "dangerous twosome," or "Bolsheviki," whom he must prevent from "getting control" of the Court.[27] Still, Taft appreciated Butler's nominal Democratic party label because the Chief thought the Court top heavy with seven Republicans. He also worked to block the nomination of Benjamin Cardozo for fear that the gifted New York jurist would join Brandeis and Holmes to form a radical trio. After Butler's successful appointment, Taft's former Attorney General wrote to the Chief: "I congratulate *you* on the President's selection of Pierce Butler for the existing vacancy in your Court."[28] Taft and Associate Justice Willis Van Devanter had also worked behind the scenes to attract support from the Catholic hierarchy for Butler's nomination. Although the Chief treated a nominee's religion as an irrelevancy, with Chief Justice White's death, and Justice Joseph McKenna's anticipated demise, no Catholics would remain on the Bench.[29] Harding's fourth and last nomination to the Court, Edward Sanford, in 1923, attracted Taft's consent, although Sanford was not his first choice. In 1925, however, the "Big Chief" enthusiastically recommended Attorney General Harlan Stone to Harding's successor, President Calvin Coolidge.[30]

When Justice Holmes stepped off the high Court as he neared his 91st birthday in 1932, his colleague, Justice Harlan Fiske Stone, urged President Herbert Hoover to name New York Court of Appeals Judge Benjamin Cardozo. As Attorney General, Stone had pronounced Cardozo "the outstanding jurist of our times" and unsuccessfully advocated his appointment by Coolidge. Now a Justice himself, Stone, a New Yorker, even offered to resign from the Court in case of objections to Cardozo's becoming its third member from the Empire State.[31] Stone's offer earns the award for most selfless support by a sitting Supreme Court Justice for a nominee. Hoover finally relented to the wide acclaim Cardozo received and nominated him in early 1932. He would serve only a half-dozen years before his premature death, but Cardozo is uniformly considered among the "greats" to have graced the nation's highest Court.

The Cardozo vacancy put Hoover's successor, Franklin D. Roosevelt in a political bind. He wanted to nominate his loyal New Deal lieutenant, Harvard law professor and Justice Brandeis's protégé, Felix Frankfurter. But the western states still were without representation on the Court since the resignation of Californian, Justice Joseph McKenna. Yet FDR thought that Frankfurter, a native of Austria, would be the perfect replacement for Brandeis because of their shared religion. The Jewish seat tradition was in its infancy, but certainly gaining strength, while geographic considerations were beginning to wane as Supreme Court selection criteria.[32] Justice Stone was among a host of Frankfurter supporters lobbying the president on Frankfurter's behalf, telling FDR to ignore the geographic factor and focus on merit alone. President Roosevelt ultimately followed the recommendations, nominating Frankfurter in early 1939. One month later, Frankfurter's mentor, Justice Brandeis, resigned at the age of eighty-three. These two stellar Harvard-trained Justices, who had combined to support a plethora of progressive policies, had, by that time, fallen out over Brandeis' opposition to

FDR's ill-conceived and highly partisan Court-packing scheme. In a personal visit with the president, Brandeis recommended William O. Douglas as his successor. Douglas, in turn, along with Justice Hugo L. Black, another FDR appointee, advocated the president's selection of Wiley Rutledge in 1942.[33]

Roosevelt had packed the Court by attrition, rather than through his aborted plan to add up to six seats on the Bench, but he did make one bi-partisan nomination, in which Justice Frankfurter played a key role. Charles Evans Hughes, the Court's leader through the fractious fight over the New Deal, announced at age eighty that he was stepping down in 1941. FDR wanted to appoint Attorney General Robert H. Jackson. As Roosevelt deliberated, the outgoing Chief and all of the Associate Justices urged him to act with dispatch. He called Hughes to a White House meeting where the Chief declared that "[Justice] Stone's record gave him first claim on the honor."[34] The retiring Chief advocated Stone's promotion in light of his eleven years of outstanding service as an Associate Justice. Roosevelt consulted Justice Frankfurter for one more comparison of the Stone/Jackson candidacies. Frankfurter noted that he preferred the Attorney General because of their close friendship, but the sitting Justice observed the obvious—Stone had seniority and judicial experience in his favor. An official Independent, yet staunch New Dealer, Frankfurter nonetheless asserted that Stone's Republican credentials were an asset. As America's entry into World War II seemed a near certainty in the summer of 1941, Frankfurter advised FDR that a bipartisan pick for Chief Justice would serve both the President and Court well in the turbulent days ahead. FDR advised Jackson that he could inform Stone of his elevation to Chief but promised a future Supreme Court appointment to the disappointed Jackson. Frankfurter had been right: Stone's nomination met with unanimous acclaim.[35]

For his nomination recommendations, both as Chief and as an Associate Justice,

When Chief Justice Charles Evans Hughes (above with his wife, Mary) retired in 1941, he urged President Franklin D. Roosevelt to promote Associate Justice Harlan Fiske Stone in light of his eleven years of outstanding service as an Associate Justice.

Harlan Stone earns another award. Not surprisingly, it is the "Most Bi-partisan Prize." In the three documented illustrations of his suggestions to Presidents, Stone, a Republican, recommended a Democrat (Cardozo) to a Republican (Hoover); an Independent (Frankfurter) to a Democrat (FDR); and a Republican (Senator Harold Burton) to a Democrat (President Harry S. Truman). Though Truman knew all four of his Supreme Court appointees well, Chief Justice Stone added his support for Burton, believing that his senatorial experience would serve the Court well in statutory construction cases.[36] Perhaps the award to Stone should instead be labeled "Most Non-partisan."

Stricken by a fatal cerebral hemorrhage while presiding over oral argument in 1946, Chief Justice Stone was replaced by Truman appointee Fred Vinson. As Chief, Vinson strongly recommended Tom C. Clark, President Truman's Attorney General, to succeed the deceased Frank Murphy in 1949.[37]

Justice Frankfurter continued his appointment influence even as his tenure on the High Court moved toward its conclusion in the early 1960s. The Jewish seat, now a tradition, would be vacant with his departure. President John F. Kennedy told his journalist friend Ben Bradlee that replacing Frankfurter with another Jewish Justice was too "obvious and cute"; nevertheless, JFK did so in

1962, with Arthur Goldberg, when ill health forced Frankfurter off the Court.[38] According to President Kennedy's counsel, Meyer Feldman, JFK had consulted about his choice with both Justice Frankfurter and Chief Justice Earl Warren.[39]

Kennedy's successor, Lyndon Johnson, the former Senate majority leader, always had his own ideas about judicial appointments, but he did look to sitting Justices to *affirm* his choices. LBJ's long-time friend and political ally, Abe Fortas did not want to ascend to the Bench, preferring his lucrative private practice in Washington as well as his continued partisan support for his "dear friend," the President. Johnson, however, twisted the arms of two reluctant men: sending Justice Goldberg to the United Nations as the U.S. ambassador and Fortas to the High Court as Associate Justice. LBJ had enlisted Justices Hugo Black and William Douglas to cajole Fortas.[40] The "Jewish seat," therefore, remained intact.

Chief Justice Earl Warren supported Johnson's unsuccessful attempt to promote Fortas to the center chair after Warren alerted LBJ in 1968 that he wanted to retire. The Chief remained on the Bench until the new Republican President Richard Nixon named Warren Burger to replace him in 1969. In that position, Burger would rival Chief Justice Taft for the label, "most active participant in presidential selection of justices." In fact, during his first months as Chief Justice, Burger received an inquiry from the Nixon administration: Could the President discuss Supreme Court appointments with him? The Chief's pithy response: "Entirely appropriate."[41] After Nixon's first two nominees to replace Fortas, southerners Clement Haynesworth and G. Harold Carswell, were defeated in the Senate, the frustrated President searched for a third nominee who was a northern strict constructionist. On Nixon's original short list was Burger's childhood friend and best man at his wedding, 8th U.S. Circuit Judge Harry Blackman. By all accounts, the Chief eagerly endorsed and advocated his fellow Minnesotan, who would for-

ever refer to himself as "Old Number Three," to indicate that he was Nixon's third choice to replace Fortas in 1970.[42]

Just before the Court began its October 1971 Term, Nixon faced two additional openings when Justices Hugo L. Black and John Marshall Harlan, suffering terminal illnesses, retired in close succession. Chief Justice Burger expressed concern over the Court's diminished membership. Deciding cases with seven Justices, instead of nine, was problematic. The Chief grew especially anxious when he discovered that the administration had submitted the following three names to the ABA for evaluation: Arkansas municipal bond lawyer Herschel Friday, California Court of Appeals judge Mildred Lillie, and Senator Robert Byrd of West Virginia. Although Lillie represented the first serious consideration of a female candidate, Nixon had told Attorney General John Mitchell that women should not serve in government because they were "erratic" and "emotional."[43] "Thank God, we don't have any in the Cabinet!" he exclaimed. "Friday and Lillie fell from obscurity into derision" when the press learned of their consideration.[44] Fearing a repeat of the Haynesworth/Carswell debacle, Chief Justice Burger fired off a "personal and confidential" letter to Attorney General Mitchell, repeating his previous recommendation that distinguished attorney, Lewis F. Powell, Jr., should be the next nominee. The sixty-four-year-old Virginia gentleman had already asked that his name be removed from consideration, first in 1969; and he was no more interested two years later. Even after President Nixon called him directly and told Powell it was his "duty" to accept the nomination, the ever-cautious lawyer said only that he would reconsider the offer. Next, Chief Justice Burger phoned Powell, who wanted to discuss his concerns over financial investments, conflicts of interest with former clients, and insurance benefits for Justices. Powell found the Chief reassuring about all of his doubts and worries. When he announced the possibility of going

Having already asked that his name be removed from consideration for a seat on the Supreme Court in 1969, Lewis F. Powell, Jr. begrudgingly told President Nixon that he would reconsider the offer when a vacancy opened two years later. Chief Justice Warren Burger (seated, third from left) phoned Powell (standing directly behind Burger in this 1981 photo taken with President Reagan), who wanted to discuss his concerns over financial investments, conflicts of interests with former clients, and insurance benefits for Justices.

to the High Court to his law partners in Richmond, Powell felt disappointed that no one expressed regret that he might be leaving! In fact, it occurred to him that they might be relishing the prospect of carving up his lucrative share of the Hunton, Williams, Gay, Powell & Gibson practice. Benjamin Franklin had been right about the Scottish system of judicial appointments. At least it led to the naming of the best lawyers to the Bench. And, indeed, Powell represented the finest qualities of the bar. Still less than certain about leaving his beloved Richmond home and career, and with Mrs. Powell in tears, he called John Mitchell and reluctantly agreed to accept the President's nomination.[45]

Patterns of Court Involvement in Appointments

The Court's Early History

Court involvement in nominations to its Bench is primarily a post-bellum phenomenon. Lit-

tle, if any, evidence points to Justices making successful recommendations to Presidents for appointments to the Court during its first half-century. Why might that be the case? Several facts about the Court's early years arguably played a role. First, Justices in the initial decades of the Court's history were simply closer in time to the birth of the Constitution and its clearly delineated process for judicial appointments, which created no formal role for incumbent judges. Second, the Court's initial rank among the three branches was clearly third. Prior to the Great Chief Justice John Marshall's ascent to the Court in 1801, "it could not, in fact, claim parity with the executive or legislative branch of the federal government in either prestige or power. During the first ten years of the Court's existence, no one, including members of the Court itself, appeared impressed with the authority of the federal judiciary."[46] The very lack of a building to call its own symbolized the Court's status as "the *third* branch." Why would a sitting member of the Court recommend the nomination of a colleague, ally, or friend to an institution that had so little clout, and whose duties included the arduous and understandably despised circuit-riding? Moreover, presiding in their assigned circuits, and living in their home states, took the Justices far afield from the nation's capital, where they might have had the most direct contact with the President. It is probably more than coincidental that the Justices' informal role in nominations increased steadily after their circuit-riding requirements ended in the 1890s. Third, historian Michael Kammen has accurately and eloquently observed that, although Chief Justice Marshall "lacked a temple of justice, his greatest legacy may very well have been a template of justice," consisting of "credible and consensual judgments" that could constitute "a gauge and a guide that successors might use in rendering judgments that achieve legitimacy and endure."[47] Marshall's "template of justice" obviously increased the Court's influence. Yet the Presidents whose tenures Marshall overlapped were of a different political party and ideology than the "Great Chief," and they were not very likely to welcome his advice on Supreme Court nominees. Professor Kent Newmyer has also noted that "the painful lesson driven home by the Chase impeachment [of 1803], was the need for justices to avoid personal involvement in the world of politics."[48] Although the Senate did not convict Justice Chase, his indictment must have distressed federal jurists, particularly Federalists. The Court went out of its way to avoid precipitating political attacks.[49] Plunging into nomination politics may have seemed too risky.

A Brief Statistical Profile

Of the 104 successful appointments to the U.S. Supreme Court, from its establishment to 1974, sitting Justices or Chief Justices, by my count, have had a role in roughly 1/3 (that is, 27). Of those 27 nominations, a little more than 1/3 (10), were supported by Chief Jus-

tices and more than half of those 10 (6) by two Chiefs in particular (Taft and Burger). They gave all but one of their suggested nominees to the respective Presidents who had appointed them to the Court's center chair. Earl Warren, a Republican when he assumed the Chief Justiceship, consulted with two Presidents who had not appointed him (JFK and LBJ) and who were from the opposite party from his appointing President, Republican Dwight D. Eisenhower. Of course, Chief Justice Warren had embraced, much to Ike's dismay, the Democratic party's liberal ideology, which had become his "real politics," as Theodore Roosevelt labeled true political colors.

What would the Founders think of this extra-constitutional record compiled by sitting Justices? Would the Framers conclude that it depicts occasional departures from their 1787 debates over Supreme Court appointments or how they described the process in the post-Convention period? In a way, the recommendation of Supreme Court nominees by incumbent Justices comports with one point that Madison asserted in *Federalist Paper #51*. He focused on the need for federal judges to possess "peculiar qualifications." That is why "the people" could not select them; rather, the executive, with the advice and consent of the Senate, would presumably understand and apply the proper criteria for selecting jurists. Yet wouldn't incumbent Court members know better than anyone which qualities their colleagues should possess? So how do the Justices, recommended by Justices, rank? Three Greats, five Near Greats, twelve Average, two Below Average, and two Failures. The distribution skews to the qualified side of the ledger. In fact, the three Greats supported by sitting Justices constitute one quarter of the twelve total Justices in that highest category. (See attached table.)

Conclusion

Finally, how does such sporadic activity by incumbent Justices in the selection process square with separation of powers? To the extent that it potentially compromises the Court's traditional "priestly" image,[50] which places the tribunal above partisan politics, Justices' involvement in Supreme Court nominations may be a gamble they prefer not to take. The tradeoff for dependence on the other two branches for appointments is judicial independence, a treasured element of the American governmental system. Better to remain aloof from the political process for the sake of judicial autonomy, unless the latter is at stake, as in the 1937 Court-packing fight with FDR. Chief Justice Charles Evans Hughes identified this venerable institution's strength in a simple pronouncement at the laying of the Court's cornerstone in 1932 during the depths of the Great Depression: "The Republic endures, and this is the symbol of its faith." If the Court has indeed helped to preserve the nation, it is the separation of powers principle, with its exquisite corollary of checks and balances, that has preserved the Supreme Court of the United States.

Examples of Incumbent Supreme Court Justices Supporting Nominees to the Court (1853–1974)

Incumbent Justice	Nominee	President	Year	Senate Party Majority
John Catron (D) [Avg] & Benjamin R. Curtis (W) [NG]	John A. Campbell (D) [Avg]	Franklin Pierce (D)	1853	D
Robert C. Grier (D) [Avg]	William Strong (R) [Avg] & Joseph P. Bradley (R) [NG]	Ulysses S. Grant (R)	1870	R
Noah H. Swayne (R) [Avg]	Joseph P. Bradley [NG]	Grant	1870	R
Morrison R. Waite, C.J. (R) [Avg]	William B. Woods (R) [BAvg]	Rutherford B. Hayes (R)	1880	D
Swayne	Stanley Matthews (R) [Avg]	Hayes and James A. Garfield (R)	1881	Tied
Samuel F. Miller (R) [NG]	David Brewer (R) [Avg]	Benjamin Harrison (R)	1889	R
Henry B. Brown (R) [Avg]	Howell E. Jackson (D) [BAvg]	Harrison	1893	R
William H. Taft, C.J. (R) [NG]	George Sutherland (R) [NG]	Warren G. Harding (R)	1922	R
Taft	Pierce Butler (D) [F]	Harding	1922	R
Taft	Edward T. Sanford (R) [Avg]	Harding	1923	R
Harlan F. Stone (R) [G]	Benjamin Cardozo (D) [G]	Herbert Hoover (R)	1932	D
Stone	Felix Frankfurter (I) [G]	Franklin D. Roosevelt (D)	1939	D
Charles E. Hughes (R) [G]	Stone [G]	Roosevelt	1941	D
Stone, C.J.	Harold Burton (R) [F]	Harry Truman (D)	1945	D
Earl Warren, C.J. (R) [G] & Frankfurter (I)	Arthur Goldberg (D) [Avg]	John F. Kennedy (D)	1962	D
Hugo Black (D) [G] and William O. Douglas (D) [NG]	Abe Fortas (D) [NG]	Lyndon Johnson (D)	1965	D

(continued)

Continued

Incumbent Justice	Nominee	President	Year	Senate Party Majority
Earl Warren	Fortas (to C.J, unsuccessful)	Johnson	1968	D
Warren E. Burger, C.J. (R)	Harry Blackmun (R)	Richard Nixon (R)	1970	D
Burger	Lewis F. Powell, Jr. (D)	Nixon	1972	D

Sources: The above list of incumbent Justices who have recommended/supported nominations is based on the narrative history of appointments in Henry J. Abraham's **Justices, Presidents, and Senators: A History of U.S. Supreme Court Appointments from Washington to Bush II**, 5th ed. (Lanham, MD: Rowman & Littlefield, 2008), as well as research compiled in Henry J. Abraham and Bruce Allen Murphy, "The Influence of Sitting and Retired Justices on Presidential Supreme Court Nominations," 3 *Hastings Constitutional Law Quarterly* (Winter 1976). Partisan categories for Justices at their time of appointment may be found in Craig R. Ducat's **Constitutional Interpretation: Rights of the Individual, Vol. II**, (Belmont, CA: Wadsworth/Thomson Learning, 2000), pp. E17-E21: (R) = Republican, (D) = Democrat, (I) = Independent, (W) = Whig. Rankings of Justices may be found in Roy M. Mersky and William David Bader's **The First One Hundred Eight Justices** (Buffalo, NY: William S. Hein & Co., 2004). The authors compiled results from surveys of law school deans and professors of law, history, and political science, who rated Justices' performances on the High Court. The categories provided for ranking were "great" [G], "near great [NG], "average" [Avg], "below average" [BAvg], and "failure" [F]. (Justice Thurgood Marshall was the last to be ranked in the Mersky/Bader survey; thus, Chief Justice Burger and Justices Powell and Blackmun are not rated in the above table.) William A. Degregorio's **The Complete Book of U.S. Presidents**, 4th ed. (New York: Barricade Books, 1993), pp. 729–732, delineates the partisan majorities of the U.S. Senate. My thanks to Sweet Briar College student Cris Gonzalez for providing research assistance. This article is dedicated to Professor Henry J. Abraham, without whom our knowledge of U.S. Supreme Court appointments would be meager indeed.

ENDNOTES

[1] Stephen Zack, "Time for America to Stop Flunking Civics Ed," *ABA Now*, April 29, 2011, http://www.abanow.org/2011/04/time-for-america-to-stop-flunking-civics-ed-op-ed-by-aba-president-stephen-zack/http://www.abanow.org/2011/04/time-for-america-to-stop-flunking-civics-ed-op-ed-by-aba-president-stephen-zack/.

[2] M. J. C. Vile, **Constitutionalism and the Separation of Powers** (Oxford, England: Clarendon Press, 1967), v.

[3] *Id.*, 13.

[4] James Madison, *The Federalist Papers, #51* (New York: Mentor, 1961), 320.

[5] *Id.*, 321.

[6] *Id.*

[7] James Madison, **Notes of Debates in the Federal Convention of 1787** (Athens, Ohio: Ohio University Press, 1966), 67.

[8] Henry J. Abraham, **Justices, Presidents, and Senators: A History of the U.S. Supreme Court Appointments from Washington to Bush II**, 5th ed. (Lanham, MD: Rowman and Littlefield, 2008), 58–59.

[9] Madison, **Notes**, 68.

[10] *Id.*

[11] *Id.*

[12] *Id.*, 314.

[13] *Id.*, 316.

[14] Madison, *Federalist Paper #51*, pp. 321–22.

[15] Madison, *Notes*, pp. 598–99.

[16] Alexander Hamilton, *Federalist Paper #78*, 471.

[17] Abraham, 90.

[18] *Id.*, 90–91.

[19] Henry J. Abraham and Bruce Allen Murphy, "The Influence of Sitting and Retired Justices on Presidential Supreme Court Nominations," 3 *Hastings Constitutional Law Quarterly* 1 (Winter 1976): 40.

[20] Abraham, 102–103.

[21] Abraham and Murphy, 41.

[22] Abraham, 113.

[23] *Id.*, 117–18, 120.

[24] Abraham and Murphy, 41.

[25] Barbara A. Perry, **A "Representative" Supreme Court? The Impact of Race, Religion, and Gender on Appointments** (New York: Greenwood Press, 1991), 28.

[26] Abraham, 148.

[27] *Id.*, 146.

[28] Alpheus T. Mason, **William Howard Taft: Chief Justice** (New York: Simon and Schuster, 1965), 169. Original emphasis.

[29] Perry, 32.

[30] Abraham and Murphy, 45.

[31] Abraham, 153, 160.

[32] Perry, 13–14.

[33] Abraham and Murphy, 47.

[34] Abraham, 182.

[35] *Id.*, 183.

[36] *Id.*, 188–89.

[37] Abraham and Murphy, 48. See Mimi Clark Gronlund's superb biography of her father, **Justice Tom C. Clark: A Life of Service** (Austin: University of Texas Press, 2009).

[38] Perry, 75.

[39] Abraham, 221.

[40] *Id.*, 224.

[41] John C. Jeffries, Jr., **Justice Lewis F. Powell, Jr.** (New York: Scribner's, 1994), 3.

[42] David Alistair Yalof, **Pursuit of Justices** (Chicago: University of Chicago Press, 2001), 113.

[43] Abraham, 245.

[44] Jeffries, 3.

[45] *Id.*, 4–6.

[46] James F. Simon, **What Kind of Nation: Thomas Jefferson, John Marshall, and the Epic Struggle to Create a United States** (New York: Simon and Schuster, 2002), 139.

[47] Michael Kammen, "Temples of Justice: The Iconography of Judgment and American Culture," in **Origins of the Federal Judiciary: Essays on the Judiciary Act of 1789**, ed. Maeva Marcus (New York: Oxford University Press, 1992), 276.

[48] R. Kent Newmyer, **John Marshall and the Heroic Age of the Supreme Court** (Baton Rouge: Louisiana State University Press, 2001), 402.

[49] *Id.*

[50] Barbara A. Perry, **The Priestly Tribe: The Supreme Court's Image in the American Mind** (Westport, CT: Praeger, 1999).

The Judicial Bookshelf

DONALD GRIER STEPHENSON, JR.

Commenting on appointments to the Supreme Court barely two years after her own, Justice Sandra O'Connor observed that someone's selection for the High Bench "is probably a classic example of being the right person in the right spot at the right time. Stated simply, you must be lucky."[1] Nearly three decades later, her comment suggests that luck may indeed take different forms.

For O'Connor, a Republican, it was truly the right time in that a vacancy opened when a Republican occupied the White House. From the outset of the party system in the very late eighteenth and very early nineteenth centuries, appointment of Supreme Court Justices has been party-driven. John Adams looked within his nascent Federalist party when naming Bushrod Washington and John Marshall, as did Thomas Jefferson in selecting William Johnson and Henry Brockholst Livingston from the ranks of Democratic-Republicans. With only occasional exceptions, the practice has persisted. Indeed, the last President to cross party lines was Republican Richard Nixon in his choice of Democrat Lewis F. Powell, Jr., to replace Hugo L. Black in 1971.

O'Connor was also the right person in that she successfully navigated the shoals of Senate confirmation politics. Equally fortuitous, she was in the right place in that O'Connor had followed what has lately become the favored career path. Without judicial experience it seems highly improbable that she would have been chosen. This is because the tendency of most recent Presidents has been overwhelmingly to prefer nominees who are themselves sitting judges or who have had experience as a judge, a practice which seems to discount Justice Felix Frankfurter's unequivocal, if self-approving, assertion over a half-century ago that "the correlation between prior judicial experience and fitness for the Supreme Court is zero."[2]

Soon after Justice Elena Kagan took her seat on the Court in 2010, I shared some data in the form of a table with a group of students and asked for comments about anything that struck them as noteworthy. The table depicted the roster of the Court at that time, the year of appointment of each of the Justices, their current age, the name of the appointing President, and the position held by the Justice at the time of her or his nomination.

As one might imagine, reactions ranged across the board. Several noted the presence of three women. A few commented on the fact that the Court of 2010 was the handiwork of five Presidents. Two thought a few of the Justices seemed very old. Only one student seemed to find it remarkable that every Justice but Elena Kagan reached the High Bench from one of the circuits of the U.S. Court of Appeals. Their assumption, it turned out, was that if you want to pitch and bat at Nationals Park, you must first pitch and bat in the minor leagues. And that assumption seems to have been held by most recent Presidents too. In fact, had I laid out the same table arranged to reflect the Court before Justice Stevens, departure and Justice Kagan's arrival, we would have seen a Bench where *every* Justice stepped to the top from one of the courts of appeals. Moreover, Justice O'Connor's retirement—she had come to the Supreme Court from the Arizona Court of Appeals, the intermediate appellate court within the Arizona state court system—and Justice Samuel Alito's arrival in 2006 created an unprecedented situation: for the first time since the federal courts of appeal were created in 1891, every Justice had seen prior judicial service on one of the federal courts of appeal, most often on the Court of Appeals for the District of Columbia Circuit.

Even the failed nominations of recent decades overwhelmingly involved sitting judges: Judge John Parker, Justice Abe Fortas, Judge Homer Thornberry, Judge Clement Haynsworth, Judge Harrold Carswell, Judge Robert Bork, and Judge Douglas Ginsburg.[3] Among failed nominees since 1930, Harriet Miers remains the only non-judge in the group. Moreover, between Fortas in 1965 and Kagan in 2010, William H. Rehnquist (for Associate Justice), Powell, and Miers are the only nominees without judicial experience.

Yet the Court of 2010, or even the Court of early 2012, is decidedly atypical of many courts of the past, where there are abundant examples of Benches composed heavily or even

largely of individuals who never sat as a judge. For example, consider the Court of 1963 when John F. Kennedy was President and Earl Warren was Chief Justice.

Without question, the career paths of the Justices of 1963 were very different from today's Court. If we discount Hugo Black's brief service as a minor police court magistrate in Birmingham, Alabama, only three of the Justices reached the Court with any judicial experience—one with experience on a state supreme court and two on the federal courts of appeal. Of the remaining six, one was a governor, two were Cabinet department heads, another a Senator, and one the chair of an independent regulatory agency.

What picture emerges from the Bench of nearly a decade earlier—the Bench that decided *Brown* v. *Board of Education*[4] in 1954?

In contrast to the Court of 2012, and more akin to the Court of 1963, the Bench of 1954 was also not populated mainly by former judges. In fact, one finds only one member of the *Brown* Court with any significant judicial experience. Instead we find a Bench staffed by one governor who had also been vice-presidential candidate on his party's ticket in 1948, three United States Senators, one regulatory agency chair, one law school professor, two Attorneys General, and one Solicitor General.

These comparisons display at least two models of judicial selection: the political and the judicial. In turn, they pose the question whether a Bench dominated by Justices chosen under the first model yields a Bench substantially different in its decisions from a Bench chosen under the second. For instance, does one conclude that a Bench staffed heavily by those with broad political experience, as opposed to a mainly judicial background, may be more inclined to adopt a politically progressive posture? That might be tempting to say, especially because the Bench of 1963, like the Bench of 1954, was hardly a bashful group. By 1963, the Court was already knee-deep into the redistricting cases, literally

halfway between *Baker v. Carr*[5] and *Reynolds.
v. Sims*.[6] But we would then have to reconsider
that hypothesis upon examination of the Justices who were sitting in 1937. This was the
Bench whose anti–New Deal decisions in 1935
and 1936 precipitated a constitutional crisis.
Its roster included one special prosecutor and
part-time law professor, two Attorneys General, one federal appeals judge, one state high
court judge, and a Chief Justice who had been
an Associate Justice, a presidential candidate,
and a Secretary of State. But this roster with
broad political experience was hardly on balance a politically progressive group. Or, do
the comparisons suggest that a broader political background might incline a Justice to a
more activist style? Yet even that conclusion
would be risky. Given recent examples, one
would be hesitant to lay claim to the reverse—
that a Bench molded from the judicial model
would usually lean toward restraint. Ironically,
the assumption that judicial experience breeds
restraint was precisely the assumption of those
in the 1950s who were so distressed over Warren Court decisions and accordingly proposed
making such experience a qualification for
Supreme Court service. It was in an attempt to
rebut this criticism that Frankfurter made his
claim about judicial experience and fitness for
the Supreme Court. So the comparisons illustrate different paths to the Supreme Court. Different paths bring different experiences, col-
orations, and perspectives to the Bench but
seem not necessarily to lead to predictable legal and political outcomes or temperaments.
Other factors are surely at work.

To be sure, beginning with George Washington, most Presidents and their closest ad-
visers have taken Supreme Court nominations
very seriously. That recent Presidents have
tended heavily to adhere to the judicial model
in picking nominees is entirely understandable
when one considers two factors. First, at least
since the Warren Court (1953–1969) the Court
has been continuously engaged with politically
salient issues. Second, and as a partial consequence of the first, the Court itself has been an

issue in almost all presidential elections since
1968. As a result, candidates and campaigns
have linked judicial selection with the out-
come of elections. In combination these factors have meant that Presidents—discounting
the boilerplate disclaimer issued by mutual
funds that past performance is no guarantee
of future results—have often viewed appointments as a tool to hasten, reverse, or retard
certain doctrinal trends in the Court's decisions. It thus should come as no surprise that
Presidents today look to those with judicial experience when a vacancy appears. Moreover,
the nature of the contemporary Senate's confirmation hearings strongly argues for selection of judicially experienced nominees. Beginning at least with the failed nomination of
Robert Bork in 1987, hearings have tended
to be lengthy affairs that are intellectually as
well as emotionally challenging and draining.
Nominees are expected to respond to a variety of questions on matters related to constitutional interpretation. One suspects that sitting
judges (or someone such as a Solicitor General who has presented arguments to and has
been questioned by the Justices) would be especially well equipped, by virtue of their experience with federal legal issues, to adroitly
engage in constitutional and statutory dialogue
with members of the Judiciary Committee.
So if it is not particularly difficult to offer
reasons why recent Presidents have preferred
nominees with judicial experience, perhaps the
more interesting question is why earlier Presidents often adhered to a very different nominating model.

Accordingly, one finds that recent books
about the Supreme Court, covering as they
do different periods, depict Justices where the
appointing Presidents adhered to the political or judicial models or some combination
of the two. One such book is **Scorpions**[7] by
Noah Feldman of Harvard Law School. This
insight-rich volume is truly several studies in
one and falls into the must-read category for
anyone interested in the Supreme Court during the middle third of the twentieth century.

Noah Feldman's new book, *Scorpions*, is a jurisprudential examination of four individuals whom Franklin D. Roosevelt named to the High Court: Hugo L. Black, William O. Douglas, Felix Frankfurter, and Robert H. Jackson. Douglas (above) represented judicial realism, while Jackson (below) was a judicial pragmatist.

At one level, it is an overview of the presidency of Franklin D. Roosevelt. At another level, it is a review of major constitutional issues that confronted the Court between 1933, when Roosevelt took office, and 1945, when he died. At a third and surely most important level, it is a jurisprudential examination of four individuals whom Roosevelt named to the High Court: Hugo L. Black, William O. Douglas, Felix Frankfurter, and Robert H. Jackson. These four were not only legacy appointees, with each serving long after the Roosevelt administration ended, but game-changing ones too. Each Justice developed and asserted a distinctive interpretative style and understanding of the Supreme Court's role in American government that in turn has had effects lasting even into the twenty-first century. Finally, at a fourth level, and because of the third, **Scorpions** is partly biographical of this quartet too.[8]

The Roosevelt presidency is the outlying example of the political truism that any President's impact on the Supreme Court is directly related not merely to how long he remains in office—and FDR's twelve years stand as the record—but to how many vacancies open during any particular administration. We know when a Representative's or a Senator's term ends. We know not when the next Supreme Court vacancy will occur or, indeed, whose departure will create that vacancy. The result is judicial tenure that is indeterminate. There is a strong element present of what can only be called randomness.

Thus, it seems highly unlikely that any President will ever surpass George Washington's eleven appointments, only six of which constituted the initial staffing of the institution that, in its infancy, experienced frequent turnover in membership. Similarly, and only because of the Twenty-Second Amendment, it seems highly improbable that any President will ever surpass Roosevelt's record of nine appointments that yielded eight new faces on the Bench.[9] Indeed, of the Roosevelt nine, the pattern shows that the President typically followed the political, not the judicial, model of selection. Overwhelmingly he looked within the administration or within the ranks of elected officials. Only twice did he go to a bench for his Justices: Black[10] arrived from the United States Senate; Stanley F. Reed was Solicitor General when he was named; Felix Frankfurter was a professor at Harvard Law School and represented only the second time in the twentieth century—Warren Harding's selection of Yale Law School's William Howard Taft was the first—that a President plucked a Justice directly from the professoriate; Douglas was chairman of the Securities and Exchange Commission; Frank Murphy, former Detroit mayor and Michigan governor, was Attorney General of the United States; James F. Byrnes, like Black, came from the Senate; Harlan F. Stone had been Associate Justice since 1925; former Solicitor General Jackson was FDR's Attorney General. Not until the nomination of Wiley B. Rutledge, former dean and professor at the State University of Iowa College of Law, did the President resort again to the judicial model when he turned to the Court of Appeals for the District of Columbia Circuit for the person who would prove to be the last addition to the Roosevelt Court.

In light of recent appointment patterns and outcomes, it seems unlikely that any President today, even if handed half as many vacancies over several years, would nominate persons with backgrounds similar to Black, Frankfurter, Douglas, and Jackson's. And, if he did, it's equally unlikely that those choices would be easily confirmed by the Senate, if at all. Consider for example Hugo Black, about whom there were already well-founded rumors about his former membership in the Ku Klux Klan even prior to his confirmation in 1937. Or consider Felix Frankfurter, who, by the time of his nomination in 1939, was practically the poster professor for many left wing American causes and who, as would become widely known only well after the deaths of both Brandeis and Frankfurter, had been on a retainer from sitting Justice Louis Brandeis in order to extend and amplify Brandeis's influence into various realms of policy including Zionism.[11] As Feldman explains, "Both men justified the arrangement on the grounds that Frankfurter would gladly have done what he did for free, that they were almost like family, and that Frankfurter needed the money. As he wrote to Brandeis in 1924, Frankfurter had to pay for the psychoanalysis of his wife Marion, who had suffered her first nervous breakdown."[12] Frankfurter was also a confidant of the President, although the extent of that relationship was not fully grasped at the time. As for Douglas, when he was nominated in 1939, he had already acquired a deserved reputation as a rambunctious regulator. Indeed in a press photograph that Feldman includes as an illustration, the future Justice is seen in his office at the Securities and Exchange Commission wearing a cowboy hat with a six-shooter revolver resting on his desk.[13] Were one to assess Black, Frankfurter, Douglas, and Jackson by contemporary selection standards, perhaps only the highly accomplished, if also partly legally self-taught, Jackson might actually be nominated.[14] In other words, viewed through any present-day lens, the Roosevelt experience should stimulate much thinking on both the opportunities that any President encounters in staffing the Supreme Court as well as the limitations such opportunities impose.

These four Justices, as well as the other Roosevelt appointees, were selected with the same overriding objective: to effectuate and consolidate a political and constitutional revolution. As Feldman's story unfolds, however, it becomes clear that the Roosevelt Justices were hardly drawn from the same mold and, therefore, often did not act in harmony. Hence the title the author chose for his book. For most readers, the very mention of scorpions—those eight-legged venomous Arachnids—conjures up a mental image of ambition, aggressiveness, and conflict. The title derives from a remark often attributed to Justice Oliver Wendell Holmes, Jr. likening the Supreme Court to nine scorpions in a bottle although, as Feldman insists, there is no evidence that Holmes ever made that or any similar statement.[15] Yet, even if Holmes never compared the Court collectively to scorpions cooped up in a bottle, we do know with certainty that Holmes also did not think of the Court as an intellectually cozy repose: "We are very quiet there," he remarked to the Harvard Law School Association of New York in 1913, "but it is the quiet of a storm center."[16]

Other authors have drawn on the same conflict theme or have focused on the Roosevelt era Justices. In fact Max Lerner converted Holmes reputed remark into a title: **Nine Scorpions in a Bottle: Great Justices and Cases of the Supreme Court** (1994). Similarly, one remembers **Battles on the Bench** (1995) by Philip J. Cooper, **New Deal Justice** (1996) by Jeffrey D. Hockett, Melvin I. Urofsky's **Division and Discord: The Supreme Court under Stone and Vinson, 1941–1953** (1997), and James F. Simon's **Antagonists: Hugo Black, Felix Frankfurter, and Civil Liberties in Modern America** (1990). In some respects, therefore, the field seems already well-plowed.

The reader can better appreciate the conflicts that arose among Black, Frankfurter, Douglas, and Jackson by keeping in mind the components of liberalism as they had developed by the time each Justice reached the Court. Political liberalism seized the reins of power in the New Deal, a victory that was secured by the Constitutional Revolution of 1937 and then was consummated by Roosevelt's appointments. The dominant question that remained, however, was, which liberalism? Liberalism was hardly monolithic.

At the time, the strand of modern liberalism with the longest pedigree was *economic liberalism*. Inspired by the Progressive movement of the very early twentieth century, economic liberalism stressed workplace reforms, a social safety net, rights of labor, and measures generally designed to reduce sharp income disparities. In many ways economic liberalism typified the legislative heart of the New Deal. Moreover, by its very nature, economic liberalism depended upon the power of popular majorities in state legislatures and in Congress for its implementation. Some of economic liberalism's policies, however, met stiff headwinds in the courts, at least before 1937. This judicial opposition in turn gave rise to a second component that might be called *constitutional liberalism*. Indeed, constitutional liberalism was necessitated by economic liberalism. To insulate or to preserve the fruits of economic liberalism from judicial attack, an intellectual defense was needed. Finding judicial power practically an embarrassment to democratic government, constitutional liberalism therefore advocated a passive role for the judiciary, which in its proper role would defer to legislative policies designed to implement economic liberalism. Constitutional liberalism, therefore, was not so much policy-centered as it was role-centered in that adherence by judges to this restrictive role fostered desirable public policy. That is, constitutional liberalism appealed to liberals and was a handmaiden to economic liberalism because faithfulness to the former increased the probability that reform measures, having been enshrined by the majority into law, would in turn be sustained by the courts. Feldman explains that liberalism in this form became the doctrine of judicial restraint that remains so closely identified with Felix Frankfurter. It was his "most important intellectual accomplishment during his years as a professor. Indeed it would shape Frankfurter's entire career."[17]

Frankfurter accomplished this by drawing first on the restraint-oriented writing of James Bradley Thayer of Harvard Law School, who had died shortly before Frankfurter enrolled there as a student. For Thayer, judges were on solid ground in striking down legislation only if the law embodied a clear transgression of the Constitution.[18] "From Frankfurter's perspective," writes Feldman in **Scorpions**, "one of the greatest advantages of Thayer's essay was almost no one else had ever read it."[19] Frank-

furter then coupled Thayer's message with views articulated by Justice Oliver Wendell Holmes in dissents in cases such as *Lochner v. New York*[20] and transformed Holmes into a saint of judicial restraint.

> Holmes, a believer in minimal government who thought little of the progressive laws he voted unsuccessfully to uphold, did embody this ideal. But Holmes favored restraint less because he thought it was the judge's proper role than because he thought it was generally pointless to stand in the way of rising classes or social movements. Brandeis, by contrast, voted to uphold progressive laws because he believed in the improved working conditions and increased wages that the laws promised.

Frankfurter thus joined the "diverse trinity" of Brandeis, Holmes, and Thayer into a "single godhead of judicial restraint."[21]

Contemporaneously, many liberals preferred not just the policy outcomes of economic liberalism but had long favored civil liberties such as free speech and expanded safeguards for persons accused of crimes, as well as civil rights to promote racial equality and a broader franchise. These goals that might be promoted by judges constituted liberalism's third strand: *programmatic liberalism*. Advocates of those aims found themselves in a bind, however. Restrictions on civil liberties and civil rights that liberals abhorred usually were the product of local or state law–making bodies that were themselves reflecting majority sentiment or at least the indifference of a majority. In such situations, constitutional liberalism— calling as it did for deference to decisions made by popular majorities—therefore tended to yield policy outcomes that were unacceptable to programmatic liberals.

If Frankfurter's judicial outlook reflected the approaches of Thayer and Holmes, Douglas began at a very different point and so ventured down a very different road. Douglas's law school years, both as student and teacher, had saturated him with legal realism, which posited "judges inevitably make law in their own image."[22] By this view, it was foolish for a judge to defer to legislators who were themselves making policy choices because judges routinely were doing the same thing when they decided cases. Engaging in a bit of law-scholar psychoanalysis, Feldman explains that after 1948 Douglas's jurisprudential leanings began to reveal themselves once "a presidential future was no longer a realistic possibility."[23] Rather than following public opinion with an eye to a ballot box in the future, as Feldman suggests he did in the Japanese-American internment cases,[24] Douglas would no longer compromise political principle for political gain. The result in the late 1940s was the adoption "of a unifying constitutional goal: the pursuit of individual freedom."[25] Accordingly, the Constitution "should be interpreted to give each person the greatest room possible to shape his or her life autonomously, without the intervention of the government." For Douglas, the Constitution properly understood "was a blueprint for personal liberty."[26] Feldman finds that, in virtually every opinion Douglas wrote after 1948, he "sought to give individuals the maximum degree of personal freedom relative to the government." From then until he retired in 1975, "Douglas steadily expanded the boundaries of constitutional rights in the crucial areas of free speech, privacy, and reproductive and sexual freedom."[27] For Douglas, therefore, the judge's task was decidedly rights-centered: the expansion of constitutional protections for the individual. Moreover, he had ample time in which to achieve that objective. His record-setting tenure of thirty-six years, beginning when he was confirmed at age forty, "is likely to stand even in this era of increasing life expectancy, because it is correspondingly difficult to get appointed to the Supreme Court so young."[28]

In a Supreme Court career that rivaled Douglas's in length and impact, Hugo L. Black, Roosevelt's first Supreme Court appointee, defined the art of judging in constitutional cases very differently: The text of the Constitution meant what it was originally intended to mean. Black, of course, was not the first Justice to work this idea into opinions. One recalls, for example, Chief Justice Roger Taney's reliance on it in the *Dred Scott* case: The Constitution, he wrote, "must be construed now as it was understood at the time of its adoption." He continues:

> It is not only the same in words, but the same in meaning, and delegates the same powers to the Government, and reserves and secures the same rights and privileges to the citizen; and as long as it continues to exist in its present form, it speaks not only in the same words, but with the same meaning and intent with which it spoke when it came from the hands of its framers, and was voted on and adopted by the people of the United States. Any other rule of construction would abrogate the judicial character of this court, and make it the mere reflex of the popular opinion or passion of the day.[29]

If less bluntly, Justice George Sutherland made a similar point in a dissent he wrote only a year before Black joined the Bench in *West Coast Hotel v. Parrish*:

> [T]he meaning of the Constitution does not change with the ebb and flow of economic events. We frequently are told in more general words that the Constitution must be construed in the light of the present. If by that it is meant that the Constitution is made up of living words that apply to every new condition which they include, the statement is quite true. But to say, if that be intended, that the words of the Constitution mean today what they did not mean when written—that is, that they do not apply to a situation now to which they

would have applied then—is to rob that instrument of the essential element which continues it in force as the people have made it until they, and not their official agents, have made it otherwise.[30]

Eventually known as originalism, this interpretative approach insists that the meaning of the Constitution "should be found by looking at the text of the Constitution as it would have been publicly understood when written," writes Feldman. "Black was the first justice to frame originalism as a definitive constitutional theory and to explain why and how he was using it. In this sense Black was the inventor of originalism."[31] In fact, the author reminds the reader that Black's very first independently authored dissent contained the seeds of what would become the Justice's "immensely influential theory of constitutional law."[32] It also revealed a Justice willing to push against the weight of precedent. The occasion of this first dissent was the Court's ruling in the otherwise obscure tax case of *Connecticut General Life Insurance Co. v. Johnson*,[33] where Black insisted that a precedent[34] from 1886 had been wrongly decided. "I do not believe the word 'person' in the Fourteenth Amendment includes corporations . . . .," he declared. "Neither the history nor the language of the Fourteenth Amendment justifies the belief that corporations are included within its protection."[35] Black's originalism was thus compatible with his overall outlook on judging because, for this critic of the Court's pre-1937 activism, originalism seemingly, if deceptively, obscured the judicial discretion that had been so prominent on the "old Court" by shifting the judge to the background and thrusting intent to center stage, all the while leaving the way open for decisions consistent with Black's brand of programmatic liberalism.

Certainly unlike Douglas and diverging from Black as well, Robert H. Jackson believed that the Court's principal task was not to impose its own values but to mediate among competing interests with the goal of achieving an acceptable and workable balance. Moreover, Jackson's tenure on the High Court (1941–1954) was considerably shorter than either Douglas's (1939–1975) or Black's (1937–1971), so Feldman's conclusions about Jackson's views are drawn from a smaller number of opinions. Chiefly, the author finds Jackson most clearly revealed in **The Struggle for Judicial Supremacy**[36] which was the culmination of a four-year self-education and writing project that Jackson undertook while a member of the Roosevelt administration's Justice Department[37] with the objective of offering a historical justification of the Court-packing plan of 1937 "as well as a detailed accounting of why it had ultimately been a success."[38] Feldman believes that the book was "a mark both of the importance of the Court-packing plan to Roosevelt's perception of his own legacy, and also of the personal stake that Jackson took in the plan that had brought him into Roosevelt's inner circle. In fact, it is difficult to think of a comparably significant and sophisticated book ever written by a senior administration official while in office."[39] Far from seeing the book as a simple political manifesto, Feldman sees it as a defense of the judiciary's proper role. "[I]t was through the very act of judging pragmatically and explaining openly what he was doing that he ended up being recognized many years after his death as one of the great justices, probably the most influential for our current era."[40] Collectively, what Feldman sees as the greatness of Black, Douglas, Frankfurter, and Jackson "came to pass precisely because he went his own way, each developing a constitutional vision distinctive to his own personality and worldview."[41] Their tenures overlapped for 13 years, and during that time and amid a host of conflicts the judicial outlook of each was honed on the strongly held and asserted views of the others.

In contrast to President Franklin Roosevelt, President William Howard Taft followed mainly the judicial model for his appointments to the Supreme Court. Taft, who is the only president also to be Chief Justice as well as the only president to have sat as a judge on a lower federal court,[42] has now been the subject of two books within three years that focus mainly on his presidency. The first was **The William Howard Taft Presidency** by Lewis L. Gould (2009), and the more recent volume is **William Howard Taft**[43] by Jonathan Lurie, emeritus professor of history at the Newark campus of Rutgers University who, with Ronald Labbé, co-authored a prize-winning volume in 2003 on the *Slaughterhouse Cases*.[44]

For students of the presidency Taft is routinely not counted among the great occupants of the White House. Some in fact see him as a one-term loser. In contrast to his impressive victory in 1908 when he won thirty states and received two thirds of the electoral vote,[45] he endured a stunning defeat when he ran for a second term in 1912, carrying only the states of Utah and Vermont and finishing third in the popular vote, behind the Progressive or Bull Moose candidacy of Roosevelt and the Democratic ticket headed by Woodrow Wilson. Alongside whatever deficit he may have had in leadership and visionary qualities, the twenty-seventh Chief Executive had the misfortune for his one-term administration to be wedged between the eight years of Theodore Roosevelt and the eight years of Woodrow Wilson. Taft's four years "seem frozen in time on one side by the dynamism of TR, hunting, fighting, expounding, and exploring, and on the other side by the eloquence and moral imperatives (sometimes accompanied by leadership) of Wilson. In between them is . . . Taft."[46] The result is an administration that has "invariably been dismissed as the stale filling separating two fresh and energetic chief executives."[47] Moreover, because perceptions in turn have a way of driving research, interest in Roosevelt and Wilson has eclipsed that in Taft with those two remaining the subjects of a vast and ongoing body of scholarship. Yet Lurie believes that "when one explores and

evaluates Taft's career on its own, eschewing comparisons at least to some extent, a different picture emerges. If ever a historical portrait needed a variety of colors, shading, and conclusions to give it relevance, it would be one of William Howard Taft."[48]

The thesis of Lurie's portrayal of Taft as President is found in the subtitle of his book: "Progressive Conservative," a self-descriptive phrase Taft used in a letter he wrote in 1913 decrying Wilson's nomination of Louis D. Brandeis to the Supreme Court. Challenging the commonly held impression of Taft as a "hide-bound traditionalist,"[49] Lurie believes the characterization Taft applied to himself stands on balance as an accurate summation of his presidency if not for his nine years as Chief Justice (1921–1930). The question would then be whether this self-appraisal has any validity for Taft's selections for the High Bench.

Students of the Court have of course long been interested in *Chief Justice* Taft. Certainly his judicial legacy consists at the very least of two significant and lasting accomplishments: first, his energies in shaping and encouraging passage of the Judges' Bill of 1925, which greatly expanded the Court's certiorari or discretionary review authority over its appellate jurisdiction into something similar to what the Justices enjoy today, and second, helping to secure passage of the congressional appropriation for, and overseeing the planning for the Supreme Court Building (even though the actual cornerstone laying for the new structure fell to his successor Chief Justice Charles Evans Hughes in 1932, after Taft's death in 1930). But students of the Court have excellent reason as well to take account of *President* Taft. This is because Taft as President left a substantial Supreme Court legacy, one that derived almost wholly from his judicial appointments. During his solitary term, unfolding events allowed Taft to make a total of six appointments to the Supreme Bench. This number includes the naming of five Associate Justices and elevating a sitting Associate Justice to the Chief Justiceship. By the

Jonathan Lurie's new biography of Taft (pictured at the White House with his children) is subtitled: "Progressive Conservative," a self-descriptive phrase Taft used in a letter he wrote in 1913 decrying President Woodrow Wilson's nomination of Louis D. Brandeis to the Supreme Court. Challenging the commonly held impression of Taft as a "hide-bound traditionalist," Lurie believes the characterization Taft applied to himself stands on balance as an accurate summation of his presidency if not for his nine years as Chief Justice.

record of any other presidency, this is truly a remarkable tally. To date, except for Washington and Franklin D. Roosevelt, only Presidents Andrew Jackson, Abraham Lincoln, and Dwight Eisenhower also placed as many as five new faces on the Supreme Bench. Moreover, as Lurie's book makes clear, Taft hardly adopted a hands-off approach to judicial selection. Whether for the lower federal bench or the Supreme Court, the President acted as a kind of one-man search committee who sought out judges compatible with his views. (Moreover, as testament to the maxim that old habits die hard, it is widely known that Taft behaved similarly after he became Chief Justice in trying to

influence judicial appointments.)[50] Indeed, an affinity for the judicial process seemed to be in his blood. "I love judges, and I love courts," he said in 1911. "They are my ideals, that typify on earth what we shall meet hereafter in heaven under a just God."[51]

Taft's first opportunity to make a Supreme Court nomination occurred upon the death of Justice Rufus Peckham in the fall of 1909. The President immediately looked to an old friend, Horace H. Lurton, with whom Taft had served on the Sixth Circuit Court of Appeals. The drawback with Lurton, however, was that he was nearly sixty-six years old. Taft was torn because he preferred nominees no older than their mid-fifties on the expectation that they would be able to serve for at least a decade. The President's quandary demonstrated that where there is a will there can be a rationalization, so Taft convinced himself that Lurton's experience compensated for his age and so justified the nomination. Besides, as a Tennessee Democrat (and Confederate veteran) Lurton might aid Taft in his objective of strengthening the Republican party in the South as a sufferable alternative for Democrats for whom a vote for the Grand Old Party was still an act of sectional betrayal.

The death of Justice David J. Brewer in March 1910 opened the way for a replacement in the form of New York's progressive-minded governor, Charles Evans Hughes. Not only was Hughes widely regarded as an outstanding choice, but his selection would remove a potential rival for 1912 should Taft choose to run for a second term. The implied understanding with the nominee was that the Court's center chair would be his should it become vacant. And vacant it became upon Chief Justice Fuller's death in July. Moreover, Taft soon found that he actually had two vacancies to fill because of Justice William H. Moody's resignation in November. Yet, it was the replacement for Fuller that caused Taft real consternation.

While Mrs. Taft had been thoroughly content with Taft as President, it was the Chief Justiceship that had long been her husband's goal. "If the Chief Justice [Fuller] would only retire," Taft said before his election in 1908, "how simple everything would become."[52] Even after becoming ensconced in the White House, Taft was uncomfortable. "If I were now presiding in the Supreme Court of the United States as chief justice," he confided to a friend, "I should feel entirely at home,

Although Horace H. Lurton was considerably older than Taft thought a Supreme Court appointee should be, the President convinced himself that Lurton's experience compensated for his age. Besides, as a Tennessee Democrat (and Confederate veteran) Taft hoped Lurton might aid in his objective of strengthening the Republican party in the South.

but ... I feel just like a fish out of water." Then, while pondering Fuller's successor, he sadly acknowledged, "that the one place in the government which I would like to fill myself I am forced to give to another."[53] Furthermore, handing that nomination to Hughes, who was forty-eight, would be doubly painful in that, Taft might have reasoned, it would likely have foreclosed any possibility for Taft, who was then fifty-three, ever to be named Chief Justice as a successor to Hughes.[54] Thus, alongside other considerations Hughes's anticipated longevity made Associate Justice Edward Douglass White, who was sixty-five, an especially appealing prospect and the logical pick. With the Louisianan, Taft "might yet have an opportunity to take his place, given the vicissitudes of time."[55] More charitably, one could add that, like Lurton, White was a Democrat and a Confederate veteran, and so fit with the President's southern strategy. White was also conveniently Roman Catholic. Nominating a Catholic Democrat from the South would be consistent with the Midwestern Unitarian Republican President's "profound distaste for bigotry."[56] Adding to the decisional mix was the visit from a delegation of Senators from the Judiciary Committee reminding the President that Hughes had never appeared before the Court and had been a Justice for barely two months. When Taft asked his Attorney General to poll the Court, the clear preference for a new Chief was White.[57] Still, replacing Fuller must have been an excruciatingly painful decision for the President to make, especially given the implied understanding with Hughes. Indeed, Taft took five months finally to make up his mind, in contrast to his first two nominations, which emerged fairly promptly. Along the way the President looked seriously at Elihu Root for whom he had "genuine affection" as well as great admiration for his legal skills.[58] He ruled out Root, however, because he had just turned sixty-five. Similarly, even though Justice John Marshall Harlan, with thirty-three years of service, had been campaigning for the position, Taft dropped the Kentuckian from considera-

tion because he was even older than Root. As it was, the nomination of White was a bold move in that it marked the first time that a sitting Associate Justice had been elevated to the center chair.

For White's seat, Taft turned to U.S. appeals judge Willis Van Devanter, age fifty-one, of Wyoming. Moody's seat went to former Georgia Supreme Court justice Joseph R. Lamar who was then in private practice in Augusta. Taft had played golf with Lamar and had visited with the former judge and his wife during a national tour in 1909, contacts that must have left a favorable impression with the President. Justice John Marshall Harlan's death in late 1911 allowed the President his final Supreme Court nomination, which he extended to Judge Mahon Pitney, age fifty-four, who was chancellor of the New Jersey courts.

In Lurie's view, what was Taft's impact on the Court? Taft's selections for the Court seem to embody with "some validity"[59] the President's description of himself as a progressive conservative, the author concludes. "Party labels were not important for him, as seen in that half of his choices were Democrats .... All were able lawyers, well established in their field, and at least two—Hughes and Pitney—can be placed within the progressive purview."[60] Moreover, as matters developed, Van Devanter probably best served Taft's goal of longevity, sitting for twenty-six years and well into the New Deal era. Indeed, the retirement of this intellectual leader of the conservative bloc in 1937 would present President Franklin Roosevelt his first opportunity to send someone to the Supreme Court. Hughes truly had the presidential aspirations that Taft suspected and resigned from the Court to run against Wilson in 1916, only to be returned to the Court by Republican Herbert Hoover as Taft's successor in 1930.

Roughly two decades separated the beginning of Taft's presidency from the end of the Waite Court. **The Supreme Court under Morrison R. Waite, 1874–1888** is the latest volume to be published in a valuable series on Supreme Court history being published by the University of South Carolina Press: "The Chief Justiceships of the Supreme Court," under the general editorship of Herbert A. Johnson, who is emeritus professor at the University of South Carolina School of Law. Inspired by the scholarly convention that emerged in the first third of the twentieth century as it became commonplace to think and write about the development of the Third Branch and American constitutional law in terms of periods bearing the name of the incumbent Chief Justice, the series already includes books on the Court before Marshall,[61] the Marshall Court,[62] the Fuller Court,[63] the White Court,[64] the Hughes Court,[65] the Vinson-Stone years,[66] the Warren Court,[67] and the Burger Court.[68] This new entry on the Waite era[69] is authored by Paul Kens, who teaches political science and history at Texas State University–San Marcos. Well researched, comprehensive, and engagingly written, Kens's contribution lives up to expectations generated by its series predecessors. Not surprisingly, the author, who has already written a book on *Lochner v. New York*[70] as well as a biography of Justice Stephen J. Field, seems as comfortable with the literature of political science as with history.

It may not be too much of an exaggeration to suggest that the Waite years, although embracing one of the less familiar judicial periods, were as much as any others truly a time when politics, law, and statecraft intersected in the Supreme Court. Those years began in the wake of the Civil War, and ended as the United States was on the eve of becoming a world economic and military power. As Herbert Johnson writes in the series editor's Preface, Waite's Court was a time when "tendencies provided a key to the current work of the justices, [and] . . . pointed to future developments as yet but also little understood."[71]

During the fourteen years that Morrison Waite occupied the center chair, fifteen Justices, counting Waite himself, served on the Bench. Moreover, they were the choices

of seven Presidents, beginning with James Buchanan (who appointed Nathan Clifford) and extending through Grover Cleveland (who appointed L. Q. C. Lamar). Of the fifteen Waite Justices, nine arrived on the Court with at least some judicial experience, including Stephen Field and Ward Hunt, who had served on the high courts of California and New York, respectively. Two (Lamar and Matthews) had served in the U.S. Senate, and Lamar had been in the Cabinet. Clifford had been minister to Mexico, while others had been United States attorneys or served in their respective state legislatures and/or in local government.

Waite stood out from his colleagues for three particular reasons. Not only was he one of the six Waite Court members with no judicial experience as well as the first Chief Justice since Marshall to have had no experience as a member of the Cabinet, but he was also the last Chief Justice to be sworn in as "Chief Justice of the Supreme Court."[72] Moreover, aside from service in the Ohio legislature, Waite's principal public experience and sole national exposure prior to his nomination was as a member of the American delegation that settled the Alabama claims against Great Britain after the Civil War. Overall, therefore, the pattern of selection by the seven Presidents who made the Waite Court thus combined the political and judicial models, with a modest edge going to the latter.

Viewed in the long sweep of Supreme Court and constitutional development, the Waite period appears transitional[73] between what might be called the "classical Court" (that characterized the pre-Marshall, Marshall, and Taney Courts and persisted until soon after the end of the Civil War) and what can be termed the "modern Court" (that began to take shape in the years following 1865). The era of the classical Court was marked by (1) an exceedingly limited federal jurisdiction, (2) a structure that made the Bench mainly a court of errors, not a court of policy, and (3) onerous circuit-riding duties. In contrast, the era of the modern Court that began near the close of the Chief Justiceship of Salmon P. Chase (1864–1873) has been marked by (1) a vastly expanded federal jurisdiction, (2) an increase in cases involving individual rights, and (3) a structure that has allowed the Court to become a court of policy for the nation. Viewed alongside these developments, the Waite Court can be seen as part classical and part modern.

Organizationally, the Waite Court had far more in common with the Marshall Court (1801–1835) than with the Fuller Court (1888–1910) that succeeded it. To be sure, Waite era Justices had to do somewhat less circuit riding than their predecessors, but the country was also larger. At least Waite and his colleagues could travel by rail from state to state, in Pullman palace cars no less, instead of on horseback or by stage coach and canal or river boat. But the fact remained that the Supreme Court in Waite's day possessed virtually no control over its docket. The notion of *meriting* Supreme Court review was under discussion, but its realization lay well in the future.

Jurisdictionally, however, the Waite Court had more in common with the Fuller and later Courts than with any Court that preceded it. In this sense, the Waite Court is practically a window into the Court of the twentieth and twenty-first centuries. Looming over everything were the Reconstruction amendments, especially the Fourteenth that, with their implementing statutes, vastly expanded the kinds of cases the Supreme Court might hear. Surely not one of the subsequent twelve amendments to the Constitution, from the Sixteenth through the Twenty-seventh, has so affected the business of federal courts. Moreover, given the nature of those amendments, cases arising under them typically involved a claim by an individual or a business enterprise that constitutional rights had been violated. And in Waite's day, there were not only more people, but more laws that affected those rights. Moreover, the Waite docket had its share of juror and voting rights cases that went to the heart of the

question regarding those whom the Constitution had admitted to the political community— those to be counted among "We the People . . . ." Thus, in the Waite Court, one finds the earliest signs of a "rights culture" developing, or at least being discussed, in which, as energized much later by Justices such as William O. Douglas, Americans would learn routinely to look to the judiciary to both vindicate and sustain their liberties under the federal Constitution.

As Kens demonstrates, an irony of the Waite era, already foreshowed in the timidity of the Chase Court's decision in the *Slaughterhouse Cases*, was a profound judicial reluctance to recognize that the Reconstruction Amendments had altered the constitutional landscape very much at all. Thus, if the Waite Court was transitional, as many scholars believe it to have been, it is also traditional. Americans today are conditioned by experience to view the Supreme Court or to admire or to criticize the Court "as an instrument for bringing about social change," Kens writes. "One of the lessons learned from tracing the history of the Waite Court comes in the form of a reminder that the judiciary often functions not as an architect of change but rather as the keeper of tradition. The Waite Court was traditional, not so much in the sense that it supported the establishment but in the sense that it tended to look backward for its cues and tended to follow the path that had already been laid."[74] Accordingly, if there are glimpses, especially in some of the Waite Court dissents, of the Court's later rights-oriented role, there is also a strong presence of judicial restraint that was later picked up by Thayer and by Justices Holmes and Frankfurter. The Waite Court's resistance to expanding judicial authority derived from a principled belief held by Waite and several of his colleagues, "that the judiciary played an important but limited role in American democracy."[75]

This theme of restraint that emphasized popular sovereignty and a presumption that legislative enactments were compatible with the Constitution rested on another presumption—much later articulated in prominent dissents by Justice Frankfurter—that "popularly elected legislatures could be every bit as much a guardian of individual liberty and rights of the community as the courts."[76] Perhaps this is why relatively few of the Waite Court decisions are routinely read and studied today by students of American constitutional development. Even the restraint-driven and pro-regulatory decision in *Munn v. Illinois*[77] that sustained a state's authority to set rates of charge for property "affected with a public interest"[78] is usually studied mainly in the context of the departure from that principle during the heyday of judicial activism in defense of property rights in pre-1937 cases such as *Lochner v. New York*.[79] Similarly, decisions illustrating the Waite Court's reluctance to sustain a strong federal presence in protecting individuals against racial discrimination have largely been dropped from the teaching canon.[80]

The common thread in the Waite era's jurisprudence, Kens believes, "was driven by more than simple deference to the legislative branch"[81] even though the Bench's reaction to Congressional civil rights legislation often indicated otherwise. Rather than thinking of the Waite Court as characterized by a particular doctrine or theory regarding the role of judges, Kens finds it more fruitful to think of the Waite era in terms of a series of at least five tendencies, all linked to the idea of tradition. Viewed in this way, a majority of the Court during the Waite years tended first to "idealize the balance of federalism that existed before the Civil War"; second, "to interpret the law in a formalistic way"; third, "it hesitated to agree that the Reconstruction Amendments had created new rights"; fourth, "it was committed to the ideal of popular sovereignty"; and fifth, "it was attached to a theory of property that recognized the rights of the community. For the author, these tendencies reveal that, for better

or for worse, the Waite Court viewed its role as the keeper of tradition."[82]

Chief Justice Waite occupies a suitable place in **Courtwatchers**,[83] a gem of a volume compiled, edited, and annotated by Clare Cushman, who is the director of publications for the Supreme Court Historical Society. Her book is a unique collection of first-hand accounts of the Supreme Court and its work by Justices, journalists, oral advocates, spouses, offspring, clerks, and others stretching across roughly two centuries. Careful documentation demonstrates the depth and breadth of Cushman's research, the fruits of which are made all the more accessible by an index fittingly tailored to magnify the usefulness of all that she has knit together. As Chief Justice John G. Roberts, Jr., writes in the Foreword, **Courtwatchers** "provides what a good anecdote conveys—the sense of personality. Ms. Cushman has organized her book around topics that capture the human element of the jurists. . . . She explores both the process of becoming a judge—including appointment, confirmation, and 'learning the ropes,'—and the poignant process of stepping down from the Court. But she also sets aside the black robes and delves into the private side of life on the Court, capturing vignettes of relations among friends, family and one another."[84]

Cushman herself explains that she selected the many anecdotes for their educational or entertainment value, but cautions the reader to proceed with an obvious caveat. "Although firsthand accounts may seem to represent the historical truth because they were recorded by an observer on the spot, eyewitnesses almost always have self-serving motives, if unwittingly. In this regard, skepticism is advised. . . . Memory is tricky. Sometimes eyewitnesses just plain get their facts wrong." Another warning follows from the organization of the book. Each chapter examines elements of one thematic topic at different periods of the Court's history. "This enables one to compare, for example, how the Justices viewed their salaries or their workload at different junctures. But the norms of the Supreme Court—the institutional values and ways of conducting business—have of course evolved enormously over time (and from chamber to chamber). While historical context is usually supplied, sometime it necessarily takes a backseat to the narrative." That means that experiences that might seem similar across time "may in fact be very different given societal and cultural norms both inside and outside the Court at the time."[85]

One especially revealing passage that Cushman includes is taken from a letter Chief Justice Waite wrote to his wife Amelia after his first meeting with his new colleagues in 1874. Waite was President Grant's seventh choice for the position, and some of the Justices (more than one of whom had coveted the position that was handed to Waite) were understandably skeptical about the credentials of

In Paul Kens's new book on the Court of Chief Justice Morrison R. Waite (above), the author demonstrates that an irony of the Waite era, already foreshowed in the timidity of the Chase Court's decision in the *Slaughterhouse Cases,* was a profound judicial reluctance to recognize that the Reconstruction Amendments had altered the constitutional landscape.

this obscure lawyer from Ohio who was joining their ranks. They were surely aware of Senator Hannibal Hamlin's comment, in a last-minute attempt to forestall the nomination, that the new Chief possessed "every requisite but repute."[86] Except for the length, the excerpt is somewhat reminiscent of a college freshman's first email or phone message home after having gone through "pledge week" or met with "the Dean" the first time and survived.

> Saturday I went through my severest ordeal. It was to meet the Judges in consultation for the first time and when as a matter of course severest criticism would be in order. I got through with it very successfully I think. At any rate there was nothing to cause any uneasiness or discomfort on my part. It was a pretty easy time and my nerves were cool as it is possible to be for a wonder, and so it has been all the time since I have been here. I have been perfectly self-possessed and have made very few mistakes . . . . I cant [sic] write about my sensations as to the gown or otherwise. I will tell you at some time. They were strange sometimes, but yet I seem to take to them naturally.[87]

Even more notable for what is revealed are comments made by Lincoln appointee Samuel Miller in 1862 about meeting Chief Justice Roger B. Taney, an appointee of Andrew Jackson, for the first time.

> When I came to Washington, I had never looked on the face of Judge Taney, but I knew of him. I remembered that he had attempted to throttle the Bank of the United States, and I hated him for it. I remembered that he took his seat on the Bench, as I believed, in reward for what he had done in that connection, and I hated him for that. He had been the chief Spokesman of the Court in the Dred Scott case, and I hated him for that.

But from my first acquaintance with him, I realized that these feelings toward him were but the suggestions of the worst elements of our nature, for before the first term of my service in the Court had passed, I more than liked him; I loved him. And after all that has been said of this great, good man, I stand always ready to say that conscience was his guide and sense of duty his principle.[88]

Cushman's **Courtwatchers** brings together the new and the familiar, and sometimes the surprising. What she has compiled reflects a total of ninety-four Justices chosen by thirty-four Presidents who followed different appointment models. Yet the richness of **Courtwatchers** is made possible not only by her labors, but by the simple fact that so many individuals over so many years recorded their observations and impressions through various media and in ways that have allowed those statements to survive across the decades. In an age of text messaging, social media, and email, where letter-writing and diary-keeping have become lost arts, and where so much communication is, practically speaking, ephemeral, one wonders how a similar collection a half century or more hence might be compiled concerning the Court, its members, and its processes of today.

THE BOOKS SURVED IN THIS ARTICLE ARE LISTED ALPHABETICALLY BY AUTHOR BELOW

CUSHMAN, CLARE. **Courtwatchers: Eyewitness Accounts in Supreme Court History.** (Lanham, MD: Rowman & Littlefield, 2011). Pp. xiv, 312. ISBN: 978-1-4422-1245-9, cloth.

FELDMAN, NOAH. **Scorpions: The Battles and Triumphs of FDR's Great Supreme Court Justices.** (New York: Twelve (Hachette Book Group), 2010). Pp. xii, 513. ISBN: 978-0-446-58057-1, cloth.

KENS, PAUL. **The Supreme Court under Morrison R. Waite, 1874-1888.** (Columbia, SC: University of South Carolina Press, 2010). Pp. xvi, 219. ISBN: 978-1-57003-918-8, cloth.

LURIE, JONATHAN. **William Howard Taft: The Travails of a Progressive Conservative.** (New York: Cambridge University Press, 2012). Pp. xv, 214. ISBN: 978-0-521-51421-7, cloth.

ENDNOTES

[1] Quoted in Henry J. Abraham, **Justices, Presidents, and Senators** (1999), 3.

[2] Felix Frankfurter, "The Supreme Court in the Mirror of Justices," 105 *University of Pennsylvania Law Review*, 781, 795 (1958).

[3] Judge Ginsburg withdrew his name from consideration in 1987 before President Reagan submitted a formal nomination to the Senate.

[4] 347 U. S. 483 (1954).

[5] 369 U. S. 186 (1962).

[6] 377 U. S. 533 (1964).

[7] Noah Feldman, **Scorpions** (2010), hereafter cited as Feldman.

[8] Feldman chose an elaborate organization for his book. The work is subdivided into nine "books" plus an Epilogue. These "books" are in turn divided into chapters of which there are a total of forty-nine. *Id.*, vii-ix.

[9] Roosevelt's total of nine appointments to the Court, included the appointment of Associate Justice Harlan Stone to the Chief Justiceship.

[10] Because of Black's relatively brief service in a minor magisterial position, I do not count him among the Roosevelt appointees with judicial experience.

[11] Frankfurter's and Brandeis judicial tenures overlapped only marginally. Frankfurter, who filled Justice Benjamin Cardozo's seat, received his commission on January 20, 1939. Brandeis retired on February 13, 1939. The latter's place was taken by William O. Douglas.

[12] Feldman, 29.

[13] The cowboy hat photograph and a cluster of other photographs follow page 210.

[14] According to a posting on January 29, 2012, from the "Jackson List" (maintained, compiled, and distributed by Professor John Q. Barrett at St. John's University School of Law), Jackson enrolled at Albany Law School in fall 1911, effectively transferring into its senior class after spending the previous year as an apprentice in the office of two attorneys in Jamestown, New York. In spring 1912, Jackson completed his two semesters at Albany. To his surprise, law school officials decided that May to deny law degrees to students who were not yet twenty-one

years old. In June, the School thus awarded Jackson, who was only twenty, a "diploma of graduation" instead. In June 1941, Albany Law School changed its decision, and awarded Jackson his degree. He was by then Attorney General of the United States and only a few days from nomination to the Supreme Court. To subscribe to the list and to access selected postings, see http://www.stjohns.edu/academics/graduate/law/faculty/Profiles/Barrett/JacksonList.stj, last accessed on January 29, 2012.

[15] Feldman, 437.

[16] Holmes, "Law and the Court," in **Collected Legal Papers** (1920), 292.

[17] Feldman, 32.

[18] James Bradley Thayer, "The American Doctrine of Constitutional Law," 7 *Harvard Law Review* 129 (1893).

[19] Feldman, 31.

[20] 198 U. S. 45 (1905).

[21] Feldman, 31–32.

[22] *Id.*, 323.

[23] *Id.*

[24] See *Korematsu v. United States*, 323 U.S. 214 (1945).

[25] Feldman, 323.

[26] *Id.*

[27] *Id.*, 323–324.

[28] *Id.*, 432.

[29] *Scott v. Sandford*, 60 U. S. (19 Howard) 393, 426 (1857).

[30] 300 U. S. 379, 402 (1937).

[31] Feldman, 145.

[32] *Id.*, 144.

[33] 303 U. S. 77 (1937).

[34] *Santa Clara County v. Southern Pacific. R.R.*, 118 U. S. 394 (1886).

[35] *Id.*, 85–86 (Black, J., dissenting).

[36] Jackson's 400-page book was published in 1941.

[37] Jackson was Assistant U.S. Attorney General, Tax Division, 1936–1938, Solicitor General of the United States, 1938–1939, and Attorney General of the United States, 1940–1941.

[38] Feldman, 122.

[39] *Id.*, 122–123.

[40] *Id.*, 431.

[41] *Id.*, 423.

[42] Appointed by President Benjamin Harrison in 1891 to one of the newly created courts of appeal, Taft was confirmed in 1892 and remained a judge on the Sixth Circuit until his resignation in 1900.

[43] Jonathan Lurie, **William Howard Taft** (2012), hereafter cited as Lurie.

[44] 83 U. S. (16 Wallace) 36 (1873).

[45] Taft's campaign song for the 1908 campaign against Democrat William Jennings Bryan was "Get on the Raft with Taft." Although Taft was hardly a physical lightweight, the song helped persuade voters that Roosevelt's Secretary of War was a worthy successor to the energetic President.

[46] Lurie, ix.

[47] *Id.*, x.

[48] *Id.*

[49] *Id.*, ix.

[50] This was true both with President Harding and, after Harding's death, his successor Calvin Coolidge. As one of Taft's biographer's writes, "The wily chief justice took no chances. The train from Marion Ohio, no sooner pulled into Union Station than he was on the way to the New Willard Hotel to see President Coolidge. There, Taft went to work on the new president, and not without effect." Alpheus Thomas Mason, **William Howard Taft: Chief Justice** (1964), 185–186. Also see Walter F. Murphy, "In his Own Image: Mr. Chief Justice Taft and Supreme Court Appointments," *Supreme Court Review* (1961), 159–193.

[51] Mason, **William Howard Taft: Chief Justice**, 19.

[52] Alpheus Thomas Mason, "William Howard Taft," in Leon Friedman and Fred L. Israel, eds., **The Justices of the United States Supreme Court: Their Lives and Major Opinions** (1969), vol. 3, 2107.

[53] *Id.*

[54] Actuarially, Taft's assessment proved correct in that Hughes outlived Taft.

[55] Lurie, 126.

[56] Mason, "William Howard Taft," 2108.

[57] Lurie, 126.

[58] *Id.*, 124.

[59] *Id.*, 120.

[60] *Id.*, 120–121.

[61] William R. Casto, **The Supreme Court in the Early Republic** (1995).

[62] Herbert A. Johnson, **The Chief Justiceship of John Marshall, 1801–1835** (1997).

[63] James W. Ely, Jr., **The Chief Justiceship of Melville W. Fuller, 1888–1910** (1995).

[64] Walter F. Pratt, Jr., **The Supreme Court under Edward Douglass White, 1910–1921** (1999).

[65] William G. Ross, **The Supreme Court under Charles Evans Hughes, 1930–1941** (2007).

[66] Melvin I. Urofsky, **Division and Discord, The Supreme Court under Stone and Vinson, 1941–1953** (1997).

[67] Michal Belknap, **The Supreme Court under Earl Warren, 1953–1969** (2005).

[68] Earl M. Maltz, **The Chief Justiceship of Warren Burger, 1969–1985** (2000).

[69] Paul Kens, **The Supreme Court under Morrison R. Waite, 1874–1888** (2010), hereafter cited as Kens.

[70] 198 U. S 45 (1905).

[71] Kens, ix.

[72] Beginning with Melville Fuller, commissions for Chief Justice have read "Chief Justice of the United States." Unless one counts as Cabinet service being U.S. Minister Plenipotentiary to France (a position Oliver Ellsworth held in 1799–1800) or service by John Jay as Foreign Affairs

Secretary for the Articles Congress and later negotiator of two treaties, Johnson seems to be in error in his Preface when he writes "[w]ithout exception, all of his [Waite's] predecessors had been selected from among former members of presidential cabinets." (xii). John Marshall had served as Secretary of State, Roger Taney had served as Attorney General, and Salmon Chase had served as Treasury Secretary, but there appears to be no *Cabinet* service for Rutledge (who was never confirmed), Ellsworth, or Jay.

[73] Kens, 2.
[74] *Id.*, 14.
[75] *Id.*, 13.
[76] *Id.*, 14.
[77] 94 U.S. 113 (1877).
[78] *Id.*, 126.
[79] 198 U. S. 45 (1905).
[80] Consider for example, *United States v. Reese*, 92 U.S. 214 (1876); *United States v. Cruikshank*, 92 U.S 542 (1876).
[81] Kens, 172.
[82] *Id.*
[83] Clare Cushman, **Courtwatchers** (2011), hereafter cited as Cushman.
[84] *Id*, ix.
[85] *Id.*, xiii-xiv.
[86] Quoted in Donald Grier Stephenson, Jr., **The Waite Court: Justices, Rulings, and Legacy** (2003), 27.
[87] Cushman, 92.
[88] *Id.*, 91.

INDEX TO THE *JOURNAL OF SUPREME COURT HISTORY* VOLUMES 1-35 (1976-2010)

By

JOEL FISHMAN, Ph.D.[1]

TABLE OF CONTENTS

[1] Joel Fishman, Ph.D., University of Wisconsin–Madison; Assistant Director for Lawyer Services, Duquesne University Center for Legal Information/Allegheny County Law Library, Pittsburgh, PA. I wish to thank Clare Cushman for her encouragement, support, and assistance of this project.

I. CHRONOLOGICAL INDEX

Belknap, Michal. Frankfurter and the Nazi Saboteurs. 7:66-71 (1982).

Black, Elizabeth S. Hugo Black: A Memorial Portrait. 7:72-94 (1982).

Pusey, Merlo J. The Nomination of Charles Evans Hughes as Chief Justice. 7:95-99 (1982).

"De Minimis" or, Judicial Potpourri. 7:101-108 (1982).

Swindler, William F. Toward 1987: Between War and Peace in 1782. 7:101-103 (1982).

McGurn, Barrett. Slogans to Fit the Occasion. 7:104-108 (1982).

[Vol. 8] YEARBOOK 1983

Lee, Rex. In Memoriam: Abe Fortas. 8:7-9 (1983).

Perry, James R. and James M. Buchanan. Admission to the Supreme Court Bar, 1790 -1800: A Case Study of Institutional Change. 8:10-16 (1983).

Christensen, George A. Here Lies the Supreme Court: Gravesites of the Justices. 8:17-30 (1983).

Gordan, John D., III. The Trial of the Officers and Crew of the Schooner "Savannah." 8:31-45 (1983).

Swindler, William F. Roscoe Conkling and the Fourteenth Amendment. 8:46-52 (1983).

Urofsky, Melvin I. Myth and Reality: The Supreme Court and Protective Legislation in the Progressive Era. 8:53-72 (1983).

Beth, Loren P. Justice Harlan and the Chief Justiceship, 1910. 8:73-79 (1983).

Morris, Jeffrey B. What Heaven Must Be Like: William Howard Taft as Chief Justice, 1921-30. 8:80-101 (1983).

Pusey, Merlo J. Justice Roberts' 1937 Turnaround. 8:102-107 (1983).

Judicial Potpourri. 8:108-116 (1983).

Daniel, Josiah M., III. "Chief Justice of the United States:" History and Historiography of the Title. 8:109-112 (1983).

Swindler, William F. Toward 1987: A "Pre-Constitutional Law Case." 8:113-116 (1983).

[Vol. 9] YEARBOOK 1984

Morris, Jeffrey B. In Memoriam: William F. Swindler. 9:5-6 (1984).

Nordham, George Washington. President George Washington and the First Supreme Court. 9:7-11 (1984).

Swindler, William F. Seditious Aliens and Native "Seditionists." 9:12-19 (1984).

McCurdy, Charles W. The Roots of "Liberty of Contract" Reconsidered: Major Premises in the Law of Employment, 1867-1937. 9:20-33 (1984).

Knox, John. Some Comments on Chief Justice Hughes. [PORTFOLIO]. 9:34-44 (1984).

Pusey, Merlo J. The Hughes Biography: Some Personal Reflections. [PORTFOLIO]. 9:45-52 (1984).

Bork, Judge Robert H. Styles in Constitutional Theory. 9:53-60 (1984).

Wiecek, William M. The "Imperial Judiciary" in Historical Perspective. 9:61-89 (1984).

O'Brien, David M. The Supreme Court: A Co-Equal Branch of Government. 9:90-105 (1984).

"De Minimis" or, Judicial Potpourri. 9:106-116 (1984).

Swindler, William F. Toward 1987: Consequences of Independence. 9:107-111 (1984).

Griswold, Erwin N. The Pentagon Papers Case: A Personal Footnote. 9:112-116 (1984).

Marcus, Maeva, James R. Perry, James M. Buchanan, Christine R. Jordan, and Steven L. Tull. "It is my wish as well as my Duty to attend the court": The Hardships of Supreme Court Service, 1790-1800. 9:118-126 (1984).

Stephenson, D. Grier, Jr. On Review: Recent Books About the Supreme Court, the Justices, and the Constitution. 9:127-143 (1984).

[Vol. 10] YEARBOOK 1985

Handler, Milton. The 1926 Term: My Clerkship with Mr. Justice Stone. 10:5-7 (1985).

Langran, Robert W. Why Are Some Supreme Court Justices Rated as "Failures?" 10:8-14 (1985).

Lee, Rex E. Lawyering in the Supreme Court: The Role of the Solicitor General. 10:15-21 (1985).

Shapiro, Stephen M. Oral Argument in the Supreme Court: The Felt Necessities of the Time. 10:22-34 (1985).

Joyce, Craig. *Wheaton v. Peters*: The Untold Story of the Early Reporters. 10:35-92 (1985).

Brodhead, Michael J. Justice David J. Brewer: A Voice for Peace on the Supreme Court. 10:93-102 (1985).

Scalia, Antonin. Historical Anomalies in Administrative Law. 10:103-111 (1985).

Kennedy, Cornelius Bryant. Toward 1987: A Dramatic Change in Goals, 1785-1787. 10:112-116 (1985).

Eisenberg, David. A Consideration of Extra-Judicial Activities in the Pre-Marshall Era. 10:117-126 (1985).

Judicial Potpourri. 10:128-145 (1985).

Stephenson, D. Grier, Jr. The Judicial Bookshelf. 10:128-145 (1985).

Millgramm, Karl-Heinz. Comparative Law: The Federal Constitutional Court of Germany and the Supreme Court of the United States. 10:146-154 (1985).

[Vol. 11] YEARBOOK 1986

Powell, Lewis F., Jr. In Memoriam: Justice Potter Stewart. 11:5-7 (1986).

Markey, Howard T. Chief Justice Burger as Chairman of the Judicial Conference of the United States. 11:8-10 (1986).

[Vol. 15] JOURNAL OF SUPREME COURT HISTORY 1990

Mikva, Abner. Arthur J. Goldberg, The Practitioner. 15:1-3 (1990).

Breyer, Stephen. Clerking for Justice Goldberg. 15:4-7 (1990).

Burger, Warren E., Rex E. Lee, Kenneth W. Starr, William H. Rehnquist. Remarks on the Bicentennial of the Supreme Court. 15:8-16 (1990).

Rotunda, Ronald D. and John E. Nowak. Joseph Story: A Man for All Seasons. 15:17-24 (1990).

Powell, Lewis F., Jr. George Wythe. 15:25-28 (1990).

Maxey, David W. The Translation of James Wilson. 15:29-43 (1990).

Tushnet, Mark. Dual Office Holding and the Constitution: A View from Hayburn's Case. 15:44-58 (1990).

Wheeler, Russell R. Judging What Justices Do Off the Bench. 15:59-68 (1990).

Ching, Miriam. Extrajudicial Writings of Supreme Court Justices. 15:69-78 (1990).

Stern, Robert L. The Rosenberg Case in Perspective—Its Present Significance. 15:79-92 (1990).

Rauh, Joseph L., Jr. A Personalized View of the Court-Packing Episode. 15:93-98 (1990).

Gardner, Warner W. Court Packing: The Drafting Recalled. 15:99-103 (1990).

Brennan, William J., Jr. Richard W. Benka, Richard H. Chambers, Ramsey Clark, Milton V. Freeman, Thomas J. Klitgaard, Simon H. Rifkind, Gerhard A. Gesell, Erwin N. Griswold, Milton Handler, Leonard F. Jansen, William A. Reppy, Marshall L. Small, Jay Kelly Wright, and Eric Sevareid. Remembrances of William O. Douglas on the 50th Anniversary of His Appointment to the Supreme Court. 15:104-124 (1990).

Olken, Samuel R. John Marshall and Spencer Roane: An Historical Analysis of Their Conflict over U. S. Supreme Court Appellate Jurisdiction. 15:125-141 (1990).

Palmer, Jan and Saul Brenner. Determinants of the Amount of Time Taken by the Vinson Court to Process its Full-Opinion Cases. 15:142-151 (1990).

Stephenson, D. Grier, Jr. The Judicial Bookshelf. 15:152-177 (1990).

[Vol. 16] JOURNAL OF SUPREME COURT HISTORY 1991

Rehnquist, William H. William J. Brennan, Jr. 16:1-2 (1991).

O'Neil, Robert. Clerking for Justice Brennan. 16:3-4 (1991).

Arnold, Richard S. A Remembrance: Mr. Justice Brennan October Term 1960. 16:5-8 (1991).

Goldberger, Paul. Preservation's Supreme Authority. 16:9-12 (1991).

Powell, Lewis F., Jr. Stare Decisis and Judicial Restraint. 16:13-19 (1991).

Buchanan, James M. Oliver Ellsworth, Third Chief Justice. 16:20-26 (1991).

O'Brien, David M. John Marshall Harlan's Unpublished Opinions: Reflections of a Supreme Court at Work. 16:27-49 (1991).

Dorsen, Norman. John Marshall Harlan and the Warren Court. 16:50-62 (1991).

Seddig, Robert S. John Marshall and the Origins of Supreme Court Leadership. 16:63-85 (1991).

Bloomfield, Maxwell. The Warren Court in American Fiction. 16:86-96 (1991).

Burger, Warren E. Thomas Jefferson and the Court. 16:97-104 (1991).

Stephenson, D. Grier, Jr. The Judicial Bookshelf. 16:105-131 (1991).

[Vol. 17] JOURNAL OF SUPREME COURT HISTORY 1992

Brennan, William J., Jr. A Tribute to Thurgood Marshall. 17:1-8 (1992).

O'Connor, Sandra Day. Thurgood Marshall: The Influence of a Raconteur. 17:9-13 (1992).

Carter, Robert L. Reflections on Justice Marshall. 17:15-18 (1992).

Claiborne, Louis F. The Noblest Roman of Them All: A Tribute to Justice Marshall. 17:19-21 (1992).

Bloch, Susan Low. The Privilege of Clerking for Thurgood Marshall. 17:23-25 (1992).

Baker, Liva. John Marshall Harlan I and a Color Blind Constitution The Frankfurter-Harlan II Conversations. 17:27-37 (1992).

Stern, Robert L. Chief Justice Taney and the Shadow of *Dred Scott*. 17:39-52 (1992).

Hickox, Charles F., III, and Andrew C. Laviano. William Paterson. 17:53-61 (1992).

Simpson, Brooks D. President Washington's Appointments to the Supreme Court. 17:63-74 (1992).

Prettyman, E. Barrett, Jr. Robert H. Jackson: "Solicitor General for Life." 17:75-85 (1992).

O'Hara, James B. The Supreme Court Fleet. 17:87-97 (1992).

Binion, Gayle. Justice Potter Stewart: The *Unpredictable* Vote. 17:99-108 (1992).

Stephenson, D. Grier, Jr. The Judicial Bookshelf. 17:109-135 (1992).

Cardozo, Michael H. The Judicial Bookshelf—Continued. 17:137-140 (1992).

Howard, J. Woodford, Jr. The *Cramer* Treason Case. 21-1:49-60 (1996).

Danelski, David J. The Saboteurs' Case. 21-1:61-82 (1996).

Freyer, Tony A. The First Amendment and World War II. 21-1:83-104 (1996).

Hutchinson, Dennis J. Justice Jackson and the Nuremberg Trials. 21-1:105-116 (1996).

For Further Reading. 21-1:117-120 (1996).

[Vol. 21-2] JOURNAL OF SUPREME COURT HISTORY 1996

Urofsky, Melvin I. Introduction. 21-2:i (1996).

Woolf, Lord. The Appellate Committee and the Supreme Court: Anglo-American Comparisons. 21-2:1-10 (1996).

Blackmun, Harry A. The Story-Holmes Seat. 21-2:11-16 (1996).

Sirvet, Ene and R. B. Bernstein. Documentary Editing and the Jay Court: Opening New Lines of Inquiry. 21-2:17-22 (1996).

Sirvet, Ene and R. B. Bernstein. John Jay, Judicial Independence, and Advising Coordinate Branches. 21-2:23-29 (1996).

Hobson, Charles F. John Marshall and His Papers. 21-2:30-35 (1996).

Hobson, Charles F. John Marshall and the Fairfax Litigation: The Background of *Martin v. Hunter's Lessee*. 21-2:36-50 (1996).

Marcus, Maeva. Documenting Judicial History: The Supreme Court of the United States, 1789-1800. 21-2:51-56 (1996).

Marcus, Maeva. *Georgia v. Brailsford*. 21-2:57-72 (1996).

Casto, William R. Oliver Ellsworth. 21-2:73-91 (1996).

Polenberg, Richard. Cardozo and the Criminal Law: *Palko v. Connecticut* Reconsidered. 21-2:92-105 (1996).

Kyvig, David E. Appealing Supreme Court Decisions: Constitutional Amendments as Checks on Judicial Review. 21-2:106-119 (1996).

Ely, James W., Jr. The Fuller Court and Takings Jurisprudence. 21-2:120-135 (1996).

Mosnier, Joseph. The Demise of an "Extraordinary Criminal Procedure": *Klopfer v. North Carolina* and the Incorporation of the Sixth Amendment's Speedy Trial Provision. 21-2:136-160 (1996).

Wolf, Michael Allan. *The Supreme Court in United States History*: A New Appreciation. 21-2:161-167 (1996).

Stephenson, D. Grier, Jr. The Judicial Bookshelf. 21-2:168-188 (1996).

[Vol. 22-1] JOURNAL OF SUPREME COURT HISTORY 1997

Urofsky, Melvin I. Introduction. 22-1:i (1997).

Kens, Paul. Dawn of the Conservative Era. 22-1:1-13 (1997).

Schmidt, Benno C., Jr. The Court in the Progressive Era. 22-1:14-32 (1997).

Arkes, Hadley. A Return to the Four Horsemen. 22-1:33-54 (1997).

Leuchtenburg, William E. The Nine Justices Respond to the 1937 Crisis. 22-1:55-75 (1997).

Friedman, Richard D. Chief Justice Hughes' Letter on Court-Packing. 22-1:76-86 (1997).

Currie, David P. The New Deal Court in the 1940s: Its Constitutional Legacy. 22-1:87-98 (1997).

Taylor, John B. Politics, the Court, and the Constitution: A Bibliographical Essay on the Pre- and Post-New Deal Supreme Court. 22-1:99-118 (1997).

[Vol. 22-2] JOURNAL OF SUPREME COURT HISTORY 1997

Urofsky, Melvin I. Introduction. 22-2:1 (1997).

McHugh, Michael Hudson. The High Court of Australia. 22-2:2-14 (1997).

Thomas, Clarence. The Virtue of Defeat: *Plessy v. Ferguson* in Retrospect. 22-2:15-24 (1997).

Wood, Sandra L. In the Shadow of the Chief: The Role of the Senior Associate Justice. 22-2:25-35 (1997).

Hoffer, Williamjames Hull. William Paterson and the National Jurisprudence: Two Draft Opinions on the Sedition Law of 1798 and the Federal Common Law. 22-2:36-50 (1997).

Finkelman, Paul. *Prigg v. Pennsylvania* Understanding Justice Story's Proslavery Nationalism. 22-2:51-64 (1997).

Kahn, Michael A. Abraham Lincoln's Appointments to the Supreme Court: A Master Politician at his Craft. 22-2:65-78 (1997).

Power, Garrett. Advocates at Cross-Purposes: The Briefs on Behalf of Zoning in the Supreme Court. 22-2:79-87 (1997).

Wolf, Michael Allan. "Compelled by Conscientious Duty": *Village of Euclid v. Ambler Realty Co.* as Romance. 22-2:88-100 (1997).

Johnson, John W. "Dear Mr. Justice": Public Correspondence with Members of the Supreme Court. 22-2:101-112 (1997).

Kruse, Kevin M. Personal Rights, Public Wrongs: The *Gaines* Case and the Beginning of the End of Segregation. 22-2:113-130 (1997).

Wohl, Alexander. *The Life of John Marshall* Revisited. 22-2:131-139 (1997).

Garrett, Elizabeth. Review of Mark V. Tushnet, *Making Civil Rights Law: Thurgood Marshall and the Supreme Court, 1936-1961* and *Making Constitutional Law: Thurgood Marshall and the Supreme Court, 1961-1991*. 22-2:140-149 (1997).

[Vol. 25-1] JOURNAL OF SUPREME COURT HISTORY 2000

Urofsky, Melvin I. Introduction. 25-1:1-2 (2000).

Ashkenazi, Elliott. Admiralty Law and Neutrality Policy in the 1790s: An Example of Judicial, Legislative, and Executive Cooperation. 25-1:3-16 (2000).

Graber, Mark A. The Jacksonian Origins of Chase Court Activism. 25-1:17-39 (2000).

Harring, Sidney L. and Kathryn Swedlow. "The Defendant Has Seemed to Live a Charmed Life": *Hopt v. Utah*: Territorial Justice, The Supreme Court of the United States, and Late Nineteenth-Century Death Penalty Jurisprudence. 25-1:40-71 (2000).

Connally, C. Ellen. Justice Harlan's "Great Betrayal"? A Reconsideration of *Cumming v. Richmond County Board of Education*. 25-1:72-92 (2000).

Bernstein, David E. *Plessy* versus *Lochner*: The *Berea College* Case. 25-1:93-111 (2000).

Stephenson, D. Grier, Jr. Judicial Bookshelf. 25-1:112-127 (2000).

[Vol. 25-2] JOURNAL OF SUPREME COURT HISTORY 2000

Urofsky, Melvin I. Introduction. 25-2:i (2000).

Dry, Murray. The Origins and Foundations of the First Amendment and the Alien and Sedition Acts. 25-2:129-144 (2000).

Rabban, David M. Free Speech: The Lost Years. 25-2:145-160 (2000).

Laycock, Douglas. The Clear and Present Danger Test. 25-2:161-186 (2000).

Berns, Walter and Philippa Strum. Issue: The Clear and Present Danger Test. 25-2:187-190 (2000).

BeVier, Lillian R. Free Expression in the Warren and Burger Courts. 25-2:191-212 (2000).

[Vol. 25-3] JOURNAL OF SUPREME COURT HISTORY 2000

Urofsky, Melvin I. Introduction. 25-3:v-vi (2000).

Breyer, Stephen. The Cherokee Indians and the Supreme Court. 25-3:215-227 (2000).

Przybyszewski, Linda. The Religion of a Jurist: Justice David J. Brewer and the Christian Nation. 25-3:228-242 (2000).

Flowers, Ronald B. The Naturalization of Douglas Clyde Macintosh, Alien Theologian. 25-3:243-270 (2000).

Fowler, Russell. Calvin Coolidge and the Supreme Court. 25-3:271-295 (2000).

Ward, Artemus. The Tenth Justice: The Retirement of William O. Douglas. 25-3:296-312 (2000).

Stephenson, D. Grier, Jr. Judicial Bookshelf. 25-3:313-330 (2000).

[Vol. 26-1] JOURNAL OF SUPREME COURT HISTORY 2001

Urofsky, Melvin I. Introduction. 26-1:v-vi (2001).

Newman, Jon O. Citators Beware: Stylistic Variations in Different Publisher's Versions of Early Supreme Court Opinions. 26-1:1-8 (2001).

Wagner, Frank D. The Role of the Supreme Court Reporter in History. 26-1:9-23 (2001).

Anderson, Jeffrey M. Conscience in the Court, 1931-1946: Religion as Duty and Choice. 26-1:25-52 (2001).

Wiecek, William M. Felix Frankfurter, Incorporation, and the Willie Francis Case. 26-1:53-66 (2001).

Cushman, Clare. Women Advocates before the Supreme Court. 26-1:67-88 (2001).

Urofsky, Melvin I. Revivifying Political Science: Lucas A. Powe, Jr., on the Warren Court. 26-1:89-94 (2001).

[Vol. 26-2] JOURNAL OF SUPREME COURT HISTORY 2001

Ginsburg, Ruth Bader. Foreword. 26-2:vii-viii (2001).

Przybyszewski, Linda. Introduction. 26-2:97-108 (2001).

Harlan, Malvina Shanklin. Some Memories of a Long Life, 1854-1911. 26-2:109-211 (2001).

[Vol. 26-3] JOURNAL OF SUPREME COURT HISTORY 2001

Urofsky, Melvin I. Introduction: "All the Facts That Surround." 26-3:v-vi (2001).

Frasca, Ralph. *The Helderberg Advocate*: A Public-Nuisance Prosecution a Century before *Near v. Minnesota*. 26-3:215-230 (2001).

Hohenstein, Kurt. Just What the Doctor Ordered: The Harrison Anti-Narcotic Act, the Supreme Court, and the Federal Regulation of Medical Practice, 1915-1919. 26-3:231-256 (2001).

Purcell, Edward A., Jr. Brandeis, *Erie*, and the New Deal "Constitutional Revolution." 26-3:257-278 (2001).

Stephenson, D. Grier, Jr. The Judicial Bookshelf. 26-3:279-295 (2001).

Hite, Gregory Nelson. Race, Education and the Courts: A Review of James T. Patterson's *Brown v. Board of Education: A Civil Rights Milestone and Its Troubled Legacy*. 26-3:296-304 (2001).

[Vol. 27-1] JOURNAL OF SUPREME COURT HISTORY 2002

Urofsky, Melvin I. Introduction. 27-1:v-vi (2002).

Rehnquist, William H. The Supreme Court in the Nineteenth Century. 27-1:1-13 (2002).

Owens, John B. The Clerk, the Thief, His Life as a Baker: Ashton Embry and the Supreme Court Leak Scandal. 27-1:14-44 (2002).

White, James Boyd. Human Dignity and the Claim of Meaning: Athenian Tragic Drama and Supreme Court Opinions. 27-1:45-64 (2002).

Stephenson, D. Grier, Jr. The Judicial Bookshelf. 27-1:65-82 (2002).

Urofsky, Melvin I. Review of Edward A. Purcell, Jr., *Brandeis and the Progressive Constitution*: Erie, *the Judicial Power, and the Politics of Federal Courts in the Twentieth-Century America*. 27-1:83-90 (2002).

[Vol. 27-2] JOURNAL OF SUPREME COURT HISTORY 2002

Urofsky, Melvin I. Introduction. 27-2:v-vi (2002).

Karachuk, Robert Feikema. Error or Appeal? Navigating Review under the Supreme Court's Admiralty Jurisdiction, 1789-1800. 27-2:93-113 (2002).

Wagner, Richard H. A Falling Out: The Relationship between Oliver Wendell Holmes and Theodore Roosevelt. 27-2:114-137 (2002).

Dorsen, Norman and Amelia Ames Newcomb. John Marshall Harlan II, Associate Justice of the Supreme Court 1955-1971: Remembrances by His Law Clerks. 27-2:138-175 (2002).

Ray, Laura Krugman. The History of the Per Curiam Opinion: Consensus and Individual Expression on the Supreme Court. 27-2:176-193 (2002).

Stephenson, D. Grier, Jr. The Judicial Bookshelf. 27-2:194-210 (2002).

[Vol. 27-3] JOURNAL OF SUPREME COURT HISTORY 2002

Editor's Note. 27-3:215 (2002).

Pollack, Louis H. and Sheldon Hackney. Remarks on the 200th Anniversary of the Accession of John Marshall as Chief Justice. 27-3:216-221 (2002).

Clinton, Robert Lowry. The Supreme Court before John Marshall. 27-3:222-239 (2002).

Nelson, William E. *Marbury v. Madison* and the Establishment of Judicial Autonomy. 27-3:240-256 (2002).

Illustrations [John Marshall's Court]. 27-3:257-72 (2002).

McConnell, Michael W. John Marshall and the Creation of a National Government. 27-3:273-285 (2002).

Abraham, Henry J. John Marshall's Associate Justices. 27-3:286-292 (2002).

Hobson, Charles F. Remembering the Great Chief Justice. 27-3:293-303 (2002).

Clinton, Robert Lowry. Bibliography [Books on John Marshall]. 27-3:304 (2002).

[Vol. 28-1] JOURNAL OF SUPREME COURT HISTORY 2003

Urofsky, Melvin I. Introduction. 28-1:v-vi (2003).

Frankel, Robert P., Jr. Before *Marbury: Hylton v. United States* and the Origins of Judicial Review. 28-1:1-13 (2003).

Gordon, Sarah Barringer. The Mormon Question: Polygamy and Constitutional Conflict in Nineteenth-Century America. 28-1:14-29 (2003).

Hockett, Jeffrey D. The Battle over *Brown*'s Legitimacy. 28-1:30-53 (2003).

Ferren, John M. General Yamashita and Justice Rutledge. 28-1:54-80 (2003).

Stephenson, D. Grier, Jr. The Judicial Bookshelf. 28-1:81-97 (2003).

[Vol. 28-2] JOURNAL OF SUPREME COURT HISTORY 2003

Urofsky, Melvin I. Introduction. 28-2:v-vi (2003).

Taylor, Michael J. C. "A More Perfect Union": *Ableman v. Booth* and the Culmination of Federal Sovereignty. 28-2:101-115 (2003).

Sharp, Allen. Presidents as Supreme Court Advocates: Before and after the White House. 28-2:116-144 (2003).

Urofsky, Melvin I. Wilson, Brandeis, and the Supreme Court Nomination. 28-2:145-156 (2003).

O'Connor, Sandra Day. William Howard Taft and the Importance of Unanimity. 28-2:157-164 (2003).

Fassett, John D. The Buddha and the Bumblebee: The Saga of Stanley Reed and Felix Frankfurter. 28-2:165-196 (2003).

Lemieux, Scott E. The Exception That Defines the Rule: Marshall's *Marbury* Strategy and the Development of Supreme Court Doctrine. 28-2:197-211 (2003).

[Vol. 28-3] JOURNAL OF SUPREME COURT HISTORY 2003

Urofsky, Melvin I. Introduction. 28-3:v-vi (2003).

Stone, Geoffrey R. Civil Liberties in Wartime. 28-3:215-251 (2003).

Ferren, John M. Military Curfew, Race-Based Internment, and Mr. Justice Rutledge. 28-3:252-269 (2003).

Kmiec, Douglas W. The Supreme Court in Times of Hot and Cold War: Learning from the Sounds of Silence for a War on Terrorism. 28-3:270-299 (2003).

Belknap, Michal R. Alarm Bells from the Past: The Troubling History of American Military Commissions. 28-3:300-322 (2003).

Turner, Robert F. The Supreme Court, Separation of Powers, and the Protection of Individual Rights during Periods of War or National Security Emergency. 28-3:323-338 (2003).

Scheiber, Harry N. Property Rights versus "Public Necessity": A Perspective on Emergency Powers and the Supreme Court. 28-3:339-369 (2003).

Stephenson, D. Grier, Jr. The Judicial Bookshelf. 28-3:370-386 (2003).

[Vol. 29-1] JOURNAL OF SUPREME COURT HISTORY 2004

Urofsky, Melvin I. Preface. 29-1:v-vi (2004).

Kens, Paul. Introduction. 29-1:1-21 (2004).

Field, Stephen J. Personal Reminiscences of Early Days in California, With Other Sketches. 29-1:22-119 (2004).

[Vol. 29-2] JOURNAL OF SUPREME COURT HISTORY 2004

Urofsky, Melvin I. Introduction. 29-2:v-vi (2004).

Downs, Harry. Unlikely Abolitionist: William Cushing and the Struggle against Slavery. 29-2:123-135 (2004).

Van Orden, James F. "Jehovah Will Provide": Lillian Gobitas and Freedom of Religion. 29-2:136-144 (2004).

Wallenstein, Peter. To Sit or Not to Sit: The Supreme Court of the United States and the Civil Rights Movement in the Upper South. 29-2:145-162 (2004).

Lahav, Pnina. History in Journalism and Journalism in History: Anthony Lewis and the Watergate Crisis. 29-2:163-176 (2004).

Powe, L. A., Jr. Writing the First Draft of History: Anthony Lewis as Supreme Court Correspondent. 29-2:177-190 (2004).

Strum, Philippa. The Journalist as Historian: Anthony Lewis, Civil Liberties, and the Supreme Court. 29-2:191-206 (2004).

Stephenson, D. Grier, Jr. The Judicial Bookshelf. 29-2:207-225 (2004).

[Vol. 29-3] JOURNAL OF SUPREME COURT HISTORY 2004

Urofsky, Melvin I. Introduction. 29-3:v-vi (2004).

Lightner, David L. The Supreme Court and the Interstate Slave Trade: A Study in Evasion, Anarchy, and Extremism. 29-3:229-253 (2004).

Hamilton, Daniel W. A New Right to Property: Civil War Confiscation in the Reconstruction Supreme Court. 29-3:254-285 (2004).

Sharp, Allen. Justices Seeking the Presidency. 29-3:286-307 (2004).

Lyman, Frank Interviewed by Darryl J. Gonzalez. A Voice from behind the Bench: Recollections of a Supreme Court Page. 29-3:308-322 (2004).

Blackmun, Harry A. Some Personal Reminiscences and What They Meant for Me. 29-3:323-336 (2004).

Powe, L. A., Jr. (Re)introducing Wiley Rutledge. 29-3:337-345 (2004).

Stephenson, D. Grier, Jr. The Judicial Bookshelf. 29-3:346-366 (2004).

[Vol. 30-1] JOURNAL OF SUPREME COURT HISTORY 2005

Urofsky, Melvin I. Introduction. 30-1:v-vi (2005).

Frederick, David C. Supreme Court Advocacy in the Early Nineteenth Century. 30-1:1-16 (2005).

Lurie, Jonathan. Ex-Justice Campbell: The Case of the Creative Advocate. 30-1:17-30 (2005).

Urofsky, Melvin I. Louis D. Brandeis: Advocate Before and On the Bench. 30-1:31-46 (2005).

Clark, Mary L. Women as Supreme Court Advocates, 1879-1979. 30-1:47-67 (2005).

Roberts, John G., Jr. Oral Advocacy and the Re-emergence of a Supreme Court Bar. 30-1:68-81 (2005).

[Vol. 30-2] JOURNAL OF SUPREME COURT HISTORY 2005

Kens, Paul. Introduction: The Incident at Lathrop Station. 30-2:85-104 (2005).

Gorham, George C. The Story of the Attempted Assassination of Justice Field by a Former Associate on the Supreme Bench of California. 30-2:105-194 (2005).

[Vol. 30-3] JOURNAL OF SUPREME COURT HISTORY 2005

Urofsky, Melvin I. Introduction. 30-3:v-vi (2005).

Sparrow, Bartholomew H. The Public Response to Controversial Supreme Court Decisions: The Insular Cases. 30-3:197-210 (2005).

Novak, Andrew. Courtroom to Classroom: Justice Harlan's Lectures at George Washington University Law School. 30-3:211-225 (2005).

Fakhimi, Morad. Terrorism and Habeas Corpus: A Jurisdictional Escape. 30-3:226-243 (2005).

Lawrence, Albert. Biased Justice: James C. McReynolds of the Supreme Court of the United States. 30-3:244-270 (2005).

Dyk, Timothy B. The *Graver Tank* Litigation in the Supreme Court. 30-3:271-283 (2005).

Stephenson, D. Grier, Jr. The Judicial Bookshelf. 30-3:284-302 (2005).

[Vol. 31-1] JOURNAL OF SUPREME COURT HISTORY 2006

Urofsky, Melvin I. Introduction. 31-1:v (2006).

Nannes, John M. The "Lone Dissenter." 31-1:1-4 (2006).

O'Connor, Sandra Day. Remembering Rehnquist. 31-1:5-8 (2006).

Augustyn, Noel J. The Chief I Knew. 31-1:9-14 (2006).

Roberts, John G. Jr. Tribute to William H. Rehnquist. 31-1:15-17 (2006).

Campbell, Peter Scott. The Civil War Reminiscences of John Marshall Harlan. 32-3:249-275 (2007).

Price, Barry A. The Question of Diminution of Income for Justices and Judges of the Supreme Court and the Inferior Courts of the United States. 32-3:276-281 (2007).

Cushman, Clare. Rookie on the Bench: The Role of the Junior Justice. 32-3:282-296 (2007).

Small, Marshall L. William O. Douglas Remembered: A Collective Memory by WOD's Law Clerks. 32-3:297-334 (2007).

Terris, Bruce J. Attorney General Kennedy versus Solicitor General Cox: The Formulation of the Federal Government's Position in the Reapportionment Cases. 32-3:335-345 (2007).

Stephenson, D. Grier, Jr. The Judicial Bookshelf. 32-3:346-363 (2007).

[Vol. 33-1] JOURNAL OF SUPREME COURT HISTORY 2008

Urofsky, Melvin I. Introduction. 33-1:v-vi (2008).

Sternberg, Jonathan. Deciding Not to Decide: The Judiciary Act of 1925 and the Discretionary Court. 33-1:1-16 (2008).

Christensen, George A. Here Lies the Supreme Court: Revisited. 33-1:17-41 (2008).

Martin, Constance L. The Life and Career of Justice Robert H. Jackson. 33-1:42-67 (2008).

Goldstein, Robert Justin. The Grapes of *McGrath*: The Supreme Court and the Attorney General's List of Subversive Organizations in *Joint Anti-Fascist Refugee Committee v. McGrath* (1951). 33-1:68-88 (2008).

Freyer, Tony A. *Cooper v. Aaron* (1958): A Hidden Story of Unanimity and Division. 33-1:89-109 (2008).

Ward, Artemus. The "Good Old #3 Club" Gets a New Member. 33-1:110-119 (2008).

[Vol. 33-2] JOURNAL OF SUPREME COURT HISTORY 2008

Urofsky, Melvin I. Introduction. 33-2:v-vi (2008).

O'Hara, James. The Gilded Age and the Supreme Court: An Overview. 33-2:123-133 (2008).

Ross, Michael A. Melancholy Justice: Samuel Freeman Miller and the Supreme Court during the Gilded Age. 33-2:134-148 (2008).

Kens, Paul. Justice Stephen Field of California. 33-2:149-159 (2008).

Lurie, Jonathan. Stanley Matthews: A Case Portrait of Gilded Age High Court Jurisprudence. 33-2:160-169 (2008).

Wiecek, William M. Justice David J. Brewer and "the Constitution in Exile." 33-2:170-185 (2008).

Davies, Ross E. A Tall Tale of *The Brethren*. 33-2:186-199 (2008).

Stephenson, D. Grier, Jr. The Judicial Bookshelf. 33-2:200-220 (2008).

[Vol. 33-3] JOURNAL OF SUPREME COURT HISTORY 2008

Urofsky, Melvin I. Introduction. 33-3:v-vi (2008).

Thorp, Galen N. William Wirt. 33-3:223-303 (2008).

Campbell, Peter Scott. John Marshall Harlan's Political Memoir. 33-3:304-321 (2008).

Carter, Edward L. and James C. Phillips. The Mormon Education of a Gentile Justice: George Sutherland and Brigham Young Academy. 33-3:322-340 (2008).

Altschuler, Bruce E. A Look Back at the *Steel Seizure* Case. 33-3:341-352 (2008).

Peppers, Todd C. William Thaddeus Coleman, Jr. : Breaking the Color Barrier at the U. S. Supreme Court. 33-3:353-370 (2008).

Vestal, Theodore M. Public Diplomacy in the U. S. Supreme Court: The Warren Years—Part I. 33-3:371-393 (2008).

[Vol. 34-1] JOURNAL OF SUPREME COURT HISTORY 2009

Urofsky, Melvin I. Introduction. 34-1:v-vi (2009).

Garrison, Arthur H. The Internal Security Acts of 1978: The Founding Generation and the Judiciary during America's First National Security Crisis. 34-1:1-27 (2009).

McLaughlin, Jeremy M. Henry Clay and the Supreme Court. 34-1:28-55 (2009).

Cox, Thomas H. Contesting Commerce: *Gibbons v. Ogden,* Steam Power, and Social Change. 34-1:56-74 (2009).

Peppers, Todd C. Isaiah and His Young Disciples: Justice Brandeis and His Law Clerks. 34-1:75-97 (2009).

Vestal, Theodore M. Public Diplomacy in the U. S. Supreme Court: The Warren Years, Part II. 34-1:98-124 (2009).

Stephenson, D. Grier, Jr. The Judicial Bookshelf. 34-1:125-145 (2009).

[Vol. 34-2] JOURNAL OF SUPREME COURT HISTORY 2009

Urofsky, Melvin I. Introduction. 34-2:v-vi (2009).

Waldrep, Christopher. Joseph P. Bradley's Journey: The Meaning of Privileges and Immunities. 34-2:149-163 (2009).

Rutherglen, George. Textual Corruption in the *Civil Rights Cases*. 34-2:164-169 (2009).

Kens, Paul. The Crédit Mobilier Scandal and the Supreme Court: Corporate Power, Corporate Person, and Government Control in the Mid-nineteenth Century. 34-2:170-182 (2009).

Hyman, Harold M. The Undocketed Constitutional Bridge across the War Gulf, ca. 1861-73. Sp. Ed.:63-74 (1996).

Maltz, Earl M. The Waite Court and Federal Power to Enforce the Reconstruction Amendments. Sp. Ed.:75-88 (1996).

Benedict, Michael Les. Reconstruction: The Civil War Amendments. Sp. Ed.:89-97 (1996).

Kennedy, Randall. Reconstruction: The Waite Court and the Politics of History. Sp. Ed.:99-102 (1996).

II. AUTHOR INDEX

Abraham, Henry J. John Marshall's Associate Justices. 27-3:286-292 (2002).

Abraham, Henry J. President Jefferson's Three Appointments to the Supreme Court of the United States: 1804, 1807, and 1807. 31-2:141-154 (2006).

Aichele, Gary J. Self-Preference, Competition and the Rule of Force: The Holmesian Legacy. 13:11-17 (1988).

Alito, Samuel A. Jr. The Origin of the Baseball Antitrust Exemption: *Federal Baseball Club of Baltimore, Inc. v. National League of Professional Baseball.* 34-2:183-195 (2009).

Altschuler, Bruce E. A Look Back at the *Steel Seizure* Case. 33-3:341-352 (2008).

Amestoy, Jeffrey L. The Supreme Court Argument that Saved the Union: Richard Henry Dana, Jr., and the *Prize Cases.* 35-1:10-24 (2010).

Anderson, Jeffrey M. Conscience in the Court, 1931-1946: Religion as Duty and Choice. 26-1:25-52 (2001).

Arkes, Hadley. A Return to the Four Horsemen. 22-1:33-54 (1997).

Arnold, Richard S. A Remembrance: Mr. Justice Brennan October Term 1960. 16:5-8 (1991).

Ashkenazi, Elliott. Admiralty Law and Neutrality Policy in the 1790s: An Example of Judicial, Legislative, and Executive Cooperation. 25-1:3-16 (2000).

Augustyn, Noel J. The Chief I Knew. 31-1:9-14 (2006).

Bader, William and Roy M. Mersky. Justice Levi Woodbury: A Reputational Study. 23-2:129-142 (1998).

Baker, Liva. John Marshall Harlan I and a Color Blind Constitution The Frankfurter-Harlan II Conversations. 17:27-37 (1992).

Baker, Leonard P. The Circuit Riding Justices. 2:63-69 (1977).

Barrett, C. Walker. The Miracle of the Constitution. 3:97-102 (1978).

Baynes, Thomas E. Yankee From Georgia. 3:31-42 (1978).

Belknap, Michal R. Alarm Bells from the Past: The Troubling History of American Military Commissions. 28-3:300-322 (2003).

Belknap, Michal. Frankfurter and the Nazi Saboteurs. 7:66-71 (1982).

Belknap, Michal R. *Dennis v. United States*: Great Case Or Cold War Relic? 18:41-58 (1993).

Belknap, Michal R. Why *Dennis v. United States* Is a Landmark Case. 34-3:289-302 (2009).

Belz, Herman. The Supreme Court and Constitutional Responsibility in the Civil War Era. Sp. Ed.:5-8 (1996).

Benedict, Michael Les. Reconstruction: The Civil War Amendments. Sp. Ed.:89-97 (1996).

Berns, Walter and Philippa Strum. Issue: The Clear and Present Danger Test. 25-2:187-190 (2000).

Bernstein, David E. *Plessy* versus *Lochner*: The *Berea College* Case. 25-1:93-111 (2000).

Bernstein, David E. Two Asian Laundry Cases. 24-1:95-111 (1999).

Bernstein, R. B. Hugo L. Black and the Challenges of Judicial Biography. 20:147-152 (1995).

Beth, Loren P. Justice Harlan and the Chief Justiceship, 1910. 8:73-79 (1983).

Beth, Loren P. President Hayes Appoints a Justice. 14:68-77 (1989).

BeVier, Lillian R. Free Expression in the Warren and Burger Counts. 25-2:191-212 (2000).

Binion, Gayle. Justice Potter Stewart: The *Unpredictable* Vote. 17:99-108 (1992).

Black, Elizabeth S. Hugo Black: A Memorial Portrait. 7:72-94 (1982).

Blackmun, Harry A. Some Personal Reminiscences and What They Meant for Me. 29-3:323-336 (2004).

Blackmun, Harry A. The Story-Holmes Seat. 21-2:11-16 (1996).

Bloch, Susan Low and Maeva Marcus. John Marshall's Selective Use of History in *Marbury v. Madison.* 12:82-107 (1987).

Bloch, Susan Low. The Privilege of Clerking for Thurgood Marshall. 17:23-25 (1992).

Bloomfield, Maxwell. The Warren Court in American Fiction. 16:86-96 (1991).

Bork, Judge Robert H. Styles in Constitutional Theory. 9:53-60 (1984).

Boskey, Bennett. Supreme Court Declinations. 31-3:252-261 (2006).

Danelski, David J. The Saboteurs' Case. 21-1:61-82 (1996).

Daniel, Josiah M., III. "Chief Justice of the United States": History and Historiography of the Title. 8:109-112 (1983).

Davies, Ross E. The Judicial and Ancient Games: James Wilson, John Marshall Harlan, and the Beginnings of Golf at the Supreme Court. 35-2:122-143 (2010).

Davies, Ross E. The Other Supreme Court. 31-3:221-234 (2006).

Davies, Ross E. A Tall Tale of *The Brethren*. 33-2:186-199 (2008).

Dennisont, George M. The Dorr War and Political Questions. 4:45-62 (1979).

Dierenfield, Bruce J. "The Most Hated Woman in America": Madalyn Murray and the Crusade against School Prayer. 32-1:62-84 (2007).

Doherty, Brendan J. Interpreting the Bill of Rights and the Nature of Federalism: *Baron v. City of Baltimore*. 32-3:210-228 (2007).

Dorsen, Norman. John Marshall Harlan and the Warren Court. 16:50-62 (1991).

Dorsen, Norman and Amelia Ames Newcomb. John Marshall Harlan II, Associate Justice of the Supreme Court 1955-1971: Remembrances by His Law Clerks. 27-2:138-175 (2002).

Douglas, Cathleen H. William O. Douglas: The Man. 6:6-9 (1981).

Downey, Arthur T. The Conflict between the Chief Justice and the Chief Executive: *Ex parte Merryman*. 31-3:262-278 (2006).

Downs, Harry. Unlikely Abolitionist: William Cushing and the Struggle against Slavery. 29-2:123-135 (2004).

Dry, Murray. The Origins and Foundations of the First Amendment and the Alien and Sedition Acts. 25-2:129-144 (2000).

Dudziak, Mary L. The Supreme Court and Racial Equality during World War II. 21-1:35-48 (1996).

Duetsch, Eberhard P. The Case of the Missing Bodies. 3:61-67,76 (1978).

Dumbauld, Edward. The Case of the Mutinous Mariner. 2:52-58, 69 (1977).

Dunne, Gerald T. Bushrod Washington and the Mount Vernon Slaves. 5:25-29 (1980).

Dunne, Gerald T. The Early Court Reporters. 1:61-72 (1976).

Dyk, Timothy B. The *Graver Tank* Litigation in the Supreme Court. 30-3:271-283 (2005).

Eisenberg, David. A Consideration of Extra-Judicial Activities in the Pre-Marshall Era. 10:117-126 (1985).

Ely, James W., Jr. The Fuller Court and Takings Jurisprudence. 21-2:120-135 (1996).

Ely, James W., Jr. Melville W. Fuller Reconsidered. 23-1:35-49 (1998).

Ely, James W., Jr. Property Rights and the Supreme Court in World War II. 21-1:19-34 (1996).

Evans, Patricia R. and Roger F. Jacobs. The Court in Recent Literature. 4:94-100 (1979).

Fakhimi, Morad. Terrorism and Habeas Corpus: A Jurisdictional Escape. 30-3:226-243 (2005).

Fassett, John D. The Buddha and the Bumblebee: The Saga of Stanley Reed and Felix Frankfurter. 28-2:165-196 (2003).

Fassett, John D. Mr. Justice Reed and *Brown v. The Board of Education*. 11:48-63 (1986).

Faulkner, Robert K. Lincoln and the Rebirth of Liberal Democracy. 35-3:201-212 (2010).

Ferren, John M. General Yamashita and Justice Rutledge. 28-1:54-80 (2003).

Ferren, John M. Military Curfew, Race-Based Internment, and Mr. Justice Rutledge. 28-3:252-269 (2003).

Field, Stephen J. Personal Reminiscences of Early Days in California, With Other Sketches. 29-1:22-119 (2004).

Finkelman, Paul. "Hooted Down the Page of History": Reconsidering the Greatness of Chief Justice Taney. 19:83-102 (1994).

Finkelman, Paul. Lincoln and Emancipation: Constitutional Theory, Practical Politics, and the Basic Practice of Law. 35-3:243-266 (2010).

Finkelman, Paul. *Prigg v. Pennsylvania* Understanding Justice Story's Proslavery Nationalism. 22-2:51-64 (1997).

Finley, S. W. Daniel Webster Packed 'Em In. 4:70-78, 83 (1979).

Fish, Peter G. Harper's Weekly Celebrates the Centennial of the Supreme Court of the United States: A Bicentennial Retrospective. 13:46-49 (1988).

Flowers, Ronald B. The Naturalization of Douglas Clyde Macintosh, Alien Theologian. 25-3:243-270 (2000).

For Further Reading. 21-1:117-120 (1996).

Fowler, Russell. Calvin Coolidge and the Supreme Court. 25-3:271-295 (2000).

Frank, John P. Judicial Appointments—Controversy and Accomplishment. 2:79-85 (1977).

Frankel, Robert P., Jr. Before *Marbury: Hylton v. United States* and the Origins of Judicial Review. 28-1:1-13 (2003).

Frankel, Robert P., Jr. The Supreme Court and Impartial Justice: The View from the 1790s. 19:103-116 (1994).

Frankfurter, Felix. Chief Justices I Have Known. 5:3-9 (1980).

Franklin, John Hope. A Half-Century of Presidential Race Initiatives: Some Reflections. 24-2:226-237 (1999).

Franz, Patricia L. Ohio v. The Bank: An Historical Examination of *Osborn v. The Bank of the United States*. 24-1:112-137 (1999).

Hickox, Charles F., III, and Andrew C. Laviano. William Paterson. 17:53-61 (1992).

Hite, Gregory Nelson. Race, Education and the Courts: A Review of James T. Patterson's *Brown v. Board of Education: A Civil Rights Milestone and Its Troubled Legacy.* 26-3:296-304 (2001).

Hobson, Charles F. John Marshall and the Fairfax Litigation: The Background of *Martin v. Hunter's Lessee.* 21-2:36-50 (1996).

Hobson, Charles F. Remembering the Great Chief Justice. 27-3:293-303 (2002).

Hobson, Charles F. John Marshall and His Papers. 21-2:30-35 (1996).

Hockett, Jeffrey D. Justice Robert H. Jackson and Segregation: A Study of the Limitations and Proper Basis of Judicial Action. 14:52-67 (1989).

Hockett, Jeffrey D. The Battle over *Brown's* Legitimacy. 28-1:30-53 (2003).

Hoffer, Williamjames Hull. William Paterson and the National Jurisprudence: Two Draft Opinions on the Sedition Law of 1798 and the Federal Common Law. 22-2:36-50 (1997).

Hoffheimer, Michael H. Justice Holmes: Law and the Search for Control. 14:98-118 (1989).

Hohenstein, Kurt. Just What the Doctor Ordered: The Harrison Anti-Narcotic Act, the Supreme Court, and the Federal Regulation of Medical Practice, 1915-1919. 26-3:231-256 (2001).

Howard, J. Woodford, Jr. The *Cramer* Treason Case. 21-1:49-60 (1996).

Huebner, Timothy S. Divided Loyalties: Justice William Johnson and the Rise of Disunion in South Carolina, 1822-1834. 20:19-30 (1995).

Hutchinson, Dennis J. Justice Jackson and the Nuremberg Trials. 21-1:105-116 (1996).

Hylton, Joseph Gordon. David Josiah Brewer: A Conservative Justice Reconsidered. 19:45-64 (1994).

Hyman, Harold M. The Undocketed Constitutional Bridge across the War Gulf, ca. 1861-73. Sp. Ed.:63-74 (1996).

In Memoriam: Tom C. Clark as the Court Remembers Him. 3:1-2 (1978).

In Memoriam: Elizabeth Hughes Gossett 1907-1981. 7:[5] (1982).

Irvine, Alexander Andrew Mackay. Constitutional Change in the United Kingdom: British Solutions to Universal Problems. 23-2:26-39 (1998).

Johnson, Calvin H. The Four Good Dissenters in *Pollock.* 32-2:162-177 (2007).

Johnson, Herbert A. Chief Justice John Marshall (1801-1835). 23-1:3-20 (1998).

Johnson, John W. "Dear Mr. Justice": Public Correspondence with Members of the Supreme Court. 22-2:101-112 (1997).

Johnson, Ludwell H., III. No Faith in Parchment. Sp. Ed.:9-14 (1996).

Jones, John Paul. *The Business of the Supreme Court* Revisited. 20:131-136 (1995).

Jordan, Christine. The Last of the Jacksonians. 5:78-88 (1980).

Joyce, Craig. "A Good Judge." 31-2:100-106 (2006).

Joyce, Craig. *Wheaton v. Peters*: The Untold Story of the Early Reporters. 10:35-92 (1985).

Kahn, Michael A. Abraham Lincoln's Appointments to the Supreme Court: A Master Politician at His Craft. 22-2:65-78 (1997).

Kahn, Michael A. The Appointment of John McLean to the Supreme Court: Practical Presidential Politics in the Jacksonian Era. 18:59-72 (1993).

Kaminski, John P. and Jennifer Lawton. Duty and Justice at "Every Man's Door": The Grand Jury Charges of Chief Justice John Jay, 1790-1794. 31-3:235-251 (2006).

Karachuk, Robert Feikema. Error or Appeal? Navigating Review under the Supreme Court's Admiralty Jurisdiction, 1789-1800. 27-2:93-113 (2002).

Kaufman, Andrew L. Judging New York Style: A Brief Retrospective of Two New York Judges. 13:60-65 (1988).

Kennedy, Cornelius Bryant. Toward 1987: A Dramatic Change in Goals, 1785-1787. 10:112-116 (1985).

Kennedy, Cornelius B. Toward 1987: The Foundation for the Constitution. 11:96-102 (1986).

Kennedy, Randall. Reconstruction: The Waite Court and the Politics of History. Sp. Ed.:99-102 (1996).

Kens, Paul. The Crédit Mobilier Scandal and the Supreme Court: Corporate Power, Corporate Person, and Government Control in the Mid-nineteenth Century. 34-2:170-182 (2009).

Kens, Paul. Dawn of the Conservative Era. 22-1:1-13 (1997).

Kens, Paul. Introduction. 29-1:1-21 (2004).

Kens, Paul. Introduction: The Incident at Lathrop Station. 30-1:85-104 (2005).

Kens, Paul. Justice Stephen Field of California. 33-2:149-159 (2008).

Kens, Paul. *Lochner v. New York*: Rehabilitated and Revised, but Still Reviled. 20:31-46 (1995).

Kersch, Ken I. The *Gompers v. Buck's Stove* Saga: A Constitutional Case Study in Dialogue, Resistance, and the Freedom of Speech. 31-1:28-57 (2006).

Kmiec, Douglas W. The Supreme Court in Times of Hot and Cold War: Learning from the Sounds of Silence for a War on Terrorism. 28-3:270-299 (2003).

Knowles, Helen J. May It Please the Court? The Solicitor General's Not-So-"Special" Relationship: Archibald Cox and the 1963-1964 Reapportionment Cases. 31-3:279-297 (2006).

Knox, John. Some Comments on Chief Justice Hughes. [PORTFOLIO]. 9:34-44 (1984).

Maxey, David W. The Translation of James Wilson. 15:29-43 (1990).

McAllister, Stephen R. *Wheaton v. Greenleaf*: A (Story) Tale of Three Reporters. 23-2:53-64 (1998).

McConnell, Michael W. John Marshall and the Creation of a National Government. 27-3:273-285 (2002).

McCurdy, Charles W. The Roots of "Liberty of Contract" Reconsidered: Major Premises in the Law of Employment, 1867-1937. 9:20-33 (1984).

McDonald, Kevin D. Antitrust and Baseball: Stealing Holmes. 23-2:88-128 (1998).

McGurn, Barrett. The Court's Officers. 4:87-93 (1979).

McGurn, Barrett. Downstairs at the Court. 2:93-100 (1977).

McGurn, Barrett. Law Clerks—A Professional Elite. 5:98-99 (1980).

McGurn, Barrett. Slogans to Fit the Occasion. 7:104-108 (1982).

McGurn, Barrett. Small Fry and the Court's Mailbag. 3:106-109 (1978).

McHugh, Michael Hudson. The High Court of Australia. 22-2:2-14 (1997).

McLaughlin, Jeremy M. Henry Clay and the Supreme Court. 34-1:28-55 (2009).

Meador, Daniel J. Lamar to the Court: Last Step to National Reunion. 11:27-47 (1986).

Merritt, Deborah Jones. Justice Sandra Day the Framers' "First Woman." 31-2:107-108 (2006).

Mersky, Roy and Jenni Parrish. The Court in Recent Literature. 2:102-113 (1977).

Messinger, I. Scott. Legitimating Liberalism: The New Deal Image-Makers and Oliver Wendell Holmes, Jr. 20:57-72 (1995).

Mikva, Abner. Arthur J. Goldberg, The Practitioner. 15:1-3 (1990).

Millgramm, Karl-Heinz. Comparative Law: The Federal Constitutional Court of Germany and the Supreme Court of the United States. 10:146-154 (1985).

Monagan, John S. The Grand Panjandrum: Mellow Years of Justice Holmes. 13:26-36 (1988).

Monroe, Elizabeth Brand. The Influence of the *Dartmouth College* Case on the American Law of Educational Charities. 32-1:1-21 (2007).

Morel, Lucas E. The *Dred Scott* Dissents: McLean, Curtis, Lincoln, and the Public Mind. 32-2:133-151 (2007).

Morel, Lucas E. Lincoln and the Constitution: A Unionist for the Sake of Liberty. 35-3:213-224 (2010).

Morgan, Richard. The *Flag Salute Cases* Reconsidered. 34-3:273-288 (2009).

Morris, Jeffrey B. Chief Justice Edward Douglass White and President Taft's Court. 7:27-45 (1982).

Morris, Jeffrey B. The Era of Melville Weston Fuller. 6:37-51 (1981).

Morris, Jeffrey B. In Memoriam: William F. Swindler. 9:5-6 (1984).

Morris, Jeffrey B. Morrison Waite: Reconstruction and After. [PORTFOLIO]. 5:39-48 (1980).

Morris, Jeffrey B. Niles Register and the Supreme Court. 3:50-60 (1978).

Morris, Jeffrey B. What Heaven Must Be Like: William Howard Taft as Chief Justice, 1921-30. 8:80-101 (1983).

Morris, Richard B., Paul A. Freund and Herbert Wechsler. Columbians as Chief Justices: John Jay, Charles Evans Hughes and Harlan Fiske Stone. 13:66-77 (1988).

Mosnier, Joseph. The Demise of an "Extraordinary Criminal Procedure": *Klopfer v. North Carolina* and the Incorporation of the Sixth Amendment's Speedy Trial Provision. 21-2:136-160 (1996).

Mullin, Connor. Edward Bennett Williams for the Petitioner: Profile of a Supreme Court Advocate. 34-2:204-223 (2009).

Myers, Minor, III. The Judicial Service of Retired United States Supreme Court Justices. 32-1:46-61 (2007).

Nannes, John M. The "Lone Dissenter." 31-1:1-4 (2006).

Neely, Mark E., Jr. Justice Embattled: The Lincoln Administration and the Constitutional Controversy over Conscription in 1863. Sp. Ed.:47-61 (1996).

Nelson, William E. *Marbury v. Madison* and the Establishment of Judicial Autonomy. 27-3:240-256 (2002).

Newman, Jon O. Citators Beware: Stylistic Variations in Different Publisher's Versions of Early Supreme Court Opinions. 26-1:1-8 (2001).

Newmyer, R. Kent. Chief Justice John Marshall's Last Campaign: Georgia, Jackson, and the Cherokee Cases. 24-1:76-94 (1999).

Newmyer, R. Kent. Thomas Jefferson and the Rise of the Supreme Court. 31-2:126-140 (2006).

Nordham, George Washington. President George Washington and the First Supreme Court. 9:7-11 (1984).

Norgren, Jill. Before It Was Merely Difficult: Belva Lockwood's Life in Law and Politics. 24-1:16-42 (1999).

Norgren, Jill. The Cherokee Nation Cases of the 1830s. 19:65-82 (1994).

Norgren, Jill. Ladies of Legend: The First Generation of American Women Attorneys. 35-1:71-90 (2010).

Novak, Andrew. Courtroom to Classroom: Justice Harlan's Lectures at George Washington University Law School. 30-3:211-225 (2005).

O'Brien, David M. Filling Justice William O. Douglas's Seat: President Gerald R. Ford's Appointment of Justice John Paul Stevens. 14:20-39 (1989).

Stevens, John Paul. Tribute to Justice O'Connor. 31-2:99 (2006).

Stone, Lauson H. My Father the Chief Justice. 3:7-17 (1978).

Stone, Geoffrey R. Civil Liberties in Wartime. 28-3:215-251 (2003).

Strickland, Rennard I. and William R. Strickland. The Court and the Trail of Tears. 4:20-30 (1979).

Strum, Philippa. The Journalist as Historian: Anthony Lewis, Civil Liberties, and the Supreme Court. 29-2:191-206 (2004).

Strum, Philippa. Louis D. Brandeis as Lawyer and Judge. 18:29-40 (1993).

Swindler, William F. Another Early College Charter Case. 2:38, 113 (1977).

Swindler, William F. Books by Justices—A Representative List. 4:38-39 (1979).

Swindler, William F. The Court in the Age of the Marshall. [PORTFOLIO]. 2:44-50 (1977).

Swindler, William F. The Court under Chief Justice Taney. [PORTFOLIO]. 3:43-49 (1978).

Swindler, William F. Documentary Films on the Supreme Court. 3:25-30 (1978).

Swindler, William F. W.F.S. His Honor and the Field of Honor. 4:84-85 (1979).

Swindler, William F. Justices in Academe. 4:31-37 (1979).

Swindler, William F. Mr. Chisholm and the Eleventh Amendment. 6:14-18 (1981).

Swindler, William F. The Eighteenth Century Court and Bar. [PORTFOLIO]. 1:45-50 (1976).

Swindler, William F. The Era of Salmon P. Chase. [PORTFOLIO]. 4:40-44 (1979).

Swindler, William F. The Numbers Game. 2:87-92 (1977).

Swindler, William F. Of Revolution, Law and Order. 1:16-24 (1976).

Swindler, William F. "Robin Hood," Congress and the Court. 2:39-43 (1977).

Swindler, William F. Roscoe Conkling and the Fourteenth Amendment. 8:46-52 (1983).

Swindler, William F. Seditious Aliens and Native "Seditionists." 9:12-19 (1984).

Swindler, William F. The Selling of the Constitution. 5:49-54 (1980).

Swindler, William F. Toward 1987: A "Pre-Constitutional Law Case." 8:113-116 (1983).

Swindler, William F. Toward 1987: Between War and Peace in 1782. 7:101-103 (1982).

Swindler, William F. Toward 1987: Consequences of Independence. 9:107-111 (1984).

Swindler, William F. Toward 1987: Lessons from the Centennial. 5:94-97 (1980).

Swindler, William F. Toward 1987—Two Milestones in 1781. 6:117-120 (1981).

Swindler, William F. The Trials of Aaron Burr. 3:18-24 (1978).

Taft, Charles P. My Father the Chief Justice. 2:5-10 (1977).

Taylor, John B. Hail to the Chief: A Bibliographical Essay on Six Chief Justices of the United States. 23-1:133-165 (1998).

Taylor, John B. Politics, the Court, and the Constitution: A Bibliographical Essay on the Pre- and Post-New Deal Supreme Court. 22-1:99-118 (1997).

Taylor, Michael J. C. "A More Perfect Union": *Ableman v. Booth* and the Culmination of Federal Sovereignty. 28-2:101-115 (2003).

Ten Year Index: S. C. H. S. *YEARBOOK*. 11:122-132 (1986).

Terris, Bruce J. Attorney General Kennedy versus Solicitor General Cox: The Formulation of the Federal Government's Position in the Reapportionment Cases. 32-3:335-345 (2007).

Thomas, Clarence. The Virtue of Defeat: *Plessy v. Ferguson* in Retrospect. 22-2:15-24 (1997).

Thorp, Galen N. William Writ. 33-3:223-303 (2008).

Turner, Charles C., Lori Beth Way and Nancy Maveety. Beginning to Write Separately: The Origins and Development of Concurring Judicial Opinions. 35-2:93-109 (2010).

Turner, Robert F. The Supreme Court, Separation of Powers, and the Protection of Individual Rights during Periods of War or National Security Emergency. 28-3:323-338 (2003).

Tushnet, Mark. Dual Office Holding and the Constitution: A View from Hayburn's Case. 15:44-58 (1990).

Tushnet, Mark. Writing Supreme Court Histories. 18:11-20 (1993).

Urofsky, Melvin I. Beyond the Bottom Line: The Value of Judicial Biography. 23-2:143-156. (1998).

Urofsky, Melvin I. The Court at War, and the War at the Court. 21-1:1-18 (1996).

Urofsky, Melvin I. The Court Diary of Justice William O. Douglas: Introduction. 20:78-79 (1995).

Urofsky, Phillip E. The Diary of Wm. O. Douglas. 20:80-112 (1995).

Urofsky, Melvin I. Editor's Note. 27-3:215 (2002).

Urofsky, Melvin I. Editorial Foreword. 18:1 (1993).

Urofsky, Melvin I. Editorial Foreword. 20:i (1995).

Urofsky, Melvin I. Editorial Introduction. 19:i (1994).

Urofsky, Melvin I. Introduction. 21-2:i (1996).

Urofsky, Melvin I. Introduction. 22-1:i (1997).

Urofsky, Melvin I. Introduction. 22-2:1 (1997).

Urofsky, Melvin I. Introduction. 23-1:1-2 (1998).

III. TITLE INDEX

The Judicial Bookshelf. D. Grier Stephenson, Jr. 15:152-177 (1990).

The Judicial Bookshelf. D. Grier Stephenson, Jr. 16:105-131 (1991).

The Judicial Bookshelf. D. Grier Stephenson, Jr. 17:109-135 (1992).

The Judicial Bookshelf. D. Grier Stephenson, Jr. 18:90-117 (1993).

The Judicial Bookshelf. D. Grier Stephenson, Jr. 19:147-170 (1994).

The Judicial Bookshelf. D. Grier Stephenson, Jr. 20:153-172 (1995).

The Judicial Bookshelf. D. Grier Stephenson, Jr. 21-2:168-188 (1996).

The Judicial Bookshelf. D. Grier Stephenson, Jr. 22-2:150-169 (1997).

The Judicial Bookshelf. D. Grier Stephenson, Jr. 23-2:157-181 (1998).

Judicial Bookshelf. D. Grier Stephenson, Jr. 24-1:138-152 (1999).

Judicial Bookshelf. D. Grier Stephenson, Jr. 24-3:333-347 (1999).

Judicial Bookshelf. D. Grier Stephenson, Jr. 25-1:112-127 (2000).

Judicial Bookshelf. D. Grier Stephenson, Jr. 25-3:313-330 (2000).

The Judicial Bookshelf. D. Grier Stephenson, Jr. 26-3:279-295 (2001).

The Judicial Bookshelf. D. Grier Stephenson, Jr. 27-1:65-82 (2002).

The Judicial Bookshelf. D. Grier Stephenson, Jr. 27-2:194-210 (2002).

The Judicial Bookshelf. D. Grier Stephenson, Jr. 28-1:81-97 (2003).

The Judicial Bookshelf. D. Grier Stephenson, Jr. 28-3:370-386 (2003).

The Judicial Bookshelf. D. Grier Stephenson, Jr. 29-2:207-225 (2004).

The Judicial Bookshelf. D. Grier Stephenson, Jr. 29-3:346-366 (2004).

The Judicial Bookshelf. D. Grier Stephenson, Jr. 30-3:284-302 (2005).

The Judicial Bookshelf. D. Grier Stephenson, Jr. 31-2:199-218 (2006).

The Judicial Bookshelf. D. Grier Stephenson, Jr. 31-3:298-315 (2006).

The Judicial Bookshelf. D. Grier Stephenson, Jr. 32-1:96-112 (2007).

The Judicial Bookshelf. D. Grier Stephenson, Jr. 32-2:190-208 (2007).

The Judicial Bookshelf. D. Grier Stephenson, Jr. 32-3:346-363 (2007).

The Judicial Bookshelf. D. Grier Stephenson, Jr. 33-3:200-220 (2008).

The Judicial Bookshelf. D. Grier Stephenson, Jr. 34-1:125-145 (2009).

The Judicial Bookshelf. D. Grier Stephenson, Jr. 34-2:224-240 (2009).

The Judicial Bookshelf. D. Grier Stephenson, Jr. 34-3:315-331 (2009).

The Judicial Bookshelf. D. Grier Stephenson, Jr. 35-2:177-192 (2010).

The Judicial Bookshelf. D. Grier Stephenson, Jr. 35-3:267-283 (2010).

The Judicial Bookshelf—Continued. Michael H. Cardozo. 17:137-140 (1992).

Judicial Management and Judicial Disinterest: The Achievements and Perils of Chief Justice William Howard Taft. Robert Post. 23-1:50-78 (1998).

Judicial Potpourri. 2:86 (1977).

Judicial Potpourri. 3:103-112 (1978).

Judicial Potpourri. 4:79-93 (1979).

Judicial Potpourri. 5:89-99 (1980).

Judicial Potpourri. 8:108-116 (1983).

Judicial Potpourri 10:127-145 (1985).

Judicial Potpourri. 11:95-121 (1986).

Judicial Robes. S. James Clarkson. 5:90-93 (1980).

The Judicial Service of Retired United States Supreme Court Justices. Minor Myers, III. 32-1:46-61 (2007).

The Judicial and Ancient Games: James Wilson, John Marshall Harlan, and the Beginnings of Golf at the Supreme Court. Ross E. Davies. 35-2:122-143 (2010).

Just What the Doctor Ordered: The Harrison Anti-Narcotic Act, the Supreme Court, and the Federal Regulation of Medical Practice, 1915-1919. Kurt Hohenstein. 26-3:231-256 (2001).

The Justice and the Lady. Robert H. Kroninger. 2:11-19 (1977).

The Justice and the Lady: A Postscript. Alfred J. Schweppe. 6:114-116 (1981).

Justice Cardozo: One-Ninth of the Supreme Court Milton C. Handler and Michael Ruby. 13:50-59 (1988).

Justice David J. Brewer: A Voice for Peace on the Supreme Court. Michael J. Brodhead. 10:93-102 (1985).

Justice David J. Brewer and "The Constitution in Exile." William M. Wiecek. 33-2:170-185 (2008).

Justice Embattled: The Lincoln Administration and the Constitutional Controversy over Conscription in 1863. Mark E. Neely, Jr. Sp. Ed.:47-61 (1996).

Justice Frank Murphy: A Reexamination Margaret H. Potts. 7:57-65 (1982).

Justice George Sutherland and the Status Quo: A Biographical and Review Essay. Gary C. Leedes. 20:137-146 (1995).

A Remembrance: Mr. Justice Brennan October Term 1960. Richard S. Arnold. 16:5-8 (1991).

Remembrances of William O. Douglas on the 50th Anniversary of his Appointment to the Supreme Court. William J. Brennan, Jr. Richard W. Benka, Richard H. Chambers, Ramsey Clark, Milton V. Freeman, Thomas J. Klitgaard, Simon H. Rifkind, Gerhard A. Gesell, Erwin N. Griswold, Milton Handler, Leonard F. Jansen, William A. Reppy, Marshall L. Small, Jay Kelly Wright, and Eric Sevareid. 15:104-124 (1990).

Reminiscences of the Solicitor General's Office. Robert L. Stern 20:123-130 (1995).

Res Gestae 1976, The Society Report. William H. Press. 2:115-118 (1977).

Res Gestae: The Society in 1977. 3:121-125 (1978).

Res Gestae: The Society in 1978. 4:101-104 (1979).

A Return to the Four Horsemen. Hadley Arkes. 22-1:33-54 (1997).

Review of Edward A. Purcell, Jr., *Brandeis and the Progressive Constitution*: Erie, *the Judicial Power, and the Politics of Federal Courts in the Twentieth-Century America*. Melvin I. Urofsky. 27-1:83-90 (2002).

Review of Mark V. Tushnet, *Making Civil Rights Law: Thurgood Marshall and the Supreme Court, 1936-1961 and Making Constitutional Law: Thurgood Marshall and the Supreme Court, 1961-(1991)*. Elizabeth Garrett. 22-2:140-149 (1997).

Reviewed: *Failing Justice: Charles Evans Whittaker of the Supreme Court*, by Craig Alan Smith. Alan C. Kohn. 3-1:91-96 (2006).

Revivifying Political Science: Lucas A. Powe, Jr., on the Warren Court. Melvin I. Urofsky. 26-1:89-94 (2001).

A Revolution Runs Wild. Charles Leonard. 5:55-61 (1980).

Robbing the Poor to Aid the Rich: Roger B. Taney and the Bank of Maryland Swindle. David Grimsted. 12:38-81 (1987).

Robert H. Jackson: "Solicitor General for Life." E. Barrett Prettyman, Jr. 17:75-85 (1992).

Robin Hood, Congress and the Court. William F. Swindler. 2:39-43 (1977).

The Role of the Supreme Court Reporter in History. Frank D. Wagner. 26-1:9-23 (2001).

Rookie on the Bench: The Role of the Junior Justice. Clare Cushman. 32-3:282-296 (2007).

The Roots of "Liberty of Contract" Reconsidered: Major Premises in the Law of Employment, 1867-1937. Charles W. McCurdy. 9:20-33 (1984).

Roscoe Conkling and the Fourteenth Amendment. William F. Swindler. 8:46-52 (1983).

The Rosenberg Case in Perspective: Its Present Significance. Robert L. Stern. 15:79-92 (1990).

The Saboteurs' Case. David J. Danelski. 21-1:61-82 (1996).

Salmon Portland Chase and the Judicial Culture of the Supreme Court in the Civil War Era. G. Edward White. Sp. Ed.:37-45 (1996).

Seditious Aliens and Native "Seditionists." William F. Swindler. 9:12-19 (1984).

Self-Preference, Competition and the Rule of Force: The Holmesian Legacy. Gary J. Aichele. 13:11-17 (1988).

The Selling of the Constitution. William F. Swindler. 5:49-54 (1980).

Skeleton in Mr. Jay's Closet? Maeva Marcus and Christine Jordan. 4:81-83 (1979).

Slogans to Fit the Occasion. Barrett McGurn. 7:104-108 (1982).

Some Personal Reminiscences and What They Meant for Me. Harry A. Blackmun. 29-3:323-336 (2004).

Stanley F. Reed. Warren E. Burger. 6:10-13 (1981).

Stanley Matthews: A Case Portrait of Gilded Age High Court Jurisprudence. Jonathan Lurie. 33-2:160-169 (2008).

Stare Decisis and Judicial Restraint. Lewis F. Powell, Jr. 16:13-19 (1991).

The Story-Holmes Seat. Harry A. Blackmun. 21-2:11-16 (1996).

The Story of the Attempted Assassination of Justice Field by a Former Associate on the Supreme Bench of California. Hon. George C. Gorham. 30-2:105-194 (2005).

Styles in Constitutional Theory. Judge Robert H. Bork. 9:53-60 (1984).

Suits against States: Diversity of Opinion in the 1790s. Maeva Marcus and Natalie Wexler. 18:73-89 (1993).

The Supreme Court, Separation of Powers, and the Protection of Individual Rights during Periods of War or National Security Emergency. Robert F. Turner. 28-3:323-338 (2003).

The Supreme Court: A Co-Equal Branch of Government. David M. O'Brien. 9:90-105 (1984).

Supreme Court Activism in Economic Policy in the Waning Days of the New Deal: Interpreting the Fair Labor Standards Act, 1941-1946. Jerold Waltman. 31-1:58-80 (2006).

Supreme Court Advocacy in the Early Nineteenth Century. David C. Frederick. 30-1:1-16 (2005).

The Supreme Court Argument that Saved the Union: Richard Henry Dana, Jr., and the *Prize Cases*. Jeffrey L. Amestoy. 35-1:10-24 (2010).

The Supreme Court Bar's First Black Member. Clarence G. Gontee. 1:82-85 (1976).

The Supreme Court before John Marshall. Robert Lowry Clinton. 27-3:222-239 (2002).

Supreme Court Declinations. Bennett Boskey. 31-3:252-261 (2006).

The Supreme Court Fleet. James B. O'Hara. 17:87-97 (1992).

A Voice from behind the Bench: Recollections of a Supreme Court Page. Frank Lyman. Interviewed by Darryl J. Gonzalez. 29-3:308-322 (2004).

The Waite Court and Federal Power to Enforce the Reconstruction Amendments. Earl M. Maltz. Sp. Ed.:75-88 (1996).

The Warren Court in American Fiction. Maxwell Bloomfield. 16:86-96 (1991).

Warren E. Burger and the American Bar Association. Justin A. Stanley. 11:14-17 (1986).

The Warren Tapes: Oral History and the Supreme Court. Amelia Roberts Fry. 7:10-22 (1982).

Welcome Back, Justice Harrison? Maeva Marcus and Christine Jordan. 4:80-81 (1979).

What Heaven Must Be Like: William Howard Taft as Chief Justice, 1921-30. Jeffrey B. Morris. 8:80-101 (1983).

Wheaton v. Greenleaf: A (Story) Tale of Three Reporters. Stephen R. McAllister. 23-2:53-64 (1998).

Wheaton v. Peters: The Untold Story of the Early Reporters. Craig Joyce. 10:35-92 (1985).

Why Are Some Supreme Court Justices Rated as "Failures?" Robert W. Langran. 10:8-14 (1985).

Why *Dennis v. United States* is a Landmark Case. Michal R. Belknap. 34-3:289-302 (2009).

William Howard Taft and the Importance of Unanimity. Sandra Day O'Connor. 28-2:157-164 (2003).

William J. Brennan, Jr. William H. Rehnquist. 16:1-2 (1991).

William O. Douglas: The Man. Cathleen H. Douglas. 6:6-9 (1981).

William O. Douglas Remembered: A Collective Memory by WOD's Law Clerks. Marshall L. Small. 32-3:297-334 (2007).

William Paterson. Charles F. Hickox, III and Andrew C. Laviano. 17:53-61 (1992).

William Paterson and the National Jurisprudence: Two Draft Opinions on the Sedition Law of 1798 and the Federal Common Law. Williamjames Hull Hoffer. 22-2:36-50 (1997).

William Pinkney: The Supreme Court's Greatest Advocate. Stephen M. Shapiro. 13:40-45 (1988).

William Thaddeus Coleman, Jr. : Breaking the Color Barrier at the U. S. Supreme Court. Todd C. Peppers. 33-3:353-370 (2008).

William Wirt. Galen N. Thorp. 33-3:223-303 (2008).

Wilson, Brandeis, and the Supreme Court Nomination. Melvin I. Urofsky. 28-2:145-156 (2003).

Women Advocates before the Supreme Court. Clare Cushman. 26-1:67-88 (2001).

Women and Other Strangers at the Bar. Alice O'Donnell. 2:59-62,114 (1977).

Women as Supreme Court Advocates, 1879-1979. Mary L. Clark. 30-1:47-67 (2005).

Writing Supreme Court Biography: A Single Lens View of a Nine-Sided Image. Stephen J. Wermlel. 19:9-18 (1994).

Writing Supreme Court Histories. Mark Tushnet. 18:11-20 (1993).

Writing the First Draft of History: Anthony Lewis as Supreme Court Correspondent. L. A. Powe, Jr. 29-2:177-190 (2004).

Yankee from Georgia. Thomas E. Baynes. 3:31-42 (1978).

IV. SUBJECT INDEX

1. Introductions

Burger, Warren E. Introduction. 1:5-6 (1976).

Gossett, Elizabeth Hughes. Introduction. 2:[ii] (1977).

Gossett, Elizabeth Hughes. Introduction. 3:[iii] (1978).

Gossett, Elizabeth Hughes. Introduction. 4:[ii] (1979).

Gossett, Elizabeth Hughes. Introduction. 5:[ii] (1980).

Urofsky, Melvin I. Editorial Foreword. 18:1 (1993).

Urofsky, Melvin I. Editorial Foreword. 20:i (1995).

Urofsky, Melvin I. Editorial Introduction. 19:i (1994).

Urofsky, Melvin I. Introduction. 21-2:i (1996).

Urofsky, Melvin I. Introduction. 22-1:i (1997).

Urofsky, Melvin I. Introduction. 22-2:1 (1997).

Urofsky, Melvin I. Introduction. 23-1:1-2 (1998).

Urofsky, Melvin I. Introduction. 23-2: v (1998).

Urofsky, Melvin I. Introduction. 24-1:1-2 (1999).

Urofsky, Melvin I. Introduction. 24-2:i (1999).

Urofsky, Melvin I. Introduction. 24-3:i (1999).

Urofsky, Melvin I. Introduction. 25-1:1-2 (2000).

Urofsky, Melvin I. Introduction. 25-2:i (2000).

Urofsky, Melvin I. Introduction. 25-3:v-vi (2000).

Urofsky, Melvin I. Introduction. 26-1:v-vi (2001).

Urofsky, Melvin I. Introduction: "All the Facts That Surround." 26-3:v-vi (2001).

Urofsky, Melvin I. Introduction. 27-1:v-vi (2002).

Urofsky, Melvin I. Introduction. 27-2:v-vi (2002).

Urofsky, Melvin I. Editor's Note. 27-3:215 (2002).

Urofsky, Melvin I. Introduction. 28-1:v-vi (2003).

Urofsky, Melvin I. Introduction. 28-2:v-vi (2003).

Urofsky, Melvin I. Introduction. 28-3:v-vi (2003).

Urofsky, Melvin I. Preface. 29-1:v-vi (2004).

Urofsky, Melvin I. Introduction. 29-2:v-vi (2004).

Urofsky, Melvin I. Introduction. 29-3:v-vi (2004).

Urofsky, Melvin I. Introduction. 30-1:v-vi (2005).

Urofsky, Melvin I. Introduction. 30-3:v-vi (2005).

Urofsky, Melvin I. Introduction. 31-1:v (2006).

Urofsky, Melvin I. Introduction. 31-2:v (2006).

Urofsky, Melvin I. Introduction. 31-3:v (2006).

Urofsky, Melvin I. Introduction. 32-1:v-vi (2007).

Urofsky, Melvin I. Introduction. 32-2:v-vi (2007).

Urofsky, Melvin I. Introduction. 32-3:v-vii (2007).

Urofsky, Melvin I. Introduction. 33-1:v-vi (2008).

Urofsky, Melvin I. Introduction. 33-2:v-vi (2008).

Urofsky, Melvin I. Introduction. 33-3:v-vi (2008).

Urofsky, Melvin I. Introduction. 34-1:v-vi (2009).

Urofsky, Melvin I. Introduction. 34-2:v-vi (2009).

Urofsky, Melvin I. Introduction. 34-3:v-vi (2009).

Urofsky, Melvin I. Introduction. 35-2:v-vi (2010).

Urofsky, Melvin I. Introduction. 35-3:v-vi (2010).

2. Articles

Administrative Law

Hohenstein, Kurt. Just What the Doctor Ordered: The Harrison Anti-Narcotic Act, the Supreme Court, and the Federal Regulation of Medical Practice, 1915-1919. 26-3:231-256 (2001).

Scalia, Antonin. Historical Anomalies in Administrative Law. 10:103-111 (1985).

Admiralty Law

Ashkenazi, Elliott. Admiralty Law and Neutrality Policy in the 1790s: An Example of Judicial, Legislative, and Executive Cooperation. 25-1:3-16 (2000).

Karachuk, Robert Feikema. Error or Appeal? Navigating Review under the Supreme Court's Admiralty Jurisdiction, 1789-1800. 27-2:93-113 (2002).

African-American Justices, Judges, Lawyers

Bloch, Susan Low. The Privilege of Clerking for Thurgood Marshall. 17:23-25 (1992).

Brennan, William J., Jr. A Tribute to Thurgood Marshall. 17:1-8 (1992).

Carter, Robert L. Reflections on Justice Marshall. 17:15-18 (1992).

Claiborne, Louis F. The Noblest Roman of Them All: A Tribute to Justice Marshall. 17:19-21 (1992).

Contee, Clarence G. The Supreme Court Bar's First Black Member. 1:82-85 (1976).

O'Connor, Sandra Day. Thurgood Marshall: The Influence of a Raconteur. 17:9-13 (1992).

Peppers, Todd C. William Thaddeus Coleman, Jr.: Breaking the Color Barrier at the U. S. Supreme Court. 33-3:353-370 (2008).

American Bar Association

Segal, Bernard G. Lewis F. Powell and the American Bar Association. 12:7-9 (1987).

Stanley, Justin A. Warren E. Burger and the American Bar Association. 11:14-17 (1986).

Antitrust Law

Alito, Samuel A., Jr. The Origin of the Baseball Antitrust Exemption: *Federal Baseball Club of Baltimore, Inc. v. National League of Professional Baseball.* 34-2:183-195 (2009).

McDonald, Kevin D. Antitrust and Baseball: Stealing Holmes. 23-2:88-128 (1998).

Wagner, Richard H. A Falling Out: The Relationship Between Oliver Wendell Holmes and Theodore Roosevelt. 27-2:114-137 (2002).

Attorney General

Robert, Joseph C. The Many-Sided Attorney General. 1:51-60 (1976).

Terris, Bruce J. Attorney General Kennedy versus Solicitor General Cox: The Formulation of the Federal Government's Position in the Reapportionment Cases.32-3:335-345 (2007).

Thorp, Galen N. William Wirt. 33-3:223-303 (2008).

Australia

McHugh, Michael Hudson. The High Court of Australia. 22-2:2-14 (1997).

Banking

Franz, Patricia L. Ohio v. The Bank: An Historical Examination of *Osborn v. The Bank of the United States.* 24-1:112-137 (1999).

Baseball

Alito, Samuel A., Jr. The Origin of the Baseball Antitrust Exemption: *Federal Baseball Club of Baltimore, Inc. v. National League of Professional Baseball.* 34-2:183-195 (2009).

Davies, Ross E. A Tall Tale of *The Brethren.* 33-2:186-199 (2008).

McDonald, Kevin D. Antitrust and Baseball: Stealing Holmes. 23-2:88-128 (1998).

Bicentennial of the Constitution

Swindler, William F. Toward 1987: Between War and Peace in 1782. 7:101-103 (1982).

Swindler, William F. Toward 1987: Consequences of Independence. 9:107-111 (1984).

Swindler, William F. Toward 1987: Guidelines from the Centennial. 5:94-97 (1980).

Swindler, William F. Toward 1987: A "Pre-Constitutional" Law Case. 8:113-116 (1983).

Swindler, William F. Toward 1987—Two Milestones of 1781. 6:117-120 (1981).

Biography and Autobiography

Ackerman, Bruce A.

Dorsen, Norman and Amelia Ames Newcomb, Eds. John Marshall Harlan II, Associate Justice of the Supreme

Court 1955-1971: Remembrances by His Law Clerks.
27-2:138-175 (2002).

Adams, John Quincy

Sharp, Allen. Presidents as Supreme Court Advocates:
Before and after the White House. 28-2:116-144 (2003).

Alsup, William

Small, Marshall L. William O. Douglas Remembered: A
Collective Memory by WOD's Law Clerks. 32-3:297-334
(2007).

Ares, Charles

Small, Marshall L. William O. Douglas Remembered: A
Collective Memory by WOD's Law Clerks. 32-3:297-334
(2007).

Arnold, Richard S.

Arnold, Richard S. A Remembrance: Mr. Justice
Brennan October Term 1960. 16:5-8 (1991).

Price, Polly J. *Mapp v. Ohio* Revisited: A Law Clerk's
Diary. 35-1:54-70 (2010).

Austin, Alan

Small, Marshall L. William O. Douglas Remembered: A
Collective Memory by WOD's Law Clerks. 32-3:297-334
(2007).

Baldwin, Henry

Robertson, Lyndsay G. Justice Henry Baldwin's "Lost
Opinion" in *Worcester v. Georgia*. 24-1:50-75 (1999).

Barnett, Wayne G.

Dorsen, Norman and Amelia Ames Newcomb, Eds. John
Marshall Harlan II, Associate Justice of the Supreme
Court 1955-1971: Remembrances by His Law Clerks.
27-2:138-175 (2002).

Benka, Richard W.

Brennan, William J., Jr. Richard W. Benka, Richard H.
Chambers, Ramsey Clark, Milton V. Freeman, Thomas J.
Klitgaard, Simon H. Rifkind, Gerhard A. Gesell, Erwin
N. Griswold, Milton Handler, Leonard F. Jansen, William
A. Reppy, Marshall L. Small, Jay Kelly Wright, and Eric
Sevareid. Remembrances of William O. Douglas on the
50th Anniversary of His Appointment to the Supreme
Court. 15:104-124 (1990).

Beveridge, Albert

Wohl, Alexander. *The Life of John Marshall* Revisited.
22-2:131-139 (1997).

Bieke, James R.

Dorsen, Norman and Amelia Ames Newcomb, Eds. John
Marshall Harlan II, Associate Justice of the Supreme
Court 1955-1971: Remembrances by His Law Clerks.
27-2:138-175 (2002).

Black, Elizabeth S.

Black, Elizabeth S. Hugo Black: A Memorial Portrait.
7:72-94 (1982).

Black, Hugo L.

Bernstein, R. B. Hugo L. Black and the Challenges of
Judicial Biography. 20:147-152 (1995).

Black, Elizabeth S. Hugo Black: A Memorial Portrait.
7:72-94 (1982).

Johnson, John W. "Dear Mr. Justice": Public
Correspondence with Members of the Supreme Court.
22-2:101-112 (1997).

Perry, Barbara A. Jefferson's Legacy to the Supreme
Court: Freedom of Religion. 31-2:181-198 (2006).

Blackmun, Harry A.

Blackmun, Harry A. Some Personal Reminiscences and
What They Meant for Me. 29-3:323-336 (2004).

Koh, Harold Hongju. The Justice Who Grew. 19:5-8
(1994).

Rehnquist, William H. A Tribute to Harry A. Blackmun.
19:1-4 (1994).

Bloch, Susan Low

Bloch, Susan Low. The Privilege of Clerking for
Thurgood Marshall. 17:23-25 (1992).

Boudin, Michael

Dorsen, Norman and Amelia Ames Newcomb, Eds. John
Marshall Harlan II, Associate Justice of the Supreme
Court 1955-1971: Remembrances by His Law Clerks.
27-2:138-175 (2002).

Bradley, Joseph P.

Waldrep, Christopher. Joseph P. Bradley's Journey: The
Meaning of Privileges and Immunities. 34-2:149-163
(2009).

Brandeis, Louis D.

Peppers, Todd C. Isaiah and His Young Disciples: Justice
Brandeis and His Law Clerks. 34-1:75-97 (2009).

Purcell, Edward A., Jr. Brandeis, *Erie*, and the New Deal
"Constitutional Revolution." 26-3:257-278 (2001).

Strum, Philippa. Louis D. Brandeis as Lawyer and Judge.
18:29-40 (1993).

Urofsky, Melvin I. Louis D. Brandeis: Advocate Before
and On the Bench. 30-1:31-46 (2005).

Urofsky, Melvin I. Wilson, Brandeis, and the Supreme
Court Nomination. 28-2:145-156 (2003).

Brennan, William J., Jr.

Arnold, Richard S. A Remembrance: Mr. Justice
Brennan October Term 1960. 16:5-8 (1991).

Brennan, William J., Jr. Richard W. Benka, Richard H.
Chambers, Ramsey Clark, Milton V. Freeman, Thomas J.
Klitgaard, Simon H. Rifkind, Gerhard A. Gesell, Erwin
N. Griswold, Milton Handler, Leonard F. Jansen, William
A. Reppy, Marshall L. Small, Jay Kelly Wright, and Eric
Sevareid. Remembrances of William O. Douglas on the
50th Anniversary of His Appointment to the Supreme
Court. 15:104-124 (1990).

Goldberger, Paul. Preservation's Supreme Authority.
16:9-12 (1991).

O'Neil, Robert. Clerking for Justice Brennan. 16:3-4
(1991).

Price, Polly J. *Mapp v. Ohio* Revisited: A Law Clerk's
Diary. 35-1:54-70 (2010).

Clark, Ramsey

Brennan, William J., Jr. Richard W. Benka, Richard H. Chambers, Ramsey Clark, Milton V. Freeman, Thomas J. Klitgaard, Simon H. Rifkind, Gerhard A. Gesell, Erwin N. Griswold, Milton Handler, Leonard F. Jansen, William A. Reppy, Marshall L. Small, Jay Kelly Wright, and Eric Sevareid. Remembrances of William O. Douglas on the 50th Anniversary of His Appointment to the Supreme Court. 15:104-124 (1990).

Clark, Tom C.

Burger, Warren E. Tom Clark Eulogies. 3:3-4 (1978).

Clark, Ramsey. Tom Clark Eulogies. 3:5-6 (1978).

In Memoriam: Tom C. Clark 1899-1997. 3:1 (1978).

Tom C. Clark. As the Court Remembers Him. 3:2 (1978).

Clay, Henry

McLaughlin, Jeremy M. Henry Clay and the Supreme Court. 34-1:28-55 (2009).

Cleveland, Grover

Sharp, Allen. Presidents as Supreme Court Advocates: Before and after the White House. 28-2:116-144 (2003).

Cohen, Louis R.

Dorsen, Norman and Amelia Ames Newcomb, Eds. John Marshall Harlan II, Associate Justice of the Supreme Court 1955-1971: Remembrances by His Law Clerks. 27-2:138-175 (2002).

Cohen, William

Small, Marshall L. William O. Douglas Remembered: A Collective Memory by WOD's Law Clerks. 32-3:297-334 (2007).

Coleman, William Thaddeus, Jr.

Peppers, Todd C. William Thaddeus Coleman, Jr.: Breaking the Color Barrier at the U. S. Supreme Court. 33-3:353-370 (2008).

Conkling, Roscoe

Swindler, William F. Roscoe Conkling and the Fourteenth Amendment. 8:46-52 (1983).

Conley, Lyda Burton

Cushman, Clare. Women Advocates Before the Supreme Court. 26-1:67-88 (2001).

Coolidge, Calvin

Fowler, Russell. Calvin Coolidge and the Supreme Court. 25-3:271-295 (2000).

Cox, Archibald

Knowles, Helen J. May It Please the Court? The Solicitor General's Not-So-"Special" Relationship: Archibald Cox and the 1963-1964 Reapportionment Cases. 31-3:279-297 (2006).

Terris, Bruce J. Attorney General Kennedy versus Solicitor General Cox: The Formulation of the Federal Government's Position in the Reapportionment Cases. 32-3:335-345 (2007).

Crafts, James F., Jr.

Small, Marshall L. William O. Douglas Remembered: A Collective Memory by WOD's Law Clerks. 32-3:297-334 (2007).

Cumming, Joseph W.

Harring, Sidney L. and Kathryn Swedlow. "The Defendant Has Seemed to Live a Charmed Life": *Hopt v. Utah*: Territorial Justice, The Supreme Court of the United States, and Late Nineteenth-Century Death Penalty Jurisprudence. 25-1:40-71 (2000).

Curtis, Benjamin

Morel, Lucas E. The *Dred Scott* Dissents: McLean, Curtis, Lincoln and the Public Mind. 32-2:133-151 (2007).

Cushing, William

Abraham, Henry J. John Marshall's Associate Justices. 27-3:286-292 (2002).

Downs, Harry. Unlikely Abolitionist: William Cushing and the Struggle against Slavery. 29-2:123-135 (2004).

Dallas, Alexander James

Dunne, Gerald T. The Early Court Reporters. 1:61-72 (1976).

Joyce, Craig. *Wheaton v. Peters*: The Untold Story of the Early Reporters. 10:35-92 (1985).

Dana, Richard Henry

Amestoy, Jeffrey L. The Supreme Court Argument that Saved the Union: Richard Henry Dana, Jr., and the *Prize Cases*. 35-1:10-24 (2010).

Daniel, Peter V.

[Swindler, William F.] W. F. S. His Honor and the Field of Honor. 4:84-85 (1979).

Davis, David

Kahn, Michael A. Abraham Lincoln's Appointments to the Supreme Court: A Master Politician at His Craft. 22-2:65-78 (1997).

Sharp, Allen. Justices Seeking the Presidency. 29-3:286-307 (2004).

Douglas, William O.

Brennan, William J., Jr. Richard W. Benka, Richard H. Chambers, Ramsey Clark, Milton V. Freeman, Thomas J. Klitgaard, Simon H. Rifkind, Gerhard A. Gesell, Erwin N. Griswold, Milton Handler, Leonard F. Jansen, William A. Reppy, Marshall L. Small, Jay Kelly Wright, and Eric Sevareid. Remembrances of William O. Douglas on the 50th Anniversary of His Appointment to the Supreme Court. 15:104-124 (1990).

Cohen, Sheldon S. The Court Diary of Justice William O. Douglas: Preface. 20:77 (1995).

Danelski, David J. Lucile Lomen: The First Woman to Clerk at the Supreme Court. 24-1:43-49 (1999).

Sharp, Allen. Justices Seeking the Presidency. 29-3:286-307 (2004).

Gessell, Gerhard A.

Brennan, William J., Jr. Richard W. Benka, Richard H. Chambers, Ramsey Clark, Milton V. Freeman, Thomas J. Klitgaard, Simon H. Rifkind, Gerhard A. Gesell, Erwin N. Griswold, Milton Handler, Leonard F. Jansen, William A. Reppy, Marshall L. Small, Jay Kelly Wright, and Eric Sevareid. Remembrances of William O. Douglas on the 50th Anniversary of His Appointment to the Supreme Court. 15:104-124 (1990).

Ginsburg, David

Small, Marshall L. William O. Douglas Remembered: A Collective Memory by WOD's Law Clerks. 32-3:297-334 (2007).

Gobitas, Lillian

Van Orden, James F. "Jehovah Will Provide": Lillian Gobitas and Freedom of Religion. 29-2:136-144 (2004).

Goldberg, Arthur J.

Breyer, Stephen. Clerking for Justice Goldberg. 15:4-7 (1990).

Mikva, Abner. Arthur J. Goldberg, The Practitioner. 15:1-3 (1990).

Gossett, Elizabeth Hughes

Gossett, Elizabeth Hughes. My Father the Chief Justice. 1:7-15 (1976).

In Memoriam: Elizabeth Hughes Gossett 1907-1981. 7:[5] (1982).

Gray, Marvin L., Jr.

Dorsen, Norman and Amelia Ames Newcomb, Eds. John Marshall Harlan II, Associate Justice of the Supreme Court 1955-1971: Remembrances by His Law Clerks. 27-2:138-175 (2002).

Greenawalt, Kent

Dorsen, Norman and Amelia Ames Newcomb, Eds. John Marshall Harlan II, Associate Justice of the Supreme Court 1955-1971: Remembrances by His Law Clerks. 27-2:138-175 (2002).

Griswold, Erwin N.

Brennan, William J., Jr. Richard W. Benka, Richard H. Chambers, Ramsey Clark, Milton V. Freeman, Thomas J. Klitgaard, Simon H. Rifkind, Gerhard A. Gesell, Erwin N. Griswold, Milton Handler, Leonard F. Jansen, William A. Reppy, Marshall L. Small, Jay Kelly Wright, and Eric Sevareid. Remembrances of William O. Douglas on the 50th Anniversary of His Appointment to the Supreme Court. 15:104-124 (1990).

Grossman, Harvey

Small, Marshall L. William O. Douglas Remembered: A Collective Memory by WOD's Law Clerks. 32-3:297-334 (2007).

Hand, Learned

Gunther, Gerald. Judge Learned Hand: The Man, the Myth, the Biography. 20:47-56 (1995).

Handler, Milton

Brennan, William J., Jr. Richard W. Benka, Richard H. Chambers, Ramsey Clark, Milton V. Freeman, Thomas J. Klitgaard, Simon H. Rifkind, Gerhard A. Gesell, Erwin N. Griswold, Milton Handler, Leonard F. Jansen, William A. Reppy, Marshall L. Small, Jay Kelly Wright, and Eric Sevareid. Remembrances of William O. Douglas on the 50th Anniversary of His Appointment to the Supreme Court. 15:104-124 (1990).

Handler, Milton. The 1926 Term: My Clerkship with Mr. Justice Stone. 10:5-7 (1985).

Handler, Milton C. Clerking for Justice Harlan Fiske Stone. 20:113-122 (1995).

Handler, Milton and Michael Ruby. Justice Holmes and the Year Books. 13:37-39 (1988).

Harlan, John Marshall

Baker, Liva. John Marshall Harlan I and a Color Blind Constitution The Frankfurter-Harlan II Conversations. 17:27-37 (1992).

Beth, Loren P. Justice Harlan and the Chief Justiceship, 1910. 8:73-79 (1983).

Beth, Loren P. President Hayes Appoints a Justice. 14:68-77 (1989).

Campbell, Peter Scott. The Civil War Reminiscences of John Marshall Harlan. 32-3:249-275 (2007).

Campell, Peter Scott. John Marshall Harlan's Political Memoir. 33-3:304-321 (2008).

Connally, C. Ellen. Justice Harlan's "Great Betrayal"? A Reconsideration of *Cumming v. Richmond County Board of Education*. 25-1:72-92 (2000).

Davies, Ross E. The Judicial and Ancient Games: James Wilson, John Marshall Harlan, and the Beginnings of Golf at the Supreme Court. 35-2:122-143 (2010).

Novak, Andrew. Courtroom to Classroom: Justice Harlan's Lectures at George Washington University Law School. 30-3:211-225 (2005).

Przybyszewski, Linda. The Dissents of John Marshall Harlan I. 32-2:152-161 (2007).

Harlan, John Marshall, II

Baker, Liva. John Marshall Harlan I and a Color Blind Constitution The Frankfurter-Harlan II Conversations. 17:27-37 (1992).

Dorsen, Norman. John Marshall Harlan and the Warren Court. 16:50-62 (1991).

Dorsen, Norman and Amelia Ames Newcomb, Eds. John Marshall Harlan II, Associate Justice of the Supreme Court 1955-1971: Remembrances by His Law Clerks. 27-2:138-175 (2002).

O'Brien, David M. John Marshall Harlan's Unpublished Opinions: Reflections of a Supreme Court at Work. 16:27-49 (1991).

Vasicko, Sally Jo. Justice Harlan and the Equal Protection Clause. 7:46-56 (1982).

Harlan, Malvina Shanklin

Ginsburg, Ruth Bader. Foreword. 26-2:vii-viii (2001).

Przybyszewski, Linda. Introduction. 26-2:97-108 (2001).

Harlan, Malvina Shanklin. Some Memories of a Long Life, 1854-1911. 26-2:109-211 (2001).

Harrison, Benjamin

Sharp, Allen. Presidents as Supreme Court Advocates: Before and after the White House. 28-2:116-144 (2003).

Harrison, Robert Hanson

Marcus, Maeva and Christine Jordan. Welcome Back, Justice Harrison? 4:80-81 (1979).

Hayes, Rutherford B.

Beth, Loren P. President Hayes Appoints a Justice. 14:68-77 (1989).

Heymann, Philip B.

Dorsen, Norman and Amelia Ames Newcomb, Eds. John Marshall Harlan II, Associate Justice of the Supreme Court 1955-1971: Remembrances by His Law Clerks. 27-2:138-175 (2002).

Hiegel, Richard J.

Dorsen, Norman and Amelia Ames Newcomb, Eds. John Marshall Harlan II, Associate Justice of the Supreme Court 1955-1971: Remembrances by His Law Clerks. 27-2:138-175 (2002).

Holmes, Oliver Wendell, Jr.

Aichele, Gary J. Self-Preference, Competition and the Rule of Force: The Holmesian Legacy. 13:11-17 (1988).

Berns, Walter and Philippa Strum. Issue: The Clear and Present Danger Test. 25-2:187-190 (2000).

Handler, Milton and Michael Ruby. Justice Holmes and the Year Books. 13:37-39 (1988).

Hoffheimer, Michael H. Justice Holmes: Law and the Search for Control. 14:98-118 (1989).

Laycock, Douglas. The Clear and Present Danger Test. 25-2:161-186 (2000).

McDonald, Kevin D. Antitrust and Baseball: Stealing Holmes. 23-2:88-128 (1998).

Messinger, I. Scott. Legitimating Liberalism: The New Deal Image-Makers and Oliver Wendell Holmes, Jr. 20:57-72 (1995).

Monagan, John S. The Grand Panjandrum: Mellow Years of Justice Holmes. 13:26-36 (1988).

O'Brien, David M. Sutherland's Recollections of Justice Holmes. 13:18-25 (1988).

Polenberg, Richard. Freedom of Speech, 1919 and 1994: Justice Holmes after Seventy-Five Years. 19:19-32 (1994).

Wagner, Richard H. A Falling Out: The Relationship Between Oliver Wendell Holmes and Theodore Roosevelt. 27-2:114-137 (2002).

Hoover, Herbert

Pusey, Merlo J. The Nomination of Charles Evans Hughes as Chief Justice. 7:95-99 (1982).

Hopt, Fred

Harring, Sidney L. and Kathryn Swedlow. "The Defendant Has Seemed to Live a Charmed Life": *Hopt v. Utah*: Territorial Justice, The Supreme Court of the United States, and Late Nineteenth-Century Death Penalty Jurisprudence. 25-1:40-71 (2000).

Hughes, Charles Evans

Cushman, Barry. The Hughes Court and Constitutional Consultation. 23-1:79-111 (1998).

Friedman, Richard D. Chief Justice Hughes' Letter on Court-Packing. 22-1:76-86 (1997).

Gossett, Elizabeth Hughes. My Father the Chief Justice. 1:7-15 (1976).

Knox, John. Some Comments on Chief Justice Hughes. [PORTFOLIO]. 9:34-44 (1984).

Morris, Richard B., Paul A. Freund and Herbert Wechsler. Columbians as Chief Justices: John Jay, Charles Evans Hughes and Harlan Fiske Stone. 13:66-77 (1988).

Pusey, Merlo J. The Hughes Biography: Some Personal Reflections. [PORTFOLIO]. 9:45-52 (1984).

Pusey, Merlo J. The Nomination of Charles Evans Hughes as Chief Justice. 7:95-99 (1982).

Sharp, Allen. Justices Seeking the Presidency. 29-3:286-307 (2004).

Hylton, Daniel

Frankel, Robert P., Jr. Before *Marbury: Hylton v. United States* and the Origins of Judicial Review. 28-1:1-13 (2003).

Jacob, Bernard

Small, Marshall L. William O. Douglas Remembered: A Collective Memory by WOD's Law Clerks. 32-3:297-334 (2007).

Jacobson, Richard

Small, Marshall L. William O. Douglas Remembered: A Collective Memory by WOD's Law Clerks. 32-3:297-334 (2007).

Jackson, Andrew

Norgren, Jill. The Cherokee Nation Cases of the 1830s. 19:65-82 (1994).

Jackson, Robert H.

Hockett, Jeffrey D. Justice Robert H. Jackson and Segregation: A Study of the Limitations and Proper Basis of Judicial Action. 14:52-67 (1989).

Hutchinson, Dennis J. Justice Jackson and the Nuremberg Trials. 21-1:105-116 (1996).

Martin, Constance L. The Life and Career of Justice Robert H. Jackson. 33-1:42-67 (2008).

Prettyman, E. Barrett, Jr. Robert H. Jackson: "Solicitor General for Life." 17:75-85 (1992).

Sharp, Allen. Justices Seeking the Presidency. 29-3:286-307 (2004).

Jansen, Leonard F.

Brennan, William J., Jr. Richard W. Benka, Richard H. Chambers, Ramsey Clark, Milton V. Freeman, Thomas J. Klitgaard, Simon H. Rifkind, Gerhard A. Gesell, Erwin N. Griswold, Milton Handler, Leonard F. Jansen, William A. Reppy, Marshall L. Small, Jay Kelly Wright, and Eric Sevareid. Remembrances of William O. Douglas on the 50th Anniversary of His Appointment to the Supreme Court. 15:104-124 (1990).

Jay, John

Freeman, Landa M. Mr. Jay Rides Circuit. 31-1:18-27 (2006).

Kaminski, John P. and Jennifer Lawton. Duty and Justice at "Every Man's Door": The Grand Jury Charges of Chief Justice John Jay, 1790-1794. 31-3:235-251 (2006).

Marcus, Maeva and Christine Jordan. Skeleton in Mr. Jay's Closet. 4:81-83 (1979).

Morris, Richard B., Paul A. Freund and Herbert Wechsler. Columbians as Chief Justices: John Jay, Charles Evans Hughes and Harlan Fiske Stone. 13:66-77 (1988).

Sirvet, Ene and R. B. Bernstein. Documentary Editing and the Jay Court: Opening New Lines of Inquiry. 21-2:17-22 (1996).

Sirvet, Ene and R. B. Bernstein. John Jay, Judicial Independence, and Advising Coordinate Branches. 21-2:23-29 (1996).

Jefferson, Thomas

Abraham, Henry J. President Jefferson's Three Appointments to the Supreme Court of the United States: 1804, 1807, and 1807. 31-2:141-154 (2006).

Bragaw, Stephen G. Thomas Jefferson and the American Indian Nations: Native American Sovereignty and the Marshall Court. 31-2:155-180 (2006).

Burger, Warren E. Thomas Jefferson and the Court. 16:97-104 (1991).

Newmyer, R. Kent. Thomas Jefferson and the Rise of the Supreme Court. 31-2:126-140 (2006).

Perry, Barbara A. Jefferson's Legacy to the Supreme Court: Freedom of Religion. 31-2:181-198 (2006).

Urofsky, Melvin I. Thomas Jefferson and John Marshall: What Kind of Constitution Shall We Have? 31-2:109-125 (2006).

Johnson, William

Abraham, Henry J. John Marshall's Associate Justices. 27-3:286-292 (2002).

Huebner, Timothy S. Divided Loyalties: Justice William Johnson and the Rise of Disunion in South Carolina, 1822-1834. 20:19-30 (1995).

VanBurkleo, Sandra F. In Defense of "Public Reason": Supreme Court Justice William Johnson. 32-2:115-132-2:(2007).

Kelley, Donald E.

Small, Marshall L. William O. Douglas Remembered: A Collective Memory by WOD's Law Clerks. 32-3:297-334 (2007).

Klitgaard, Thomas J.

Brennan, William J., Jr. Richard W. Benka, Richard H. Chambers, Ramsey Clark, Milton V. Freeman, Thomas J. Klitgaard, Simon H. Rifkind, Gerhard A. Gesell, Erwin N. Griswold, Milton Handler, Leonard F. Jansen, William A. Reppy, Marshall L. Small, Jay Kelly Wright, and Eric Sevareid. Remembrances of William O. Douglas on the 50th Anniversary of His Appointment to the Supreme Court. 15:104-124 (1990).

Small, Marshall L. William O. Douglas Remembered: A Collective Memory by WOD's Law Clerks. 32-3:297-334 (2007).

Koh, Harold Hongju

Koh, Harold Hongju. The Justice Who Grew. 19:5-8 (1994).

Krattenmaker, Thomas G.

Dorsen, Norman and Amelia Ames Newcomb, Eds. John Marshall Harlan II, Associate Justice of the Supreme Court 1955-1971: Remembrances by His Law Clerks. 27-2:138-175 (2002).

Kreindler, Peter

Small, Marshall L. William O. Douglas Remembered: A Collective Memory by WOD's Law Clerks. 32-3:297-334 (2007).

Lake, William T.

Dorsen, Norman and Amelia Ames Newcomb, Eds. John Marshall Harlan II, Associate Justice of the Supreme Court 1955-1971: Remembrances by His Law Clerks. 27-2:138-175 (2002).

Leiman, Leonard M.

Dorsen, Norman and Amelia Ames Newcomb, Eds. John Marshall Harlan II, Associate Justice of the Supreme Court 1955-1971: Remembrances by His Law Clerks. 27-2:138-175 (2002).

Lesnick, Howard

Dorsen, Norman and Amelia Ames Newcomb, Eds. John Marshall Harlan II, Associate Justice of the Supreme Court 1955-1971: Remembrances by His Law Clerks. 27-2:138-175 (2002).

Lewin, Nathan

Dorsen, Norman and Amelia Ames Newcomb, Eds. John Marshall Harlan II, Associate Justice of the Supreme Court 1955-1971: Remembrances by His Law Clerks. 27-2:138-175 (2002).

Lewis, Anthony

Lahav, Pnina. History in Journalism and Journalism in History: Anthony Lewis and the Watergate Crisis. 29-2:163-176 (2004).

Marshall, Thurgood

Bloch, Susan Low. The Privilege of Clerking for Thurgood Marshall. 17:23-25 (1992).

Brennan, William J., Jr. A Tribute to Thurgood Marshall. 17:1-8 (1992).

Carter, Robert L. Reflections on Justice Marshall. 17:15-18 (1992).

Claiborne, Louis F. The Noblest Roman of Them All: A Tribute to Justice Marshall. 17:19-21 (1992).

O'Connor, Sandra Day. Thurgood Marshall: The Influence of a Raconteur. 17:9-13 (1992).

Matthews, Stanley

Lurie, Jonathan. Stanley Matthews: A Case Portrait of Gilded Age High Court Jurisprudence. 33-2:160-169 (2008).

McKenna, Joseph

Owens, John B. The Clerk, the Thief, His Life as a Baker: Ashton Embry and the Supreme Court Leak Scandal. 27-1:14-44 (2002).

McLean, John

Kahn, Michael A. The Appointment of John McLean to the Supreme Court: Practical Presidential Politics in the Jacksonian Era. 18:59-72 (1993).

Morel, Lucas E. The *Dred Scott* Dissents: McLean, Curtis, Lincoln and the Public Mind. 32-2:133-151 (2007).

Sharp, Allen. Justices Seeking the Presidency. 29-3:286-307 (2004).

McReynolds, James C.

Arkes, Hadley. A Return to the Four Horsemen. 22-1:33-54 (1997).

Lawrence, Albert. Biased Justice: James C. McReynolds of the Supreme Court of the United States. 30-3:244-270 (2005).

Merrifield, Lewis

Small, Marshall L. William O. Douglas Remembered: A Collective Memory by WOD's Law Clerks. 32-3:297-334 (2007).

Miller, Charles

Small, Marshall L. William O. Douglas Remembered: A Collective Memory by WOD's Law Clerks. 32-3:297-334 (2007).

Miller, Samuel F.

Kahn, Michael A. Abraham Lincoln's Appointments to the Supreme Court: A Master Politician at His Craft. 22-2:65-78 (1997).

Ross, Michael A. Melancholy Justice: Samuel Freeman Miller and the Supreme Court during the Gilded Age. 33-2:134-148 (2008).

Minsker, Martin D.

Dorsen, Norman and Amelia Ames Newcomb, Eds. John Marshall Harlan II, Associate Justice of the Supreme Court 1955-1971: Remembrances by His Law Clerks. 27-2:138-175 (2002).

Mnookin, Robert H.

Dorsen, Norman and Amelia Ames Newcomb, Eds. John Marshall Harlan II, Associate Justice of the Supreme Court 1955-1971: Remembrances by His Law Clerks. 27-2:138-175 (2002).

Moody, William Henry

Heffron, Paul. Profile of a Public Man. 5:30-37, 48 (1980).

Moore, Alfred

Abraham, Henry J. John Marshall's Associate Justices. 27-3:286-292 (2002).

Murphy, Frank

Potts, Margaret H. Justice Frank Murphy: A Reexamination. 7:57-65 (1982).

Urofsky, Melvin I. The Court at War, and the War at the Court. 21-1:1-18 (1996).

Murray, Madelyn

Dierenfield, Bruce J. "The Most Hated Woman in America": Madalyn Murray and the Crusade against School Prayer. 32-1:62-84 (2007).

Nesson, Charles R.

Dorsen, Norman and Amelia Ames Newcomb, Eds. John Marshall Harlan II, Associate Justice of the Supreme Court 1955-1971: Remembrances by His Law Clerks. 27-2:138-175 (2002).

Newcomb, Amelia Ames

Dorsen, Norman and Amelia Ames Newcomb, Eds. John Marshall Harlan II, Associate Justice of the Supreme Court 1955-1971: Remembrances by His Law Clerks. 27-2:138-175 (2002).

Nimetz, Matthew

Dorsen, Norman and Amelia Ames Newcomb, Eds. John Marshall Harlan II, Associate Justice of the Supreme Court 1955-1971: Remembrances by His Law Clerks. 27-2:138-175 (2002).

Nixon, Richard

Sharp, Allen. Presidents as Supreme Court Advocates: Before and after the White House. 28-2:116-144 (2003).

Norris, William

Small, Marshall L. William O. Douglas Remembered: A Collective Memory by WOD's Law Clerks. 32-3:297-334 (2007).

O'Connor, Sandra Day

Joyce, Craig. "A Good Judge." 31-2:100-106 (2006).

Merritt, Deborah Jones. Justice Sandra Day O'Connor the Framers' "First Woman." 31-2:107-108 (2006).

O'Connor, Sandra Day. Thurgood Marshall: The Influence of a Raconteur. 17:9-13 (1992).

Stevens, John Paul. Tribute to Justice O'Connor. 31-2:99 (2006).

Rutherglen, George

Small, Marshall L. William O. Douglas Remembered: A Collective Memory by WOD's Law Clerks. 32-3:297-334 (2007).

Rutledge, Wiley

Ferren, John M. General Yamashita and Justice Rutledge. 28-1:54-80 (2003).

Ferren, John M. Military Curfew, Race-Based Internment, and Mr. Justice Rutledge. 28-3:252-269 (2003).

Guy, George F. The Defense of General Yamashita. 6:52-67 (1981).

Powe, L. A., Jr. (Re)introducing Wiley Rutledge. 29-3:337-345 (2004).

Sailer, Henry R.

Dorsen, Norman and Amelia Ames Newcomb, Eds. John Marshall Harlan II, Associate Justice of the Supreme Court 1955-1971: Remembrances by His Law Clerks. 27-2:138-175 (2002).

Schlei, Norbert A.

Dorsen, Norman and Amelia Ames Newcomb, Eds. John Marshall Harlan II, Associate Justice of the Supreme Court 1955-1971: Remembrances by His Law Clerks. 27-2:138-175 (2002).

Schwab, Evan

Small, Marshall L. William O. Douglas Remembered: A Collective Memory by WOD's Law Clerks. 32-3:297-334 (2007).

Seneker, Carl J., III

Small, Marshall L. William O. Douglas Remembered: A Collective Memory by WOD's Law Clerks. 32-3:297-334 (2007).

Severeid, Eric

Brennan, William J., Jr. Richard W. Benka, Richard H. Chambers, Ramsey Clark, Milton V. Freeman, Thomas J. Klitgaard, Simon H. Rifkind, Gerhard A. Gesell, Erwin N. Griswold, Milton Handler, Leonard F. Jansen, William A. Reppy, Marshall L. Small, Jay Kelly Wright, and Eric Severeid. Remembrances of William O. Douglas on the 50th Anniversary of His Appointment to the Supreme Court. 15:104-124 (1990).

Shapiro, David L.

Dorsen, Norman and Amelia Ames Newcomb, Eds. John Marshall Harlan II, Associate Justice of the Supreme Court 1955-1971: Remembrances by His Law Clerks. 27-2:138-175 (2002).

Shulman, Stephen

Dorsen, Norman and Amelia Ames Newcomb, Eds. John Marshall Harlan II, Associate Justice of the Supreme Court 1955-1971: Remembrances by His Law Clerks. 27-2:138-175 (2002).

Small, Marshall L.

Brennan, William J., Jr. Richard W. Benka, Richard H. Chambers, Ramsey Clark, Milton V. Freeman, Thomas J. Klitgaard, Simon H. Rifkind, Gerhard A. Gesell, Erwin N. Griswold, Milton Handler, Leonard F. Jansen, William A. Reppy, Marshall L. Small, Jay Kelly Wright, and Eric Severeid. Remembrances of William O. Douglas on the 50th Anniversary of His Appointment to the Supreme Court. 15:104-124 (1990).

Small, Marshall L. William O. Douglas Remembered: A Collective Memory by WOD's Law Clerks. 32-3:297-334 (2007).

Snyder, Allen R.

Dorsen, Norman and Amelia Ames Newcomb, Eds. John Marshall Harlan II, Associate Justice of the Supreme Court 1955-1971: Remembrances by His Law Clerks. 27-2:138-175 (2002).

Souter, David

Gerken, Heather. Clerking for Justice Souter. 35-1:4-6 (2010).

O'Connor, Sandra Day. Tribute to Justice Souter. 35-1:1-3 (2010).

Roosevelt, Kermit. David Souter: A Clerk's View. 35-1:7-9 (2010).

Steiner, Henry J.

Dorsen, Norman and Amelia Ames Newcomb, Eds. John Marshall Harlan II, Associate Justice of the Supreme Court 1955-1971: Remembrances by His Law Clerks. 27-2:138-175 (2002).

Stern, Robert L.

Stern, Robert L. Reminiscences of the Solicitor General's Office. 20:123-130 (1995).

Sternstein, Alan

Small, Marshall L. William O. Douglas Remembered: A Collective Memory by WOD's Law Clerks. 32-3:297-334 (2007).

Stevens, John Paul

O'Brien, David M. Filling Justice William O. Douglas's Seat: President Gerald R. Ford's Appointment of Justice John Paul Stevens. 14:20-39 (1989).

Sloan, Cliff. A Clerk's View. 35-3:198-200 (2010).

Souter, David H. Tribute to John Paul Stevens. 35-3:195-197 (2010).

Stewart, Potter

Binion, Gayle. Justice Potter Stewart: The *Unpredictable* Vote. 17:99-108 (1992).

Powell, Lewis F., Jr. In Memoriam: Justice Potter Stewart. 11:5-7 (1986).

Stoel, Thomas B., Jr.

Dorsen, Norman and Amelia Ames Newcomb, Eds. John Marshall Harlan II, Associate Justice of the Supreme Court 1955-1971: Remembrances by His Law Clerks. 27-2:138-175 (2002).

Stone, Harlan Fiske

Handler, Milton. The 1926 Term: My Clerkship with Mr. Justice Stone. 10:5-7 (1985).

Handler, Milton C. Clerking for Justice Harlan Fiske Stone. 20:113-122 (1995).

Fry, Amelia Roberts. The Warren Tapes: Oral History and the Supreme Court. 7:10-22 (1982).

Schwartz, Bernard. Chief Justice Earl Warren: Super Chief in Action. 23-1:112-132 (1998).

Vestal, Theodore M. Public Diplomacy in the U. S. Supreme Court: The Warren Years—Part I. 33-3:371-393 (2008).

Vestal, Theodore M. Public Diplomacy in the U. S. Supreme Court: The Warren Years—Part II. 34-1:98-124 (2009).

Warren, Earl, Jr. My Father the Chief Justice. 7:6-9 (1982).

Warren, Earl W., Jr.

Warren, Earl, Jr. My Father the Chief Justice. 7:6-9 (1982).

Washington, Bushrod

Dunne, Gerald T. Bushrod Washington and the Mount Vernon Slaves. 5:25-29 (1980).

Washington, George

Marcus, Maeva. George Washington's Appointments to the Supreme Court. 24-3:243-254 (1999).

Nordham, George Washington. President George Washington and the First Supreme Court. 9:7-11 (1984).

Simpson, Brooks D. President Washington's Appointments to the Supreme Court. 17:63-74 (1992).

Webster, Daniel

Finley, S. W. Daniel Webster Packed 'Em In. 4:70-78, 83 (1979).

Rehnquist, William H. Daniel Webster and the Oratorical Tradition. 14:5-12 (1989).

Weinreb, Lloyd L.

Dorsen, Norman and Amelia Ames Newcomb, Eds. John Marshall Harlan II, Associate Justice of the Supreme Court 1955-1971: Remembrances by His Law Clerks. 27-2:138-175 (2002).

Wheaton, Henry

Joyce, Craig. *Wheaton v. Peters*: The Untold Story of the Early Reporters. 10:35-92 (1985).

White, Byron R.

Lee, Rex E. On Greatness and Constitutional Vision: Justice Byron R. White. 18:5-10 (1993).

Rehnquist, William H. A Tribute to Justice Byron R. White. 18:2-4 (1993).

White, Edward D.

Carter, Newman and Editorial Staff. Edward D. White in Personal Retrospect. 4:5-7 (1979).

Morris, Jeffrey B. Chief Justice Edward Douglàss White and President Taft's Court. 7:27-45 (1982).

Whittaker, Charles Evan

Kohn, Alan C. Supreme Court Law Clerk, 1957-1958, A Reminiscence. 23-2:40-52 (1998).

Williams, Edward Bennett

Mullin, Connor. Edward Bennett Williams for the Petitioner: Profile of a Supreme Court Advocate. 34-2:204-223 (2009).

Wilson, James

Davies, Ross E. The Judicial and Ancient Games: James Wilson, John Marshall Harlan, and the Beginnings of Golf at the Supreme Court. 35-2:122-143 (2010).

Maxey, David W. The Translation of James Wilson. 15:29-43 (1990).

Wilson, Paul

Wilson, Paul E. A Time to Lose. 24-2:170-180 (1999).

Wilson, Woodrow

Urofsky, Melvin I. The "Outrageous" Brandeis Nomination. 4:8-19. (1979).

Urofsky, Melvin I. Wilson, Brandeis, and the Supreme Court Nomination. 28-2:145-156 (2003).

Wirt, William

Robert, Joseph C. The Many-Sided Attorney General. 1:51-60 (1976).

Thorp, Galen N. William Wirt. 33-3:223-303 (2008).

Woods, William B.

Baynes, Thomas E., Jr. A Search for Justice Woods. 3:31-42 (1978).

Wright, Jay Kelly

Brennan, William J., Jr. Richard W. Benka, Richard H. Chambers, Ramsey Clark, Milton V. Freeman, Thomas J. Klitgaard, Simon H. Rifkind, Gerhard A. Gesell, Erwin N. Griswold, Milton Handler, Leonard F. Jansen, William A. Reppy, Marshall L. Small, Jay Kelly Wright, and Eric Sevareid. Remembrances of William O. Douglas on the 50th Anniversary of his Appointment to the Supreme Court. 15:104-124 (1990).

Small, Marshall L. William O. Douglas Remembered: A Collective Memory by WOD's Law Clerks. 32-3:297-334 (2007).

Wythe, George

Powell, Lewis F., Jr. George Wythe. 15:25-28 (1990).

Yamashita, Tomoyuki

Belknap, Michal R. Alarm Bells from the Past: The Troubling History of American Military Commissions. 28-3:300-322 (2003).

Ferren, John M. General Yamashita and Justice Rutledge. 28-1:54-80 (2003).

Guy, George F. The Defense of General Yamashita. 6:52-67 (1981).

Charities

Monroe, Elizabeth Brand. The Influence of the *Dartmouth College* Case on the American Law of Educational Charities. 32-1:1-21 (2007).

Chinese-Americans

Bernstein, David E. Two Asian Laundry Cases. 24-1:95-111 (1999).

Bernstein, David E. *Plessy* versus *Lochner*: The *Berea College* Case. 25-1:93-111 (2000).

Rhee, Jeannie. In Black and White: Chinese in the Mississippi Delta. 19:117-132 (1994).

Circuit Riding

Baker, Leonard P. The Circuit Riding Justices. 2:63-69 (1977).

Clinton, Robert Lowry. The Supreme Court before John Marshall. 27-3:222-239 (2002).

Freeman, Landa M. Mr. Jay Rides Circuit. 31-1:18-27 (2006).

Kaminski, John P. and Jennifer Lawton. Duty and Justice at "Every Man's Door": The Grand Jury Charges of Chief Justice John Jay, 1790-1794. 31-3:235-251 (2006).

Marcus, Maeva, James R. Perry, James M. Buchanan, Christine R. Jordan, and Steven L. Tull. "It is my wish as well as my Duty to attend the court": The Hardships of Supreme Court Service, 1790-1800. 9:118-126 (1984).

Civil Liberties

Stone, Geoffrey R. Civil Liberties in Wartime. 28-3:215-251 (2003).

Turner, Robert F. The Supreme Court, Separation of Powers, and the Protection of Individual Rights during Periods of War or National Security Emergency. 28-3:323-338 (2003).

Civil Rights

Benedict, Michael Les. Reconstruction: The Civil War Amendments. Sp. Ed.:89-97 (1996).

Bernstein, David E. *Plessy* versus *Lochner:* The *Berea College* Case. 25-1:93 (2000).

Bressman, Jeremy. A New Standard of Review: *Craig v. Boren* and Brennan's "Heightened Scrutiny" Test in Historical Perspective. 32-1:85-95 (2007).

Connally, C. Ellen. Justice Harlan's "Great Betrayal"? A Reconsideration of *Cumming v. Richmond County Board of Education*. 25-1:72-92 (2000).

Dudziak, Mary L. The Supreme Court and Racial Equality during World War II. 21-1:35-48 (1996).

Franklin, John Hope. A Half-Century of Presidential Race Initiatives: Some Reflections. 24-2:226-237 (1999).

Greenburg, Jack. If. . . . 24-2:181-200 (1999).

Hockett, Jeffrey D. The Battle over *Brown's* Legitimacy. 28-1:30-53 (2003).

Kennedy, Randall. Reconstruction: The Waite Court and the Politics of History. Sp. Ed.:99-102 (1996).

Kull, Andrew. Post-*Plessy*, Pre-*Brown*: "Logical Exactness" in Enforcing Equal Rights. 24-2:155-169 (1999).

Levy, David W. Before *Brown*: The Racial Integration of American Higher Education. 24-3:298-313 (1999).

Rosenberg, Gerald N. African-American Rights after *Brown*. 24-2:201-225 (1999).

Rutherglen, George. Textual Corruption in the *Civil Rights Cases*. 34-2:164-169 (2009).

Thomas, Clarence. The Virtue of Defeat: *Plessy v. Ferguson* in Retrospect. 22-2:15-24 (1997).

Waldrep, Christopher. Joseph P. Bradley's Journey: The Meaning of Privileges and Immunities. 34-2:149-163 (2009).

Wallenstein, Peter. Race, Marriage, and the Supreme Court from *Pace v. Alabama* (1883) to *Loving v. Virginia* (1967). 23-2:65-87 (1998).

Wallenstein, Peter. To Sit or Not to Sit: The Supreme Court of the United States and the Civil Rights Movement in the Upper South. 29-2:145-162 (2004).

White, G. Edward. Salmon Portland Chase and the Judicial Culture of the Supreme Court in the Civil War Era. Sp. Ed.:37-45 (1996).

Wilson, Paul E. A Time to Lose. 24-2:170-180 (1999).

Civil War

Belz, Herman. The Supreme Court and Constitutional Responsibility in the Civil War Era. Sp. Ed.:5-8 (1996).

Benedict, Michael Les. Reconstruction: The Civil War Amendments. Sp. Ed.:89-97 (1996).

Hamilton, Daniel W. A New Right to Property: Civil War Confiscation in the Reconstruction Supreme Court. 29-3:254-285 (2004).

Hyman, Harold M. The Undocketed Constitutional Bridge across the War Gulf, ca. 1861-73. Sp. Ed. 63-74 (1996).

Johnson, Ludwell H., III. No Faith in Parchment. Sp. Ed.:9-14. (1996)

Kennedy, Randall. Reconstruction: The Waite Court and the Politics of History. Sp. Ed.:99-102 (1996).

Kramer, Larry. Federalism in Antebellum America: The View from the North. Sp. Ed.:15-21 (1996).

Maltz, Earl M. The Waite Court and Federal Power to Enforce the Reconstruction Amendments. Sp. Ed.:75-88 (1996).

Neely, Mark E., Jr. Justice Embattled: The Lincoln Administration and the Constitutional Controversy over Conscription in 1863. Sp. Ed.:47-61 (1996).

Paludan, Phillip. Taney, Lincoln and the Constitutional Conversation. Sp. Ed.:22-35 (1996).

Silverman, Leon. Introduction: The Supreme Court in the Civil War. Sp. Ed.:1-4. (1996).

White, G. Edward. Salmon Portland Chase and the Judicial Culture of the Supreme Court in the Civil War Era. Sp. Ed.:37-45 (1996).

Clerks

Arnold, Richard S. A Remembrance: Mr. Justice Brennan October Term 1960. 16:5-8 (1991).

Bloch, Susan Low. The Privilege of Clerking for Thurgood Marshall. 17:23-25 (1992).

Brennan, William J., Jr. Richard W. Benka, Richard H. Chambers, Ramsey Clark, Milton V. Freeman, Thomas J.

Klitgaard, Simon H. Rifkind, Gerhard A. Gesell, Erwin N. Griswold, Milton Handler, Leonard F. Jansen, William A. Reppy, Marshall L. Small, Jay Kelly Wright, and Eric Sevareid. Remembrances of William O. Douglas on the 50th Anniversary of His Appointment to the Supreme Court. 15:104-124 (1990).

Breyer, Stephen. In Memoriam Clerking for Justice Goldberg. 15:4-7 (1990).

Danelski, David J. Lucile Lomen: The First Woman to Clerk at the Supreme Court. 24-1:43-49 (1999).

Dorsen, Norman and Amelia Ames Newcomb. John Marshall Harlan II, Associate Justice of the Supreme Court 1955-1971: Remembrances by His Law Clerks. 27-2:138-175 (2002).

Gerken, Heather. Clerking for Justice Souter. 35-1:4-6 (2010).

Handler, Milton. The 1926 Term: My Clerkship with Mr. Justice Stone. 10:5-7 (1985).

Handler, Milton C. Clerking for Justice Harlan Fiske Stone. 20:113-122 (1995).

Kohn, Alan C. Supreme Court Law Clerk, 1957-1958, A Reminiscence. 23-2:40-52 (1998).

McGurn, Barrett. Law Clerks—-A Professional Elite. 5:98-102 (1980).

O'Neil, Robert. Clerking for Justice Brennan. 16:3-4 (1991).

Owens, John B. The Clerk, the Thief, His Life as a Baker: Ashton Embry and the Supreme Court Leak Scandal. 27-1:14-44 (2002).

Peppers, Todd C. Birth of an Institution: Horace Gray and the Lost Law Clerks. 32-3:229-248 (2007).

Peppers, Todd C. Isaiah and His Young Disciples: Justice Brandeis and His Law Clerks. 34-1:75-97 (2009).

Price, Polly J. *Mapp v. Ohio* Revisited: A Law Clerk's Diary. 35-1:54-70 (2010).

Roosevelt, Kermit. David Souter: A Clerk's View. 35-1:7-9 (2010).

Sloan, Cliff. A Clerk's View. 35-3:198-200 (2010).

Small, Marshall L. William O. Douglas Remembered: A Collective Memory by WOD's Law Clerks. 32-3:297-334 (2007).

Westin, David. Justice Powell and His Law Clerks. 12:16-18 (1987).

Williams, C. Dickerman. The 1924 Term: Recollections of Chief Justice Taft's Law Clerk. 14:40-51 (1989).

Communism

Belknap, Michal R. *Dennis v. United States*: Great Case Or Cold War Relic?. 18:41-58 (1993).

Belknap, Michal R. Why *Dennis v. United States* is a Landmark Case. 34-3:289-302 (2009).

Comparative Law

Cohn, Haim H. The First Fifty Years of the Supreme Court of Israel. 24-1:3-15 (1999).

Millgramm, Karl-Heinz. Comparative Law: The Federal Constitutional Court of Germany and the Supreme Court of the United States. 10:146-154 (1985).

Constitution

Barrett, C. Waller. The Miracle of the Constitution. 3:97-102 (1978).

Kennedy, Cornelius Bryant. Toward 1987: A Dramatic Change in Goals, 1785-1787. 10:112-116 (1985).

Kennedy, Cornelius B. Toward 1987: The Foundation for the Constitution. 11:96-102 (1986).

Swindler, William F. The Selling of the Constitution. 5:49-54 (1980).

Swindler, William F. Toward 1987: Guidelines from the Centennial. 5:94-97 (1980).

Court-Packing Plan

Arkes, Hadley. A Return to the Four Horsemen. 22-1:33-54 (1997).

Currie, David P. The New Deal Court in the 1940s: Its Constitutional Legacy. 22-1:87-98 (1997).

Friedman, Richard D. Chief Justice Hughes' Letter on Court-Packing. 22-1:76-86 (1997).

Gardner, Warner W. Court Packing: The Drafting Recalled. 15:99-103 (1990).

Leuchtenburg, William E. F. D. R.'s Court-Packing Plan: A Second Life, A Second Death. 13:78-90 (1988).

Pusey, Merlo J. Justice Roberts' 1937 Turnaround. 8:102-107 (1983).

Rauh, Joseph L., Jr. A Personalized View of the Court-Packing Episode. 15:93-98 (1990).

Stern, Robert L. The Court-Packing Plan and the Commerce Clause. 13:91-97 (1988).

Criminal Law & Procedure

Danelski, David J. The Saboteurs' Case. 21-1:61-82 (1996).

Fakhimi, Morad. Terrorism and Habeas Corpus: A Jurisdictional Escape. 30-3:226-243 (2005).

Harring, Sidney L. and Kathryn Swedlow. "The Defendant Has Seemed to Live a Charmed Life": *Hopt v. Utah*: Territorial Justice, The Supreme Court of the United States, and Late Nineteenth-Century Death Penalty Jurisprudence. 25-1:40-71 (2000).

Hoffer, Williamjames Hull. William Paterson and the National Jurisprudence: Two Draft Opinions on the Sedition Law of 1798 and the Federal Common Law. 22-2:36-50 (1997).

Howard, J. Woodford, Jr. The *Cramer* Treason Case. 21-1:49-60 (1996).

Mosnier, Joseph. The Demise of an "Extraordinary Criminal Procedure": *Klopfer v. North Carolina* and the Incorporation of the Sixth Amendment's Speedy Trial Provision. 21-2:136-160 (1996).

Polenberg, Richard. Cardozo and the Criminal Law: *Palko v. Connecticut* Reconsidered. 21-2:92-105 (1996).

Wiecek, William M. Felix Frankfurter, Incorporation, and the Willie Francis Case. 26-1:53-66 (2001).

Documentary History Projects

Hobson, Charles F. John Marshall and His Papers. 21-2:30-35 (1996).

Marcus, Maeva. Documenting Judicial History: The Supreme Court of the United States, 1789-1800. 21-2:51-56 (1996).

Sirvet, Ene, and R. B. Bernstein. Documentary Editing and the Jay Court: Opening New Lines of Inquiry. 21-2:17-22 (1996).

Economic Policy

Waltman, Jerold. Supreme Court Activism in Economic Policy in the Waning Days of the New Deal: Interpreting the Fair Labor Standards Act, 1941-1946. 31-1:58-80 (2006).

Education and Segregation

Bernstein, David E. *Plessy* versus *Lochner:* The *Berea College* Case. 25-1:93-111 (2000).

Brownell, Herbert. *Brown v. Board of Education*: Revisited. 18:21-28 (1993).

Connally, C. Ellen. Justice Harlan's "Great Betrayal"? A Reconsideration of *Cumming v. Richmond County Board of Education*. 25-1:72-92 (2000).

Franklin, John Hope. A Half-Century of Presidential Race Initiatives: Some Reflections. 24-2:226-237 (1999).

Greenburg, Jack. If. . . . 24-2:181-200 (1999).

Hockett, Jeffrey D. Justice Robert H. Jackson and Segregation: A Study of the Limitations and Proper Basis of Judicial Action. 14:52-67 (1989).

Kruse, Kevin M. Personal Rights, Public Wrongs: The *Gaines* Case and the Beginning of the End of Segregation. 22-2:113-130 (1997).

Kull, Andrew. Post-*Plessy*, Pre-*Brown*: "Logical Exactness" in Enforcing Equal Rights. 24-2:155-169 (1999).

Levy, David W. Before *Brown*: The Racial Integration of American Higher Education. 24-3:298-313 (1999).

Rosenberg, Gerald N. African-American Rights after *Brown*. 24-2:201-225 (1999).

Wilson, Paul E. A Time to Lose. 24-2:170-180 (1999).

England

Woolf, Lord. The Appellate Committee and the Supreme Court: Anglo-American Comparisons. 1996-2:1-10 (1996).

Free Speech

Berns, Walter and Philippa Strum. Issue: The Clear and Present Danger Test. 25-2:187-190 (2000).

BeVier, Lillian R. Free Expression in the Warren and Burger Counts. 25-2:191-212 (2000).

Dry, Murray. The Origins and Foundations of the First Amendment and the Alien and Sedition Acts. 25-2:129-144 (2000).

Laycock, Douglas. The Clear and Present Danger Test. 25-2:161-186 (2000).

Rabban, David M. Free Speech: The Lost Years. 25-2:145-160 (2000).

White, James Boyd. Human Dignity and the Claim of Meaning: Athenian Tragic Drama and Supreme Court Opinions. 27-1:45-64 (2002).

George Washington University

Novak, Andrew. Courtroom to Classroom: Justice Harlan's Lectures at George Washington University Law School. 30-3:211-225 (2005).

Germany

Millgramm, Karl-Heinz. Comparative Law: The Federal Constitutional Court of Germany and the Supreme Court of the United States. 10:146-154 (1985).

Golf

Davies, Ross E. The Judicial and Ancient Games: James Wilson, John Marshall Harlan, and the Beginnings of Golf at the Supreme Court. 35-2:122-143 (2010).

Grand Jury

Kaminski, John P. and Jennifer Lawton. Duty and Justice at "Every Man's Door": The Grand Jury Charges of Chief Justice John Jay, 1790-1794. 31-3:235-251 (2006).

Gravesites of Justices

Christensen, George A. Here Lies the Supreme Court: Gravesites of the Justices. 8:17-30 (1983).

Christensen, George A. Here Lies the Supreme Court: Revisited. 33-1:17-41 (2008).

Maxey, David W. The Translation of James Wilson. 15:29-43 (1990).

Great Britain

Irvine, Alexander Andrew Mackay. Constitutional Change in the United Kingdom: British Solutions to Universal Problems. 23-2:26-39 (1998).

Greek Tragedy

White, James Boyd. Human Dignity and the Claim of Meaning: Athenian Tragic Drama and Supreme Court Opinions. 27-1:45-64 (2002).

Human Dignity

White, James Boyd. Human Dignity and the Claim of Meaning: Athenian Tragic Drama and Supreme Court Opinions. 27-1:45-64 (2002).

Immigration

Flowers, Ronald B. The Naturalization of Douglas Clyde Macintosh, Alien Theologian. 25-3:243-270 (2000).

Israel. Supreme Court.

Cohn, Haim H. The First Fifty Years of the Supreme Court of Israel. 24-1:3-15 (1999).

Japanese-American Internment

Ferren, John M. General Yamashita and Justice Rutledge. 28-1:54-80 (2003).

Ferren, John M. Military Curfew, Race-Based Internment, and Mr. Justice Rutledge. 28-3:252-269 (2003).

Kmiec, Douglas W. The Supreme Court in Times of Hot and Cold War: Learning from the Sounds of Silence for a War on Terrorism. 28-3:270-299 (2003).

Scheiber, Harry N. Property Rights versus "Public Necessity": A Perspective on Emergency Powers and the Supreme Court. 28-3:339-369 (2003).

Stone, Geoffrey R. Civil Liberties in Wartime. 28-3:215-251 (2003).

Jehovah's Witnesses

Peters, Shawn Francis. Re-hearing "Fighting Words": *Chaplinksy v. New Hampshire* in Retrospect. 24-3:282-297 (1999).

Van Orden, James F. "Jehovah Will Provide": Lillian Gobitas and Freedom of Religion. 29-2:136-144 (2004).

Judicial Conference of the United States

Markey, Howard T. Chief Justice Burger as Chairman of the Judicial Conference of the United States. 11:8-10 (1986).

Judicial Opinions

Bork, Judge Robert H. Styles in Constitutional Theory. 9:53-60 (1984).

Ferren, John M. General Yamashita and Justice Rutledge. 28-1:54-80 (2003).

Johnson, Calvin H. The Four Good Dissenters in *Pollock*. 32-2:162-177 (2007).

Lurie, Jonathan. Chief Justice Taft and Dissents: Down with the Brandeis Briefs! 32-2:178-189 (2007).

Marsh, James M. Mr. Dooley Discovers a Unanimous Dissent. 4:85-87 (1979).

Morel, Lucas E. The *Dred Scott* Dissents: McLean, Curtis, Lincoln, and the Public Mind. 32-2:133-151 (2007).

Palmer, Jan and Saul Brenner. Determinants of the Amount of Time Taken by the Vinson Court to Process Its Full-Opinion Cases. 15:142-151 (1990).

Przybyszewski, Linda. The Dissents of John Marshall Harlan I. 32-2:152-161 (2007).

Ray, Laura Krugman. The History of the Per Curiam Opinion: Consensus and Individual Expression on the Supreme Court. 27-2:176-193 (2002).

Scalia, Antonin. The Dissenting Opinion. 19:33-44 (1994).

Turner, Charles C., Lori Beth Way and Nancy Maveety. Beginning to Write Separately: The Origins and Development of Concurring Judicial Opinions. 35-2:93-109 (2010).

Judicial Review

Frankel, Robert P., Jr. Before *Marbury: Hylton v. United States* and the Origins of Judicial Review. 28-1:1-13 (2003).

Kyvig, David E. Appealing Supreme Court Decisions: Constitutional Amendments as Checks on Judicial Review. 21-2:106-119 (1996).

Judicial Robes

Clarkson, S. James. The Judicial Robe. 5:90-93 (1980).

Labor Law

Kens, Paul. *Lochner v. New York*: Rehabilitated and Revised, but Still Reviled. 20:31-46 (1995).

Kersch, Ken I. The *Gompers v. Buck's Stove* Saga: A Constitutional Case Study in Dialogue, Resistance, and the Freedom of Speech. 31-1:28-57 (2006).

McCurdy, Charles W. The Roots of "Liberty of Contract" Reconsidered: Major Premises in the Law of Employment, 1867-1937. 9:20-33 (1984).

Waltman, Jerold. Supreme Court Activism in Economic Policy in the Waning Days of the New Deal: Interpreting the Fair Labor Standards Act, 1941-1946. 31-1:58-80 (2006).

Land Use

Goldberger, Paul. Preservation's Supreme Authority. 16:9-12 (1991).

Power, Garrett. Advocates at Cross-Purposes: The Briefs on Behalf of Zoning in the Supreme Court. 22-2:79-87 (1997).

Wolf, Michael Allan. "Compelled by Conscientious Duty": *Village of Euclid v. Ambler Realty Co.* as Romance. 22-2:88-100 (1997).

Liberty Ships

O'Hara, James B. The Supreme Court Fleet. 17:87-97 (1992).

Maritime Law

Amestoy, Jeffrey L. The Supreme Court Argument that Saved the Union: Richard Henry Dana, Jr., and the *Prize Cases*. 35-1:10-24 (2010).

Gordan, John D., III. The Trial of the Officers and Crew of the Schooner "Savannah." 8:31-45 (1983).

O'Hara, James B. The Supreme Court Fleet. 17:87-97 (1992).

Medical Jurisprudence

Hohenstein, Kurt. Just What the Doctor Ordered: The Harrison Anti-Narcotic Act, the Supreme Court, and the Federal Regulation of Medical Practice, 1915-1919. 26-3:231-256 (2001).

Military Commissions

Belknap, Michal R. Alarm Bells from the Past: The Troubling History of American Military Commissions. 28-3:300-322 (2003).

Sharp, Allen. Presidents as Supreme Court Advocates: Before and after the White House. 28-2:116-144 (2003).

Progressive Era (1890-1920)

Urofsky, Melvin I. Myth and Reality: The Supreme Court and Protective Legislation in the Progressive Era. 8:53-72 (1983).

Property Rights

Ely, James W., Jr. Property Rights and the Supreme Court in World War II. 26-1:19-34 (1996).

Hamilton, Daniel W. A New Right to Property: Civil War Confiscation in the Reconstruction Supreme Court. 29-3:254-285 (2004).

Scheiber, Harry N. Property Rights versus "Public Necessity": A Perspective on Emergency Powers and the Supreme Court. 28-3:339-369 (2003).

Reapportionment

Knowles, Helen J. May It Please the Court? The Solicitor General's Not-So-"Special" Relationship: Archibald Cox and the 1963-1964 Reapportionment Cases. 31-3: 279-297 (2006).

Terris, Bruce J. Attorney General Kennedy versus Solicitor General Cox: The Formulation of the Federal Government's Position in the Reapportionment Cases. 32-3:335-345 (2007).

Satire

Marsh, James M. Mr. Dooley Discovers a Unanimous Dissent. 4:85-87 (1979).

School Prayer

Dierenfield, Bruce J. "The Most Hated Woman in America": Madalyn Murray and the Crusade against School Prayer. 32-1:62-84 (2007).

Slavery

Breyer, Stephen G. A Look Back at the *Dred Scott* Decision. 35-2:110-121 (2010).

Downs, Harry. Unlikely Abolitionist: William Cushing and the Struggle against Slavery. 29-2:123-135 (2004).

Dunne, Gerald T. Bushrod Washington and the Mount Vernon Slaves. 5:25-29 (1980).

Finkelman, Paul. *Prigg v. Pennsylvania* Understanding Justice Story's Proslavery Nationalism. 22-2:51-64 (1997).

Lightner, David L. The Supreme Court and the Interstate Slave Trade: A Study in Evasion, Anarchy, and Extremism. 29-3:229-253 (2004).

Morel, Lucas E. The *Dred Scott* Dissents: McLean, Curtis, Lincoln, and the Public Mind. 32-2:133-151 (2007).

Paludan, Phillip. Taney, Lincoln and the Constitutional Conversation. Sp. Ed.:22-35 (1996).

Solicitor General

Cushman, Clare. Women Advocates Before the Supreme Court. 26-1:67-88 (2001).

Knowles, Helen J. May It Please the Court? The Solicitor General's Not-So-"Special" Relationship: Archibald Cox and the 1963-1964 Reapportionment Cases. 31-3:279-297 (2006).

Lee, Rex E. Lawyering in the Supreme Court: The Role of the Solicitor General. 10:15-21 (1985).

Lepore, Stefanie A. The Development of the Supreme Court Practice of Calling for the Views of the Solicitor General. 35-1:35-53 (2010).

Prettyman, E. Barrett, Jr. Robert H. Jackson: "Solicitor General for Life." 17:75-85 (1992).

Stern, Robert L. Reminiscences of the Solicitor General's Office. 20:123-130 (1995).

Terris, Bruce J. Attorney General Kennedy versus Solicitor General Cox: The Formulation of the Federal Government's Position in the Reapportionment Cases. 32-3:335-345 (2007).

Waxman, Seth P. "Presenting the Case of the United States as It Should Be": The Solicitor General in Historical Context. 23-2:3-25 (1998).

Sports Law

Alito, Samuel A., Jr. The Origin of the Baseball Antitrust Exemption: *Federal Baseball Club of Baltimore, Inc. v. National League of Professional Baseball.* 34-2:183-195 (2009).

Davies, Ross E. A Tall Tale of *The Brethren.* 33-2:186-199 (2008).

McDonald, Kevin D. Antitrust and Baseball: Stealing Holmes. 23-2:88-128 (1998).

Stare Decisis

Powell, Lewis F., Jr. Stare Decisis and Judicial Restraint. 16:13-19 (1991).

Subversive Organizations

Goldstein, Robert Justin. The Grapes of *McGrath*: The Supreme Court and the Attorney General's List of Subversive Organizations in *Joint Anti-Fascist Refugee Committee v. McGrath* (1951). 33-1:68-88 (2008).

United States Supreme Court. Advisory Opinions

Sirvet, Ene and R. B. Bernstein. John Jay, Judicial Independence, and Advising Coordinate Branches. 21-2:23-29 (1996).

United States Supreme Court. Bar

Clark, Mary L. Women as Supreme Court Advocates, 1879-1979. 30-1:47-67 (2005).

Contee, Clarence G. The Supreme Court Bar's First Black Member. 1:82-85 (1976).

Cushman, Clare. Women Advocates Before the Supreme Court. 26-1:67-88 (2001).

Frederick, David C. Supreme Court Advocacy in the Early Nineteenth Century. 30-1:1-16 (2005).

Lurie, Jonathan. Ex-Justice Campbell: The Case of the Creative Advocate. 30-1:17-30 (2005).

Norgren, Jill. Ladies of Legend: The First Generation of American Women Attorneys. 35-1:71-90 (2010).

O'Donnell, Alice. Women and Other Strangers Before the Bar. 2:59-62, 114 (1977).

Perry, James R. and James M. Buchanan. Admission to the Supreme Court Bar, 1790 -1800: A Case Study of Institutional Change. 8:10-16 (1983).

Roberts, John G., Jr. Oral Advocacy and the Re-emergence of a Supreme Court Bar. 30-1:68-81 (2005).

Sharp, Allen. Presidents as Supreme Court Advocates: Before and after the White House. 28-2:116-144 (2003).

Urofsky, Melvin I. Louis D. Brandeis: Advocate Before and On the Bench. 30-1:31-46 (2005).

United States Supreme Court. Bicentennial

Burger, Warren E., Rex E. Lee, Kenneth W. Starr, William H. Rehnquist. Remarks on the Bicentennial of the Supreme Court. 15:8-16 (1990).

United States Supreme Court. Buildings

McGurn, Barrett. Slogans to Fit the Occasion. 7:104-108 (1982).

Skefos, Catherine Hetos. The Supreme Court Gets a Home. 1:25-36 (1976).

United States Supreme Court. Centennial

Fish, Peter G. Harper's Weekly Celebrates the Centennial of the Supreme Court of the United States: A Bicentennial Retrospective. 13:46-49 (1988).

United States Supreme Court. Circuits

Swindler, William F. The Numbers Game. 2:87-92 (1977).

United States Supreme Court. Correspondence

Johnson, John W. "Dear Mr. Justice": Public Correspondence with Members of the Supreme Court. 22-2:101-112 (1997).

McGurn, Barrett. Small Fry and the Court's Mailbag. 3:106-109 (1978).

United States Supreme Court. Court Reports

Newman, Jon O. Citators Beware: Stylistic Variations in Different Publisher's Versions of Early Supreme Court Opinions. 26-1:1-8 (2001).

United States Supreme Court. Court Staff

Dunne, Gerald T. The Early Court Reporters. 1:61-72 (1976).

Joyce, Craig. *Wheaton v. Peters*: The Untold Story of the Early Reporters. 10:35-92 (1985).

Lyman, Frank Interviewed by Darryl J. Gonzalez. A Voice from behind the Bench: Recollections of a Supreme Court Page. 29-3:308-322 (2004).

McAllister, Stephen R. *Wheaton v. Greenleaf*: A (Story) Tale of Three Reporters. 23-2:53-64 (1998).

McGurn, Barrett. Downstairs at the Court. 2:93-100 (1977).

McGurn, Barrett. Small Fry and the Court's Mailbag. 3:106-109 (1978).

McGurn, Barrett. The Court's Officers. 4:87-93 (1979).

Putzel, Henry and Paul R. Baier. "Double Revolving Peripatetic Nitpicker." 5:10-24 (1980).

Wagner, Frank D. The Role of the Supreme Court Reporter in History. 26-1:9-23 (2001).

United States Supreme Court. Extra-Judicial Activities

Ching, Miriam. Extrajudicial Writings of Supreme Court Justices. 15:69-78 (1990).

Davies, Ross E. The Judicial and Ancient Games: James Wilson, John Marshall Harlan, and the Beginnings of Golf at the Supreme Court. 35-2:122-143 (2010).

Eisenberg, David. A Consideration of Extra-Judicial Activities in the Pre-Marshall Era. 10:117-126 (1985).

Swindler, William F. Books by Justices—A Representative List. 4:38-39 (1979).

Swindler, William F. Justices in Academe. 4:31-37 (1979).

Swindler, William F. The Muse at the Bar. 3:104-106 (1978).

Wheeler, Russell R. Judging What Justices Do Off the Bench. 15:59-68 (1990).

United States Supreme Court. Family Relations

Black, Elizabeth S. Hugo Black: A Memorial Portrait. 7:72-94 (1982).

Black, Hugo, Jr. My Father, A Remembrance. 2:102-113 (1977).

Ginsburg, Ruth Bader and Laura W. Brill. Remembering Great Ladies: Supreme Court Wives' Stories. 24-3:255-268 (1999).

Gossett, Elizabeth Hughes. My Father the Chief Justice. 1:7-15 (1976).

Stone, Lauson H. My Father the Chief Justice. 3:7-17 (1978).

Swindler, William F. Supreme Court Brand. 4:86 (1979).

Taft, Charles P. My Father the Chief Justice. 2:5-10 (1977).

Warren, Earl, Jr. My Father the Chief Justice. 7:6-9 (1982).

United States Supreme Court. Film

Swindler, William F. Documentary Films on the Supreme Court. 3:25-30 (1978).

Swindler, William F. Supreme Court Brand. 4:86 (1979).

United States Supreme Court. Foreign Relations and Foreign Courts

Cohn, Haim H. The First Fifty Years of the Supreme Court of Israel. 24-1:3-15 (1999).

L'Heureux-Dubé, Claire. Canadian Justice: Celebrating Differences and Sharing Problems. 20:5-10 (1995).

McHugh, Michael Hudson. The High Court of Australia. 22-2:2-14 (1997).

Millgramm, Karl-Heinz. Comparative Law: The Federal Constitutional Court of Germany and the Supreme Court of the United States. 10:146-154 (1985).

Vestal, Theodore M. Public Diplomacy in the U. S. Supreme Court: The Warren Years—Part I. 33-3:371-393 (2008).

Vestal, Theodore M. Public Diplomacy in the U. S. Supreme Court: The Warren Years—Part II. 34-1:98-124 (2009).

Woolf, Lord. The Appellate Committee and the Supreme Court: Anglo-American Comparisons. 21-2:1-10 (1996).

United States Supreme Court. Judicial Appointments, Nominations, Selection, etc.

Abraham, Henry J. John Marshall's Associate Justices. 27-3:286-292 (2002).

Abraham, Henry J. President Jefferson's Three Appointments to the Supreme Court of the United States: 1804, 1807, and 1807. 31-2:141-154 (2006).

Beth, Loren P. President Hayes Appoints a Justice. 14:68-77 (1989).

Blackmun, Harry A. The Story-Holmes Seat. 21-1:11-16 (1996).

Boskey, Bennett. Supreme Court Declinations. 31-3:252-261 (2006).

Frank, John P. Judicial Appointments: Controversy and Accomplishment. 2:79-85 (1977).

Kahn, Michael A. Abraham Lincoln's Appointments to the Supreme Court: A Master Politician at his Craft. 22-2:65-78 (1997).

Kahn, Michael A. The Appointment of John McLean to the Supreme Court: Practical Presidential Politics in the Jacksonian Era. 18:59-72 (1993).

Marcus, Maeva. George Washington's Appointments to the Supreme Court. 24-3:243-254 (1999).

Marcus, Maeva, and Christine Jordan. Welcome Back, Justice Harrison? 4:80-81 (1979).

Marcus, Maeva, and Christine Jordan. Welcome Back, Justice Harrison? 4:80-81 (1979).

Morris, Jeffrey B. Chief Justice Edward Douglass White and President Taft's Court. 7:27-45 (1982).

Nordham, George Washington. President George Washington and the First Supreme Court. 9:7-11 (1984).

O'Brien, David M. Filling Justice William O. Douglas's Seat: President Gerald R. Ford's Appointment of Justice John Paul Stevens. 14:20-39 (1989).

Pusey, Merlo J. The Nomination of Charles Evans Hughes as Chief Justice. 7:95-99 (1982).

Sanchez, Ernesto J. John J. Parker and the Beginning of the Modern Confirmation Process. 32-1:22-45 (2007).

Schroeder, David. Joining the Court: Pierce Butler. 35-2:144-165 (2010).

Simpson, Brooks D. President Washington's Appointments to the Supreme Court. 17:63-74 (1992).

Swindler, William F. "Robin Hood," Congress and the Court. 2:39-43 (1977).

Urofsky, Melvin I. The "Outrageous" Brandeis Nomination. 4:8-19 (1979).

Urofsky, Melvin I. Wilson, Brandeis, and the Supreme Court Nomination. 28-2:145-156 (2003).

Wagner, Richard H. A Falling Out: The Relationship between Oliver Wendell Holmes and Theodore Roosevelt. 27-2:114-137 (2002).

Ward, Artemus. The "Good Old #3 Club" Gets a New Member. 33-1:110-119 (2008).

Wiener, Frederick Bernays. Justice Hughes' Appointment—The Cotton Story Re-Examined. 6:78-91 (1981).

United States Supreme Court. Judicial Ratings

Langran, Robert W. Why Are Some Supreme Court Justices Rated as "Failures?" 10:8-14 (1985).

United States Supreme Court. Judicial Retirements

Christensen, George A. Here Lies the Supreme Court: Gravesites of the Justices. 8:17-30 (1983).

Christensen, George A. Here Lies the Supreme Court: Revisited. 33-1:17-41 (2008).

Myers, Minor, III. The Judicial Service of Retired United States Supreme Court Justices. 32-1:46-61 (2007).

Pusey, Merlo J. The Court Copes with Disability. 4:63-69,100 (1979).

Ward, Artemus. The Tenth Justice: The Retirement of William O. Douglas. 25-3:296-312 (2000).

United States Supreme Court. Judicial Salaries

Price, Barry A. The Question of Diminution of Income for Justices and Judges of the Supreme Court and the Inferior Courts of the United States. 32-3:276-281 (2007).

United States Supreme Court. New Deal Constitutional Revolution

Purcell, Edward A., Jr. Brandeis, *Erie*, and the New Deal "Constitutional Revolution". 26-3:257-278 (2001).

United States Supreme Court. Portfolios

Knox, John. Some Comments on Chief Justice Hughes. 9:34-44 (1984).

Morris, Jeffrey B. Morrison Waite's Court. 5: 39-48 (1980).

Pusey, Merlo J. The Hughes Biography: Some Personal Reflections. 9:45-52 (1984).

Swindler, William F. The Eighteenth Century Court and Bar. 1:45-50 (1976).

Swindler, William F. The Court in the Age of the Marshall. 2:44-51 (1977).

Swindler, William F. The Court under Chief Justice Taney. 3:43-49 (1978).

Swindler, William F. The Era of Salmon P. Chase. 4:40-44 (1979).

United States Supreme Court. Practice & Procedure

Cushman, Clare. Rookie on the Bench: The Role of the Junior Justice. 32-3:282-296 (2007).

Daniel, Josiah M., III. "Chief Justice of the United States:" History and Historiography of the Title. 8:109-112 (1983).

Davies, Ross E. The Other Supreme Court. 31-3:221-234 (2006).

Frederick, David C. Supreme Court Advocacy in the Early Nineteenth Century. 30-1:1-16 (2005).

Olken, Samuel R. John Marshall and Spencer Roane: An Historical Analysis of Their Conflict over U. S. Supreme Court Appellate Jurisdiction. 15:125-141 (1990).

Palmer, Jan and Saul Brenner. Determinants of the Amount of Time Taken by the Vinson Court to Process Its Full-Opinion Cases. 15:142-151 (1990).

Pusey, Merlo J. The "Judges' Bill" after a Century. 1:73-81 (1976).

Shapiro, Stephen M. Oral Argument in the Supreme Court: The Felt Necessities of the Time. 10:22-34 (1985).

Sternberg, Jonathan. Deciding Not to Decide: The Judiciary Act of 1925 and the Discretionary Court. 33-1:1-16 (2008).

Wood, Sandra L. In the Shadow of the Chief: The Role of the Senior Associate Justice. 22-2:25-35 (1997).

United States Supreme Court. Relationship to Executive Department & Congress

Altschuler, Bruce E. A Look Back at the *Steel Seizure* Case. 33-3:341-352 (2008).

Ashkenazi, Elliott. Admiralty Law and Neutrality Policy in the 1790s: An Example of Judicial, Legislative, and Executive Cooperation. 25-1:3-16 (2000).

Kyvig, David E. Appealing Supreme Court Decisions: Constitutional Amendments as Checks on Judicial Review. 21-2:106-119 (1996).

Langran, Robert W. Congress vs. the Court. 3:91-96,120 (1978).

Langran, Robert W. Presidents vs. the Court. 2:70-78 (1977).

Neely, Mark E., Jr. Justice Embattled: The Lincoln Administration and the Constitutional Controversy over Conscription in 1863. Sp. Ed.:47-61 (1996).

O'Brien, David M. The Supreme Court: A Co-Equal Branch of Government. 9:90-105 (1984).

Sirvet, Ene and R. B. Bernstein. John Jay, Judicial Independence, and Advising Coordinate Branches. 21-2:23-29 (1996).

Turner, Robert F. The Supreme Court, Separation of Powers, and the Protection of Individual Rights during Periods of War or National Security Emergency. 28-3:323-338 (2003).

Wiecek, William M. The "Imperial Judiciary" in Historical Perspective. 9:61-89 (1984).

United States Supreme Court. Writing About

Bernstein, R. B. Hugo L. Black and the Challenges of Judicial Biography. 20:147-152 (1995).

Bloomfield, Maxfield. The Warren Court in American Fiction. 16:86-96 (1991).

Tushnet, Mark. Writing Supreme Court Histories. 18:11-20 (1993).

Urofsky, Melvin I. Beyond the Bottom Line: The Value of Judicial Biography. 23-2:143-156. (1998).

Wermiel, Stephen J. Writing Supreme Court Biography: A Single Lens View of a Nine-Sided Image. 19:9-18 (1994).

Women—Justices, Judges, Lawyers

Clark, Mary L. Women as Supreme Court Advocates, 1879-1979. 30-1:47-67 (2005).

Cook, Beverly B. The First Woman Candidate for the Supreme Court—Florence E. Allen. 6:19-35 (1981).

Cushman, Clare. Women Advocates Before the Supreme Court. 26-1:67-88 (2001).

Danelski, David J. Lucile Lomen: The First Woman to Clerk at the Supreme Court. 24-1:43-49 (1999).

Norgren, Jill. Ladies of Legend: The First Generation of American Women Attorneys. 35-1:71-90 (2010).

O'Donnell, Alice. Women and Other Strangers Before the Bar. 2:59-62, 114 (1977).

World War I

Stone, Geoffrey R. Civil Liberties in Wartime. 28-3:215-251 (2003).

World War II

Belknap, Michal. Frankfurter and the Nazi Saboteurs. 7:66-71 (1982).

Danelski, David J. The Saboteurs' Case. 21-1:61-82 (1996).

Dudziak, Mary L. The Supreme Court and Racial Equality during World War II. 21-1:35-48 (1996).

Ely, James W., Jr. Property Rights and the Supreme Court in World War II. 21-1:19-34 (1996).

For Further Reading. 21-1:117-120 (1996).

Ferren, John M. General Yamashita and Justice Rutledge. 28-1:54-80 (2003).

Ferren, John M. Military Curfew, Race-Based Internment, and Mr. Justice Rutledge. 28-3:252-269 (2003).

Freyer, Tony A. The First Amendment and World War II. 21-1:83-104 (1996).

Howard, J. Woodford, Jr. The *Cramer* Treason Case. 21-1:49-60 (1996).

Hutchinson, Dennis J. Justice Jackson and the Nuremberg Trials. 21-1:105-116 (1996).

Kmiec, Douglas W. The Supreme Court in Times of Hot and Cold War: Learning from the Sounds of Silence for a War on Terrorism. 28-3:270-299 (2003).

Silverman, Leon. Introduction. 21-1:i (1996).

Stone, Geoffrey R. Civil Liberties in Wartime. 28-3:215-251 (2003).

Urofsky, Melvin I. The Court at War, and the War at the Court. 21-1:1-18 (1996).

Zoning

Power, Garrett. Advocates at Cross-Purposes: The Briefs on Behalf of Zoning in the Supreme Court. 22-2:79-87 (1997).

Wolf, Michael Allan. "Compelled by Conscientious Duty": *Village of Euclid v. Ambler Realty Co.* as Romance. 22-2:88-100 (1997).

3. Constitutions & Amendments & Statutes

3a. Constitutions & Amendments

Articles of Confederation

Kennedy, Cornelius Bryant. Toward 1987: A Dramatic Change in Goals, 1785-1787. 10:112-116 (1985).

Article I, Section 6, Clause 2

Tushnet, Mark. Dual Office Holding and the Constitution: A View from Hayburn's Case. 15:44-58 (1990).

Article III, Section 2

Taylor, Michael J. C. "A More Perfect Union": *Ableman v. Booth* and the Culmination of Federal Sovereignty. 28-2:101-115 (2003).

Bill of Rights

Doherty, Brendan J. Interpreting the Bill of Rights and the Nature of Federalism: *Barron v. City of Baltimore.* 32-3:210-228 (2007).

First Amendment

Anderson, Jeffrey M. Conscience in the Court, 1931-1946: Religion as Duty and Choice. 26-1:25-52 (2001).

Berns, Walter and Philippa Strum. Issue: The Clear and Present Danger Test. 25-2:187-190 (2000).

BeVier, Lillian R. Free Expression in the Warren and Burger Counts. 25-2:191-212 (2000).

Dry, Murray. The Origins and Foundations of the First Amendment and the Alien and Sedition Acts. 25-2:129-144 (2000).

Frasca, Ralph. *The Helderberg Advocate*: A Public-Nuisance Prosecution a Century before *Near v. Minnesota.* 26-3:215-230 (2001).

Freyer, Tony A. The First Amendment and World War II. 21-1:83-104 (1996).

Kersch, Ken I. The *Gompers v. Buck's Stove* Saga: A Constitutional Case Study in Dialogue, Resistance, and the Freedom of Speech. 31-1:28-57 (2006).

Laycock, Douglas. The Clear and Present Danger Test. 25-2:161-186 (2000).

Peters, Shawn Francis. Re-hearing "Fighting Words": *Chaplinsky v. New Hampshire* in Retrospect. 24-3:282-297 (1999).

Polenberg, Richard. Freedom of Speech, 1919 and 1994: Justice Holmes after Seventy-Five Years. 19:19-32 (1994).

Powe, L. A., Jr. The Obscenity Bargain: Ralph Ginzburg for *Fanny Hill.* 35-2:166-176 (2010).

Rabban, David M. Free Speech: The Lost Years. 25-2:145-160 (2000).

Starr, Kenneth W. The Relationship of Church and State: The Views of the Founding Fathers. 12:24-37 (1987).

Van Orden, James F. "Jehovah Will Provide": Lillian Gobitas and Freedom of Religion. 29-2:136-144 (2004).

Fifth Amendment

Ely, James W., Jr. The Fuller Court and Takings Jurisprudence. 21-2:120-135 (1996).

Sixth Amendment

Mosnier, Joseph. The Demise of an "Extraordinary Criminal Procedure": *Klopfer v. North Carolina* and the Incorporation of the Sixth Amendment's Speedy Trial Provision. 21-2:136-160 (1996).

Wiecek, William M. Felix Frankfurter, Incorporation, and the Willie Francis Case. 26-1:53-66 (2001).

Eighth Amendment

Freeman, George Clemon, Jr. Justice Powell and the Eighth Amendment: The Vindication of Proportionality. 12:10-15 (1987).

Wiecek, William M. Felix Frankfurter, Incorporation, and the Willie Francis Case. 26-1:53-66 (2001).

Eleventh Amendment

Swindler, William F. Mr. Chisholm and the Eleventh Amendment. 6:14-18 (1981).

Thirteenth Amendment

Maltz, Earl M. The Waite Court and Federal Power to Enforce the Reconstruction Amendments. Sp. Ed.:75-88 (1996).

Rutherglen, George. Textual Corruption in the *Civil Rights Cases.* 34-2:164-169 (2009).

Fourteenth Amendment

Bressman, Jeremy. A New Standard of Review: *Craig v. Boren* and Brennan's "Heightened Scrutiny" Test in Historical Perspective. 32-1:85-95 (2007).

Kull, Andrew. Post-*Plessy*, Pre-*Brown*: "Logical Exactness" in Enforcing Equal Rights. 24-2:155-169 (1999).

Lemieux, Scott E. The Exception That Defines the Rule: Marshall's *Marbury* Strategy and the Development of Supreme Court Doctrine. 28-2:197-211 (2003).

***Cherokee Nation v. Georgia*, 30 (5 Pet.) U. S. 1 (1831)**

Breyer, Stephen. The Cherokee Indians and the Supreme Court. 25-3:215-227 (2000).

Norgren, Jill. The Cherokee Nation Cases of the 1830s. 19:65-82 (1994).

***Civil Rights Cases*, 109 U. S. 3 (1883)**

Rutherglen, George. Textual Corruption in the *Civil Rights Cases*. 34-2:164-169 (2009).

***Cohen v. California*, 403 U. S. 15 (1971)**

White, James Boyd. Human Dignity and the Claim of Meaning: Athenian Tragic Drama and Supreme Court Opinions. 27-1:45-64 (2002).

***Cooper v. Aaron*, 358 U. S. 1 (1958)**

Freyer, Tony A. *Cooper v. Aaron* (1958): A Hidden Story of Unanimity and Division. 33-1:89-109 (2008).

***Cotton v. Wallace*, 3 U. S. (3 Dall.) 302 (1796)**

Karachuk, Robert Feikema. Error or Appeal? Navigating Review under the Supreme Court's Admiralty Jurisdiction, 1789-1800. 27-2:93-113 (2002).

***Craig v. Boren*, 429 U. S. 190 (1976)**

Bressman, Jeremy. A New Standard of Review: *Craig v. Boren* and Brennan's "Heightened Scrutiny" Test in Historical Perspective. 32-1:85-95 (2007).

***Cramer v. United States*, 325 U. S. 1 (1945)**

Howard, J. Woodford, Jr. The *Cramer* Treason Case. 21-1:49-60 (1996).

***Cumming v. Richmond County Board of Education*, 175 U. S. 528 (1899)**

Connally, C. Ellen. Justice Harlan's "Great Betrayal"? A Reconsideration of *Cumming v. Richmond County Board of Education*. 25-1:72-92 (2000).

***Cummings v. Missouri*, 71 U. S. 277 (1967)**

Rau, Donald. Three Cheers for Father Cummings. 2:20-28 (1977).

***Dartmouth College v. Woodward*, 17 U. S. (4 Wheat.) 518 (1819)**

Lewis, Walker. Backstage at Dartmouth College. 2:29-37 (1977).

Monroe, Elizabeth Brand. The Influence of the *Dartmouth College* Case on the American Law of Educational Charities. 32-1:1-21 (2007).

***Dennis v. United States*, 341 U. S. 494 (1951)**

Belknap, Michal R. *Dennis v. United States*: Great Case or Cold War Relic?. 18:41-58 (1993).

Belknap, Michal R. Why *Dennis v. United States* is a Landmark Case. 34-3:289-302 (2009).

Laycock, Douglas. The Clear and Present Danger Test. 25-2:161-186 (2000).

***Dick v. New York Life Insurance Company*, 359 U. S. 437 (1959)**

Bright, Myron H. The Case of William Dick: Ransom County, North Dakota. 35-1:25-34 (2010).

***Dred Scott v. Sandford*, 60 U. S. (19 How.) 393 (1857)**

Breyer, Stephen G. A Look Back at the *Dred Scott* Decision 35-2:110-121 (2010).

Finkelman, Paul. "Hooted Down the Page of History": Reconsidering the Greatness of Chief Justice Taney. 19:83-102 (1994).

Morel, Lucas E. The *Dred Scott* Dissents: McLean, Curtis, Lincoln, and the Public Mind. 32-2:133-151 (2007).

Paludan, Phillip. Taney, Lincoln and the Constitutional Conversation. Sp. Ed.:22-35 (1996).

Stern, Robert L. Chief Justice Taney and the Shadow of *Dred Scott*. 17:39-52 (1992).

***Engel v. Vitale*, 370 U. S. 421 (1962)**

Dierenfield, Bruce J. "The Most Hated Woman in America": Madalyn Murray and the Crusade against School Prayer. 32-1:62-84 (2007).

***Erie Railroad v. Tompkins*, 304 U. S. 64 (1938)**

Freyer, Tony A. *Swift* and *Erie*: The Trials of an Ephemeral Landmark Case. 34-3:261-274 (2009).

Purcell, Edward A., Jr. Brandeis, *Erie*, and the New Deal "Constitutional Revolution." 26-3:257-278 (2001).

***Everson v. Board of Education of Ewing Township*, 330 U. S. 1 (1947)**

Lemieux, Scott E. The Exception That Defines the Rule: Marshall's *Marbury* Strategy and the Development of Supreme Court Doctrine. 28-2:197-211 (2003).

***Ex Parte McCardle*, 74 U. S. (7 Wall.) 506 (1869)**

Yoo, John. *Merryman* and *M*illigan and (*McCardle*). 34-3:243-260 (2009).

***Ex Parte Merryman*, 17 F. Cas. 144 (C. C. D. Md. 1861) (No. 9487)**

Downey, Arthur T. The Conflict between the Chief Justice and the Chief Executive: *Ex parte Merryman*. 31-3:262-278 (2006).

Yoo, John. *Merryman* and *M*illigan and (*McCardle*). 34-3:243-260 (2009).

***Ex Parte Milligan*, 71 U. S. (4 Wall.) 2 (1866)**

Belknap, Michal R. Alarm Bells from the Past: The Troubling History of American Military Commissions. 28-3:300-322 (2003).

Yoo, John. *Merryman* and *M*illigan and (*McCardle*). 34-3:243-260 (2009).

***Ex Parte Mitsuye Endo*, 323 U. S. 283 (1944)**

Kmiec, Douglas W. The Supreme Court in Times of Hot and Cold War: Learning from the Sounds of Silence for a War on Terrorism. 28-3:270-299 (2003).

***Ex Parte Quirin*, 317 U. S. 1 (1942)**

Belknap, Michal R. Alarm Bells from the Past: The Troubling History of American Military Commissions. 28-3:300-322 (2003).

Belknap, Michal. Frankfurter and the Nazi Saboteurs. 7:66-71 (1982).

Danelski, David J. The Saboteurs' Case. 21-1:61-82 (1996).

***Ex Parte Vallandigham*, 68 U. S. (1 Wall.) 243 (1864)**

Belknap, Michal R. Alarm Bells from the Past: The Troubling History of American Military Commissions. 28-3:300-322 (2003).

Belknap, Michal. Frankfurter and the Nazi Saboteurs. 7:66-71 (1982).

Danelski, David J. The Saboteurs' Case. 21-1:61-82 (1996).

***Ex Parte Virginia*, 100 U. S. 339 (1879)**

Maltz, Earl M. The Waite Court and Federal Power to Enforce the Reconstruction Amendments. Sp. Ed.:75-88 (1996).

***Federal Baseball Club of Baltimore, Inc. v. National League of Professional Baseball*, 259 U. S. 200 (1922)**

Alito, Samuel A., Jr. The Origin of the Baseball Antitrust Exemption: *Federal Baseball Club of Baltimore, Inc. v. National League of Professional Baseball*. 34-2:183-195 (2009).

***Fikes v. Alabama*, 352 U. S. 191 (1957)**

Prettyman, E. Barrett, Jr. The Unconstitutional Conviction of "Baby." 3:68-78 (1978).

Flag Salute Cases

Morgan, Richard. The *Flag Salute Cases* Reconsidered. 34-3:273-288 (2009).

***Flood v. Kuhn*, 407 U. S. 258 (1972)**

Davies, Ross E. A Tall Tale of *The Brethren*. 33-2:186-199 (2008).

***Fox v. Washington*, 235 U. S. 273 (1915)**

Rabban, David M. Free Speech: The Lost Years. 25-2:145-160 (2000).

***Georgia v. Brailsford*, 3 U. S. (3 Dall.) 1 (1794)**

Marcus, Maeva. *Georgia v. Brailsford*. 26-2:57-72 (1996).

***Gibbons v. Ogden*, 22 U. S. (9 Wheat.) 1 (1824)**

Cox, Thomas H. Contesting Commerce: *Gibbons v. Ogden,* Steam Power, and Social Change. 34-1:56-74 (2009).

***Ginzburg v. United States*, 383 U. S. 463 (1966)**

Powe, L. A., Jr. The Obscenity Bargain: Ralph Ginzburg for *Fanny Hill*. 35-2:166-176 (2010).

***Girouard v. United States*, 328 U. S. 61 (1946)**

Anderson, Jeffrey M. Conscience in the Court, 1931-1946: Religion as Duty and Choice. 26-1:25-52 (2001).

***Glass v. Sloop Betsey*, 3 U. S. (3 Dall.) 6 (1794)**

Karachuk, Robert Feikema. Error or Appeal? Navigating Review under the Supreme Court's Admiralty Jurisdiction, 1789-1800. 27-2:93-113 (2002).

***Gompers v. Buck's Stove & Range Co.*, 221 U. S. 418 (1911)**

Kersch, Ken I. The *Gompers v. Buck's Stove* Saga: A Constitutional Case Study in Dialogue, Resistance, and the Freedom of Speech. 31-1:28-57 (2006).

***Gong Lum v. Rice*, 275 U. S. 78 (1927)**

Rhee, Jeannie. In Black and White: Chinese in the Mississippi Delta. 19:117-132 (1994).

***Graver Tank & Mfg. Co. v. Linde Air Products*, 336 U. S. 271 (1949) adhered to on reh'g, 339 U. S. 605 (1950)**

Dyk, Timothy B. The *Graver Tank* Litigation in the Supreme Court. 30-3:271-283 (2005).

***Hamdi v. Rumsfeld*, 296 F. 3d 278 (4ᵗʰ Cir. 2002)**

Kmiec, Douglas W. The Supreme Court in Times of Hot and Cold War: Learning from the Sounds of Silence for a War on Terrorism. 28-3:270-299 (2003).

***Hayburn's Case*, 2 U. S. 409 (1792)**

Tushnet, Mark. Dual Office Holding and the Constitution: A View from *Hayburn's Case*. 15:44-58 (1990).

***Hills v. Ross*, 3 U. S. (3 Dall.) 184 (1796)**

Karachuk, Robert Feikema. Error or Appeal? Navigating Review under the Supreme Court's Admiralty Jurisdiction, 1789-1800. 27-2:93-113 (2002).

***Hirabayashi v. United States*, 320 U. S. 81 (1943)**

Ferren, John M. Military Curfew, Race-Based Internment, and Mr. Justice Rutledge. 28-3:252-269 (2003).

Kmiec, Douglas W. The Supreme Court in Times of Hot and Cold War: Learning from the Sounds of Silence for a War on Terrorism. 28-3:270-299 (2003).

***Hopt v. United States*, 120 U. S. 430 (1887)**

Harring, Sidney L. and Kathryn Swedlow. "The Defendant Has Seemed to Live a Charmed Life": *Hopt v. Utah*: Territorial Justice, The Supreme Court of the United States, and Late Nineteenth-Century Death Penalty Jurisprudence. 25-1:40-71 (2000).

***Humphreys Executor v. United States*, 295 U. S. 602 (1935)**

Scalia, Antonin. Historical Anomalies in Administrative Law. 10:103-111 (1985).

***Hylton v. United States*, 3 U. S. (3 Dall.) 171 (1796)**

Frankel, Robert P., Jr. Before *Marbury*: *Hylton v. United States* and the Origins of Judicial Review. 28-1:1-13 (2003).

***In re Yamashita*, 327 U. S. 1 (1946)**

Ferren, John M. General Yamashita and Justice Rutledge. 28-1:54-80 (2003).

Insular Cases

Sparrow, Bartholomew H. The Public Response to Controversial Supreme Court Decisions: *The Insular Cases*. 30-3:197-210 (2005).

Tsukamoto v. Lackman, 187 U. S. 635 (1902)

Bernstein, David E. Two Asian Laundry Cases. 24-1:95-111 (1999).

United States v. Bland, 283 U. S. 636 (1931)

Anderson, Jeffrey M. Conscience in the Court, 1931-1946: Religion as Duty and Choice. 26-1:25-52 (2001).

United States v. Caltex of the Phillipines, Inc., 344 U. S. 149 (1952)

Scheiber, Harry N. Property Rights versus "Public Necessity": A Perspective on Emergency Powers and the Supreme Court. 28-3:339-369 (2003).

United States v. Carolene Products Co., 304 U. S. 144 (1938)

Lemieux, Scott E. The Exception That Defines the Rule: Marshall's *Marbury* Strategy and the Development of Supreme Court Doctrine. 28-2:197-211 (2003).

Purcell, Edward A., Jr. Brandeis, *Erie*, and the New Deal "Constitutional Revolution." 26-3:257-278 (2001).

United States v. Cruikshank, 92 U. S. 542 (1876)

Maltz, Earl M. The Waite Court and Federal Power to Enforce the Reconstruction Amendments. Sp. Ed.:75-88 (1996).

United States v. Curtiss-Wright Export Corp., 299 U. S. 304 (1936)

Kmiec, Douglas W. The Supreme Court in Times of Hot and Cold War: Learning from the Sounds of Silence for a War on Terrorism. 28-3:270-299 (2003).

United States v. Doremus, 249 U. S. 86 (1919)

Hohenstein, Kurt. Just What the Doctor Ordered: The Harrison Anti-Narcotic Act, the Supreme Court, and the Federal Regulation of Medical Practice, 1915-1919. 26-3:231-256 (2001).

United States v. Jim Fuey Moy, 241 U. S. 394 (1916)

Hohenstein, Kurt. Just What the Doctor Ordered: The Harrison Anti-Narcotic Act, the Supreme Court, and the Federal Regulation of Medical Practice, 1915-1919. 26-3:231-256 (2001).

United States v. Macintosh, 283 U. S. 605 (1931)

Anderson, Jeffrey M. Conscience in the Court, 1931-1946: Religion as Duty and Choice. 26-1:25-52 (2001).

Flowers, Ronald B. The Naturalization of Douglas Clyde Macintosh, Alien Theologian. 25-3:243-270 (2000).

United States v. Peters, 9 U. S. (5 Cranch) 115 (1819)

Dumbauld, Edward. The Case of the Mutinous Mariner. 2:52-58, 69 (1977).

United States v. Reese, 92 U. S. 214 (1876)

Maltz, Earl M. The Waite Court and Federal Power to Enforce the Reconstruction Amendments. Sp. Ed.:75-88 (1996).

United States v. Schwimmer, 279 U. S. 644 (1929)

Anderson, Jeffrey M. Conscience in the Court, 1931-1946: Religion as Duty and Choice. 26-1:25-52 (2001).

United States v. Union Pacific Railroad Company, 98 U. S. 569 (1879)

Kens, Paul. The Crédit Mobilier Scandal and the Supreme Court: Corporate Power, Corporate Person, and Government Control in the Mid-nineteenth Century. 34-2:170-182 (2009).

Village of Euclid v. Ambler Realty Co., 272 U. S. 365 (1926)

Handler, Milton. Letter to the Editor. 23-2:1-2 (1998).

Power, Garrett. Advocates at Cross-Purposes: The Briefs on Behalf of Zoning in the Supreme Court. 22-2:79-87 (1997).

Wolf, Michael Allan. "Compelled by Conscientious Duty": *Village of Euclid v. Ambler Realty Co.* as Romance. 22-2:88-100 (1997).

Wallace v. Brig Caesar, Unreported Case (1795)

Karachuk, Robert Feikema. Error or Appeal? Navigating Review under the Supreme Court's Admiralty Jurisdiction, 1789-1800. 27-2:93-113 (2002).

Webb v. United States, 249 U. S. 96 (1919)

Hohenstein, Kurt. Just What the Doctor Ordered: The Harrison Anti-Narcotic Act, the Supreme Court, and the Federal Regulation of Medical Practice, 1915-1919. 26-3:231-256 (2001).

West Virginia v. Barnette, 319 U. S. 624 (1943)

Morgan, Richard. The *Flag Salute Cases* Reconsidered. 34-3:273-288 (2009).

Wheaton v. Peters, 33 U. S. (8 Pet.) 591 (1834)

Joyce, Craig. *Wheaton v. Peters*: The Untold Story of the Early Reporters. 10:35-92 (1985).

McAllister, Stephen R. Wheaton v. Greenleaf: A (Story) Tale of Three Reporters. 23-2:53-64 (1998).

Wiscart v. Dauchy, 3 U. S. (3 Dall.) 321 (1796)

Karachuk, Robert Feikema. Error or Appeal? Navigating Review under the Supreme Court's Admiralty Jurisdiction, 1789-1800. 27-2:93-113 (2002).

Worcester v. Georgia, 31 U. S. (6 Pet.) 515 (1832)

Breyer, Stephen. The Cherokee Indians and the Supreme Court. 25-3:215-227 (2000).

Newmyer, R. Kent. Chief Justice John Marshall's Last Campaign: Georgia, Jackson, and the Cherokee Cases. 24-1:76-94 (1999).

Norgren, Jill. The Cherokee Nation Cases of the 1830s. 19:65-82 (1994).

Robertson, Lyndsay G. Justice Henry Baldwin's "Lost Opinion" in *Worcester v. Georgia*. 24-1:50-75 (1999).

Wyoming Valley Case (1782)

Swindler, William F. Toward 1987: A "Pre-Constitutional" Law Case. 8:113-116 (1983).

***Yick Wo v. Hopkins*, 118 U. S. 356 (1886)**

Bernstein, David E. Two Asian Laundry Cases. 24-1:95-111 (1999).

***Youngstown Sheet & Tube v. Sawyer*, 343 U. S. 579 (1952)**

Altschuler, Bruce E. A Look Back at the *Steel Seizure* Case. 33-3:341-352 (2008).

Kmiec, Douglas W. The Supreme Court in Times of Hot and Cold War: Learning from the Sounds of Silence for a War on Terrorism. 28-3:270-299 (2003).

Scheiber, Harry N. Property Rights versus "Public Necessity": A Perspective on Emergency Powers and the Supreme Court. 28-3:339-369 (2003).

5. "De Minimis" or Judicial Potpourri

"De Minimis" or Judicial Potpourri. 2:86-100 (1977).

"De Mimimis," or Judicial Potpourri. 3:103-112 (1978).

"De Minimis," or Judicial Potpourri. 4:79-93 (1979).

"De Minimis," or Judicial Potpourri. 5:89-102 (1980).

"De Minimis," or Judicial Potpourri. 8:109-116 (1983).

"De Minimis" or,Judicial Potpourri. 9:107-116 (1984).

Judicial Potpourri. 2:86 (1977).

Judicial Potpourri. 3:103-112 (1978).

Judicial Potpourri. 4:79-93 (1979).

Judicial Potpourri. 5:89-99 (1980).

Judicial Potpourri. 8:108-116 (1983).

Judicial Potpourri 10:127-145 (1985).

Judicial Potpourri. 11:95-121 (1986).

V. BIBLIOGRAPHIES & BOOK REVIEWS

1. Cumulative Articles

Evans, Patricia R. and Roger F. Jacobs. The Supreme Court in Current Literature. 4:94-100 (1979).

Jacobstein, J. Myron and Joan S. Howland. The Supreme Court in Current Literature. 3:113-120 (1978).

Mersky, Roy and Jenni Parrish. The Supreme Court in Current Literature. 2:102-113 (1977).

Stephenson, D. Grier, Jr. The Judicial Bookshelf. 10:128-145 (1985).

Stephenson, D. Grier, Jr. The Judicial Bookshelf. 11:103-121 (1986).

Stephenson, D. Grier, Jr. The Judicial Bookshelf. 12:108-126 (1987).

Stephenson, D. Grier, Jr. The Judicial Bookshelf. 13:98-117 (1988).

Stephenson, D. Grier, Jr. The Judicial Bookshelf. 14:119-139 (1989).

Stephenson, D. Grier, Jr. The Judicial Bookshelf. 15:152-177 (1990).

Stephenson, D. Grier, Jr. The Judicial Bookshelf. 16:105-131 (1991).

Stephenson, D. Grier, Jr. The Judicial Bookshelf. 17:109-135 (1992).

Stephenson, D. Grier, Jr. The Judicial Bookshelf. 18:90-117 (1993).

Stephenson, D. Grier, Jr. The Judicial Bookshelf. 19:147-170 (1994).

Stephenson, D. Grier, Jr. The Judicial Bookshelf. 20:153-172 (1995).

Stephenson, D. Grier, Jr. The Judicial Bookshelf. 21-2:168-188 (1996).

Stephenson, D. Grier, Jr. The Judicial Bookshelf. 22-2:150-169 (1997).

Stephenson, D. Grier, Jr. The Judicial Bookshelf. 23-2:157-181 (1998).

Stephenson, D. Grier, Jr. Judicial Bookshelf. 24-1:138-152 (1999).

Stephenson, D. Grier, Jr. Judicial Bookshelf. 24-3:333-347 (1999).

Stephenson, D. Grier, Jr. Judicial Bookshelf. 25-1:112-127 (2000).

Stephenson, D. Grier, Jr. Judicial Bookshelf. 25-3:313-330 (2000).

Stephenson, D. Grier, Jr. The Judicial Bookshelf. 26-3:279-295 (2001).

Stephenson, D. Grier, Jr. The Judicial Bookshelf. 27-1:65-82 (2002).

Stephenson, D. Grier, Jr. The Judicial Bookshelf. 27-2:194-210 (2002).

Stephenson, D. Grier, Jr. The Judicial Bookshelf. 28-1:81-97 (2003).

Stephenson, D. Grier, Jr. The Judicial Bookshelf. 28-3:370-386 (2003).

Stephenson, D. Grier, Jr. The Judicial Bookshelf. 29-2:207-225 (2004).

Stephenson, D. Grier, Jr. The Judicial Bookshelf. 29-3:346-366 (2004).

Stephenson, D. Grier, Jr. The Judicial Bookshelf. 30-3:284-302 (2005).

Stephenson, D. Grier, Jr. The Judicial Bookshelf. 31-2:199-218 (2006).

Stephenson, D. Grier, Jr. The Judicial Bookshelf. 31-3:298-315 (2006).

Stephenson, D. Grier, Jr. The Judicial Bookshelf. 32-1:96-112 (2007).

Stephenson, D. Grier, Jr. The Judicial Bookshelf. 32-2:190-208 (2007).

Stephenson, D. Grier, Jr. The Judicial Bookshelf. 32-3:346-363 (2007).

Stephenson, D. Grier, Jr. The Judicial Bookshelf. 33-2:200-220 (2008).

Stephenson, D. Grier, Jr. The Judicial Bookshelf. 34-1:125-145 (2009).

Stephenson, D. Grier, Jr. The Judicial Bookshelf. 34-2:224-240 (2009).

Stephenson, D. Grier, Jr. The Judicial Bookshelf. 34-3:315-331 (2009).

Stephenson, D. Grier, Jr. The Judicial Bookshelf. 35-2:177-192 (2010).

Stephenson, D. Grier, Jr. The Judicial Bookshelf. 35-3:267-283 (2010).

Stephenson, D. Grier, Jr. On Review: Recent Books About the Supreme Court, the Justices, and the Constitution. 9:127-143 (1984).

Taylor, John B. Hail to the Chief: A Bibliographical Essay on Six Chief Justices of the United States. 23-1:133-165 (1998).

Taylor, John B. Politics, the Court and the Constitution: A Bibliographical Essay on the Pre- and Post-New Deal Supreme Court. 22-1:99-118 (1997).

2. Single Reviews

Cardozo, Michael H. The Judicial Bookshelf—Continued. Review of D. Grier Stephenson, Jr., ed. *An Essential Safeguard: Essays on the United States Supreme Court and Its Justices.* 17:137-140 (1992).

Dorsen, Norman. *Justice Lewis F. Powell, Jr.*: A Biography: A Review Essay. 19:139-146 (1994).

Friedman, Richard D. Taking Decisions Seriously: A Review of [Barry Cushman] *Rethinking the New Deal Court: The Structure of a Constitutional Revolution.* 24-3:314-324 (1999).

Freyer, Tony A. Prophet or Example: A Review of [Linda Przybyszewski] *The Republic According to John Marshall Harlan.* 24-3:325-332 (1999).

Garrett, Elizabeth. Review of Mark V. Tushnet, *Making Civil Rights Law: Thurgood Marshall and the Supreme Court, 1936-1961* and *Making Constitutional Law: Thurgood Marshall and the Supreme Court, 1961-1991.* 22-2:140-149 (1997).

Kohn, Alan C. Reviewed: *Failing Justice: Charles Evans Whittaker of the Supreme Court,* by Craig Alan Smith. 31-1:91-96 (2006).

Levy, David W. *Learned Hand, The Man the Judge* A Review Essay. 19:133-138 (1994).

Stern, Robert L. Chief Justice Taney and the Shadow of *Dred Scott.* Review of C. Swisher. *Oliver Wendell Holmes Devise History of the Supreme Court of the United States, Vol. 5, The Taney Period* (1836-1865). 17:39-52 (1992).

Urofsky, Melvin I. Revivifying Political Science: Lucas A. Powe, Jr., on the Warren Court. Review of *The Warren Court and American Politics.* 26-1:89-94 (2001).

Urofsky, Melvin I. Review of Edward A. Purcell, Jr., *Brandeis and the Progressive Constitution: Erie, the Judicial Power, and the Politics of the Federal Courts in the Twentieth-Century America.* 27-1:83-90 (2002).

Wohl, Alexander. *The Life of John Marshall* Revisited. Review of Albert Beveridge. *The Life of John Marshall.* 22-2:131-139 (1997).

Wolf, Michael Allan. *The Supreme Court in United States History*: A New Appreciation. Review of Charles Warren. *The Supreme Court in United States History.* 21-2:161-167 (1996).

3. Book Reviews by Author Cited in the Judicial Bookshelf

Abraham, Henry J. Freedom and the Court: Civil Rights and Liberties in the United States. 3:114-120 (1978).

Abraham, Henry. The Judiciary: the Supreme Court in the Governmental Process. 3d ed. 2:102-113 (1977); 3:114-120 (1978).

Abraham, Henry J. Justices and Presidents: A Political History of Appointments to the Supreme Court. 2:102-113 (1977).

Abraham, Henry. J. Justices and Presidents: A Political History of Appointments to the Supreme Court. 2d ed. 10:128-145 (1985).

Abraham, Henry J. Justices and Presidents: A Political History of Appointments to the Supreme Court. 3d. ed. 18:90-117 (1994).

Abraham, Henry J. Justices, Presidents, and Senators. 5th ed. 34-1:125-145 (2009).

Agresto, John. The Supreme Court and Constitutional Democracy. 10:128-145 (1985).

Aichele, Gary I. Oliver Wendell Holmes. Jr.: Soldier. Scholar. Judge. 15:152-177 (1990).

Aitken, Robert and Marilyn Aitken. Law Makers, Law Breakers and Uncommon Trials. 34-2:224-240 (2009).

Anastaplo, George. The Amendments to the Constitution: A Commentary. 21-2:168-188 (1996).

Anderman, Nancy. United States Supreme Court Decisions: An Index to Their Locations. 3:114-120 (1978).

Arnold, Otto Carrol. Religious Freedom on Trial. 4:95-100 (1979).

Aslop, Joseph & Turner Catledge. The 168 Days. 24-2:314-324 (1999).

Atkinson, David N. Leaving the Bench: Supreme Court Justices at the End. 25-1:112-127 (2000).

Baker, Leonard. John Marshall: A Life in Law. 2:102-113 (1977).

Baker, Liva. The Justice from Beacon Hill: The Life and Times of Oliver Wendell Holmes. 17:109-135 (1992).

Cope, Alfred. Franklin D. Roosevelt and the Supreme Court. 2:102-113 (1977).

Cortner, Richard C. Civil Rights and Public Accommodations: *The Heart of Atlanta Motel* and *McClung Cases*. 27-2:194-210 (2002).

Cortner, Richard C. The Iron Horse and the Constitution: The Railroads and the Transformation of the Fourteenth Amendment. 20:153-172 (1995).

Cortner, Richard C. The Kingfish and the Constitution: Huey Long, the First Amendment, and the Emergence of Modern Press Freedom in America. 21-2:168-188 (1996).

Cortner, Richard C. "Scottsboro" Case in Mississippi; The Supreme Court and *Brown v. Mississippi*. 12:108-126 (1987).

Cortner, Richard C. The Supreme Court and the Second Bill of Rights: The Fourteenth Amendment and the Nationalization of Civil Liberties. 9:127-143 (1984).

Cottrol, Robert J., Raymond T. Diamond, and Leland B. Ware. *Brown v. Board of Education:* Caste, Culture, and the Constitution. 29-3:346-366 (2004).

Countryman, Vern, Ed. The Douglas Opinions. 3:114-120 (1978).

Countryman, Vern. The Judicial Record of Justice William O. Douglas. 2:102-113 (1977).

Cox, A. The Role of the Supreme Court in American Government. 11:103-121 (1986).

Cox, Archibald. The Role of the Supreme Court in American Government. 2:102-113 (1977).

Craig, Barbara Hinkson. Chadha: The Story of an Epic Constitutional Struggle. 13:98-117 (1988).

Cray, Ed. Chief Justice: A Biography of Earl Warren. 23-2:157-181 (1998).

Cullen, Charles T. and Herbert A. Johnson, eds. The Papers of John Marshall Vol. II. 4:95-100 (1979).

Curriden, Mark and Leroy Phillips, Jr. Contempt of Court: The Turn-of-the-Century Lynching That Launched a Hundred Years of Federalism. 25-3:313-330 (2000).

Currie, David P. The Constitution in the Supreme Court: The First Hundred Years 1789-1888. 12:108-126 (1987).

Currie, David P. The Constitution in the Supreme Court: The Second Century 1888-1986. 17:109-135 (1992).

Curry, Thomas J. The First Freedoms; Church and State in America to the Passage of the First Amendment. 11:103-121 (1986).

Curtis, Michael Kent. Free Speech, "The People's Darling Privilege": Struggles for Freedom of Expression in American History. 28-1:81-97 (2003).

Curtis, Michael Kent. No State Shall Abridge: The Fourteenth Amendment and the Bill of Rights. 13:98-117 (1988).

Cushman, Clare. The Supreme Court Justices: Illustrated Biographies, 1789-1993. 19:147-170 (1994).

Davis, Abraham. United States Supreme Court and the Use of Social Science Data. 2:102-113 (1977).

Davis, Michael D. and Hunter R. Clark. Thurgood Marshall: Warrior at the Bar, Rebel on the Bench. 18:90-117 (1993).

Davis, Richard. Electing Justice: Fixing the Supreme Court Nominating Process. 31-3:298-315 (2006).

Davis, Sue. Justice Rehnquist and the Constitution. 16:105-131 (1991).

Devol, Kenneth. Mass Media and the Supreme Court: the Legacy of the Warren Years. 3:114-120 (1978).

Dierenfield, Bruce J. The Battle over School Prayer: How *Engel v. Vitale* Changed America. 34-2:224-240 (2009).

Domnarski, William. The Great Justices 1941-54. 32-3:346-363 (2007).

Douglas, William O. The Douglas Letters: Selections from the Private Papers of Justice William O. Douglas. 13:98-117 (1988).

Douglas, William O. Go East, Young Man. 2:102-113 (1977).

Dunne, Gerald T. Hugo Black and the Judicial Revolution. 3:114-120 (1978).

Dunne, G. Justice Joseph Story and the Rise of the Supreme Court. 11:103-121 (1986).

Durchslag, Melvyn R. State Sovereign Immunity: A Reference Guide to the United States Constitution. 28-3:370-386 (2003).

Earyl, Stephen Tyree. Constitutional Courts of the United States: The Formal and Informal Relationships between the District Courts, the Courts of Appeals, and the Supreme Court of the U. S. 4:95-100 (1979).

Eisengruber, Christopher. L. The Next Justice: Reforming the Supreme Court Appointments Process. 35-2:177-192 (2010).

Eisler, Kim Isaac. A Justice for All: William J. Brennan, Jr. and the Decisions That Transformed America. 19:147-170 (1994).

Elliott, Ward E. Y. The Rise of Guardian Democracy: The Supreme Court's Role in Voting Rights Disputes, 1845-1969. 2:102-113 (1977).

Ellis, Richard E. Aggressive Nationalism: *McCulloch v. Maryland* and the Foundation of Federal Authority in the Young Republic. 34-2:224-240 (2009).

Ely, James W., Jr. The Chief Justiceship of Melville W. Fuller 1888-1910. 21-2:168-188 (1996).

Ely, James W., Jr. The Fuller Court: Justices, Rulings, and Legacy. 29-2:207-225 (2004).

Ely, John Hart. Democracy and Distrust: A Theory of Judicial Review. 9:127-143 (1984).

Emerson, Ralph Waldo. The Complete Works of Ralph Waldo Emerson. 22-2:140-149 (1997).

Epstein, Lee. Conservatives in Court. 11:103-121 (1986); 13:98-117 (1988).

Murphy, Bruce Allen. Fortas: The Rise and Ruin of a Supreme Court Justice. 14:119-139 (1989).

Murphy, Bruce Allen. The Brandeis/Frankfurter Connection: The Secret Political Activities of Two Supreme Court Justices. 9:127-143 (1984).

Nelson, William E. The Fourteenth Amendment: From Political Principle to Judicial Doctrine. 14:119-139 (1989).

Nelson, William E. *Marbury v. Madison:* The Origins and Legacy of Judicial Review. 28-1:81-97 (2003).

Nemacheck, Christine L. Strategic Selection: Presidential Nomination of Supreme Court Justices from Hoover through George W. Bush. 34-1:125-145 (2009).

Newman, Roger K., Ed. The Yale Biographical Dictionary of American Law. 35-2:177-192 (2010).

Newmyer, R. Kent. John Marshall and the Heroic Age of the Supreme Court. 27-2:194-210 (2002).

Newmyer, R. Kent. Supreme Court Justice Joseph Story; Statesman of the Old Republic. 11:103-121 (1986).

Newmyer, R. Kent. The Supreme Court under Marshall and Taney. 11:103-121 (1986).

Newton, Jim. Justice for All: Earl Warren and the Nation He Made. 33-2:200-220 (2008).

Newton, Merlin Owen. Armed with the Constitution: Jehovah's Witnesses in Alabama and the U. S. Supreme Court, 1939-1946. 21-2:168-188 (1996).

Niven, John. Salmon P. Chase: A Biography. 20:153-172 (1995).

Norgren, Jill. Belva Lockwood: The Woman Who Would Be President. 33-2:200-220 (2008).

Nourse, Victoria F. In Reckless Hands: *Skinner v. Oklahoma* and the New Triumph of American Eugenics. 34-3:315-331 (2009).

Novick, Sheldon M. Honorable Justice: The Life of Oliver Wendell Holmes. 15:152-177 (1990).

O'Brien, David M. Judicial Roulette; Report of the Twentieth Century Fund Task Force on Judicial Selection. 15:152-177 (1990).

O'Brien, David M. Storm Center: The Supreme Court in American Politics. 12:108-126 (1987).

O'Brien, J. Stephen and Richard S. Vacca. The Supreme Court and the Religion-Education Controversy: A Tightrope to Entanglement. 2:102-113 (1977).

O'Fallon, James, ed,. Nature's Justice: Writings of William O. Douglas. 27-1:65-82 (2002).

Pacelle, Richard L., Jr. Between Law & Politics: The Solicitor General and the Structuring of Race, Gender, and Reproductive Rights Litigation. 31-2:199-218 (2006).

Pacelle, Richard L. Jr. The Transformation of the Supreme Court's Agenda: From the New Deal to the Reagan Administration. 18:90-117 (1993).

Patterson, James T. *Brown v. Board of Education*: A Civil Rights Milestone and Its Troubled Legacy. 27-1:65-82 (2002).

Paul, Arnold M. Black Americans and the Supreme Court Since Emancipation: Betrayal or Protection? 2:102-113 (1977).

Perry, Barbara A. The Priestly Tribe: The Supreme Court's Image in the American Mind. 25-1:112-127 (2000).

Perry, H. W., Jr. Deciding to Decide: Agenda Setting in the United States Supreme Court. 17:109-135 (1992).

Perry, Michael J. The Constitution, the Courts, and Human Rights. 9:127-143 (1984).

Peters, Shawn Francis. Judging Jehovah's Witnesses: Religious Prosecution and the Dawn of the Rights Revolution. 26-3:279-295 (2001).

Peters, Shawn Francis. The *Yoder* Case: Religious Freedom, Education, and Parental Rights. 29-2:207-225 (2004).

Peppers, Todd. Courtiers of the Marble Palace: The Rise and Influence of the Supreme Court Law Clerk. 32-2:190-208 (2007).

Pfeffer, Leo. Religion, State and the Burger Court. 11:103-121 (1986).

Phillips, Michael J. The *Lochner* Court, Myth and Reality: Substantive Due Process from the 1890s to the 1930s. 27-2:194-210 (2002).

Polenberg, Richard. Fighting Faiths: The Abrams Case, The Supreme Court, and Free Speech. 13:98-117 (1988).

Polenberg, Richard. The World of Benjamin Cardoza: Personal Values and the Judicial Process. 23-2:157-181 (1998).

Powe, Lucas A., Jr. The Supreme Court and the American Elite, 1789-2008. 35-3:267-283 (2010).

Powe, Lucas A., Jr. The Warren Court and American Politics. 26-3:279-295 (2001).

Pratt, Walter F., Jr. The Supreme Court under Edward Douglass White, 1901-1921. 25-3:313-330 (2000).

Provine, Doris Marie. Case Selection in the United States Supreme Court. 10:128-145 (1985).

Przybyszewski, Linda. The Republic According the John Marshall Harlan. 24-3:325-332 (1999).

Redford E. and M. Blissett. Organizing the Executive Branch: The Johnson Presidency. 13:98-117 (1988).

Reeves, William D. Paths to Distinction: Dr. James White, Governor E. D. White and Chief Justice Edward Douglass White of Louisiana. 25-3:313-330 (2000).

Rehnquist, William H. All the Laws But One: Civil Liberties in Wartime. 24-3:333-347 (1999).

Rehnquist, William H. Grand Inquests: The Historic Impeachments of Justice Samuel Chase and President Andrew Johnson. 18:90-117 (1993).

Rehnquist, William H. The Supreme Court. 27-1:65-82 (2002).

Rehnquist, William H. The Supreme Court: How It Was, How It Is. 13:98-117 (1988).

Stephenson, D. Grier. An Essential Safeguard: Essays on the United States Supreme Court and its Justices. 17:137-140 (1992).

Stevens, Richard G., and Matthew J. Franck, eds. Sober as a Judge: The Supreme Court and Republican Liberty. 25-3:313-330 (2000).

Strum, Philippa. Brandeis: Beyond Progressivism. 19:147-170 (1994).

Strum, Philippa. Louis D. Brandeis: Justice for the People. 10:128-145 (1985).

Strum, Philippa. The Supreme Court and "Political Questions:" A Study in Judicial Evasion. 2:102-113 (1977).

Stuart, Gary L. *Miranda*: The Story of America's Right to Remain Silent. 32-2:190-208 (2007).

Suitts, Steve. Hugo Black of Alabama: How His Roots and Early Career Shaped the Great Champion of the Constitution. 31-3:298-315 (2006).

Swanson, Wayne R. The Christ Child Goes to Court. 15:152-177 (1990).

Swindler, William F. Court and Constitution in the Twentieth Century. 2:102-113 (1977).

Swisher, Carl B. The Taney Period 1836-64. 2:102-113 (1977).

Tarr, George Alan. Judicial Impact and State Supreme Courts. 4:95-100 (1979).

Thomas, William R. The Burger Court and Civil Liberties. 2:102-113 (1977).

Tomlins, Christopher, Ed. The United States Supreme Court: The Pursuit of Justice. 32-1:96-112.

Tribe, Laurence H. Constitutional Choices. 11:103-121 (1986).

Tushnet, Mark V. Making Civil Rights Law: Thurgood Marshall and the Supreme Court, 1936-1961. 19:147-170 (1994); 22-2:140-149 (1997).

Tushnet, Mark V. Making Constitutional Law: Thurgood Marshall and the Supreme Court, 1961-1991. 22-2:140-149 (1997).

Urofsky, Melvin I. Affirmative Action on Trial: Sex Discrimination in *Johnson v. Santa Clara*. 24-1:138-152 (1999).

Urofsky, Melvin I. A Conflict of Rights: The Supreme Court and Affirmative Action. 16:105-131 (1991).

Urofsky, Melvin I. Division and Discord: The Supreme Court under Stone and Vinson, 1941-1953. 23-2:157-181 (1998).

Urofsky, Melvin I. Felix Frankfurter: Judicial Restraint and Individual Liberties. 17:109-135 (1992).

Urofsky, Melvin I. Religious Freedom: Rights and Liberties under the Law. 28-3:370-386 (2003).

Urofsky, Melvin I. The Supreme Court Justices: A Biographical Dictionary. 20:153-172 (1995).

Van Alstyne, W. Interpretations of the First Amendments. 11:103-121 (1986).

Vestal, Theodore M. The Eisenhower Court and Civil Liberties. 28-1:81-97 (2003).

Vile, John R. A Companion to the United States Constitution and Its Amendments. 28-3:370-386 (2003).

Vile, John R. The Constitutional Convention of 1787: A Comprehensive Encyclopedia of America's Founding. 31-3:298-315 (2006).

Vile, John R. Great American Judges: An Encyclopedia. 29-2:207-225 (2004).

Vile, John R., ed. Great American Lawyers: An Encyclopedia. 28-1:81-97 (2003).

Vivian, James F. William Howard Taft: Collected Editorials, 1917-1921. 16:105-131 (1991).

Vose C. Caucasians Only. 13:98-117 (1988).

Walker, Mary M. The Evolution of the United States Supreme Court. 2:102-113 (1977).

Ward, Artemus and David L. Weiden. Sorcerers' Apprentices: 100 Years of Law Clerks at the United States Supreme Court. 32-2:190-208 (2007).

Warren, Earl. The Memoirs of Earl Warren. 3:114-120 (1978).

Wasby, Stephen L. Continuity and Change: From the Warren Court to the Burger Court. 2:102-113 (1977).

Wasby, Stephen L. Small Town Police and the Supreme Court: Hearing the Word. 3:114-120 (1978).

Wasby, Stephen L., Anthony D'Amato and Rosemary Metrailer. Desegregation from Brown to Alexander: An Exploration of Supreme Court Strategies. 4:95-100 (1979).

Watson, George L. and John A. Stookey. Shaping America: The Politics of Supreme Court Appointments. 22-2:150-169 (1997).

Whichard, Willis P. Justice James Iredell. 27-2:194-210 (2002).

White, G. Edward. The Constitution and the New Deal. 27-1:65-82 (2002).

White, G. Edward. Earl Warren: A Public Life. 9:127-143 (1984).

White, G. Edward. Justice Oliver Wendell Holmes: Law and the Inner Self. 19:147-170 (1994).

White, G. Edward. The Oliver Wendell Holmes History of the Supreme Court of the United States: Volumes III-IV: The Marshall Court and Cultural Change, 1815-35. 13:98-117 (1988).

Wiecek, William M. Liberty under Law; The Supreme Court in American Life. 14:119-139 (1989).

Wiecek, William M. Oliver Wendell Holmes History of the Supreme Court of the United States: Volume XII: The Birth of the Modern Constitution: The United States Supreme Court, 1941-1953. 32-1:96-112 (2006).

Wilkinson, J. Harvie, III. Serving Justice; A Supreme Court Clerk's View. 2:102-113 (1977).

Wolfe, Christopher. The Rise of Modern Judicial Review: From Constitutional Interpretation to Judge-Made Law. 12:108-126 (1987).

Wolfe, Christopher, Ed. That Eminent Tribunal: Judicial Supremacy and the Constitution. 31-2:199-218 (2006).

Wolfman, Bernard. Dissent without Opinion: The Behavior of Justice William O. Douglas in Federal Tax Cases. 2:102-113 (1977).

Woodward, B. and S. Armstrong. The Brethren. 12:108-126 (1987).

Yarbrough, Tinsley E. Harry A. Blackmun: The Outsider Justice. 34-1:125-145 (2009).

Yarbrough, Tinsley E. John Marshall Harlan: Great Dissenter of the Warren Court. 17:109-135 (1992).

Yarbrough, Tinsley E. Judicial Enigma: The First Justice Harlan. 21-2:168-188 (1996).

Yarbrough, Tinsley E. Mr. Justice Black and His Critics. 16:105-131 (1991).

Yarbrough, Tinsley E. The Rehnquist Court and the Constitution. 26-3:279-295 (2001).

4. Book Reviews by Reviewer

Evans, Patricia R. and Roger F. Jacobs

Chief Justices of the United States. 4:95-100 (1979).

Constitutional Courts of the United States: The Formal and Informal Relationships between the District Courts, the Courts of Appeals, and the Supreme Court of the U. S. 4:95-100 (1979).

Criminal Justice and the Burger Court. 4:95-100 (1979).

Desegregation from Brown to Alexander: An Exploration of Supreme Court Strategies. 4:95-100 (1979).

The First One Hundred Justices: Statistical Studies on the Supreme Court of the United States. 4:95-100 (1979).

Government by Judiciary: The Transformation of the Fourteenth Amendment. 4:95-100 (1979).

A Guide to the Supreme Court. 4:95-100 (1979).

Hugo Black and the Bill of Rights: Proceedings of the First Hugo Black Symposium in American History on "The Bill of Rights and American Democracy." 4:95-100 (1979).

Judicial Impact and State Supreme Courts. 4:95-100 (1979).

The Law, the Supreme Court and People's Rights. 4:95-100 (1979).

The Legal Principles of the Founding Fathers and the Supreme Court. 4:95-100 (1979).

The Papers of John Marshall Vol. II. 4:95-100 (1979).

Pragmatism, Statesmanship, and the Supreme Court. 4:95-100 (1979).

Religious Freedom on Trial. 4:95-100 (1979).

Stability, Security, and Continuity: Mr. Justice Burton and Decision-Making in the Supreme Court, 1945-1958. 4:95-100 (1979).

The Supreme Court and Its Publics: The Communication of Policy Decisions. 4:95-100 (1979).

Truman and the Steel Seizure Case; The Limits of Presidential Power. 4:95-100 (1979).

What Justice Holmes Wrote; and What Has Been Written about Him: A Bibliography, 1866-1976. 4:95-100 (1979).

Jacobstein, J. Myron and Joan S. Howland

Constitutional Counterrevolution? The Warren Court and the Burger Court: Judicial Policy Making in Modern America. 3:114-120 (1978).

The Douglas Opinions. 3:114-120 (1978).

Freedom and the Court; Civil Rights and Liberties in the United States. 3:114-120 (1978).

Hugo Black and the Judicial Revolution. 3:114-120 (1978).

Judicial Tyranny. 3:114-120 (1978).

The Judiciary; The Supreme Court in the Governmental Process. 3:114-120 (1978).

Mass Media and the Supreme Court: the Legacy of the Warren Years. 3:114-120 (1978).

The Memoirs of Earl Warren. 3:114-120 (1978).

Small Town Police and the Supreme Court: Hearing the Word. 3:114-120 (1978).

The Supreme Court: Does It Protect or Limit Our Freedoms. 3:114-120 (1978).

The Supreme Court and Labor-Management Relations Law. 3:114-120 (1978).

United States Supreme Court Decisions: An Index to Their Locations. 3:114-120 (1978).

The Workload of the Supreme Court. 3:114-120 (1978).

Mersky, Roy and Jenni Parrish

Against the Law: The Nixon Court and Criminal Justice. 2:102-113 (1977).

Antecedents and Beginnings to 1801. 2:102-113 (1977).

Appearance of Justice. 2:102-113 (1977).

Black Americans and the Supreme Court Since Emancipation: Betrayal or Protection? 2:102-113 (1977).

The Burger Court and Civil Liberties. 2:102-113 (1977).

By What Right? A Commentary on the Supreme Court's Power to Revise the Constitution. 2:102-113 (1977).

The Constitution and the Supreme Court. 2d ed. 2:102-113 (1977).

Continuity and Change: From the Warren Court to the Burger Court. 2:102-113 (1977).

The Correspondence and Public Papers of John Jay 1763-1826. 2:102-113 (1977).

Court and Constitution in the Twentieth Century. 2:102-113 (1977).

Cruel and Unusual: the Supreme Court and Capital Punishment. 2:102-113 (1977).

Disaster by Decree: The Supreme Court Decisions on Race and the Schools. 2:102-113 (1977).

Dissent without Opinion: The Behavior of Justice William O. Douglas in Federal Tax Cases. 2:102-113 (1977).

The Evolution of the United States Supreme Court. 2:102-113 (1977).

Franklin D. Roosevelt and the Supreme Court. 2:102-113 (1977).

From the Diaries of Felix Frankfurter. 2:102-113 (1977).

Go East, Young Man. 2:102-113 (1977).

John Marshall: A Life in Law. 2:102-113 (1977).

Judicial Crises: The Supreme Court in a Changing America. 2:102-113 (1977).

Judicial Mind Revisited. 2:102-113 (1977).

The Judicial Record of Justice William O. Douglas. 2:102-113 (1977).

The Judiciary: The Supreme Court in the Governmental Process. 3d ed. 2:102-113 (1977).

Justices and Presidents: Political History of Appointments to the Supreme Court. 2:102-113 (1977).

The Justices of the United States Supreme Court 1789-1969: Their Lives and Major Opinions. 2:102-113 (1977).

Law Enforcement Guide to United States Supreme Court Decisions. 2:102-113 (1977).

Mr. Justice Black and His Books. 2:102-113 (1977).

My Father, A Remembrance. 2:102-113 (1977).

Oliver Wendell Holmes Devise History of the Supreme Court of the United States. 2:102-113 (1977).

Our American Leviathan Unbound: The Judicial Perversion of American Freedom. 2:102-113 (1977).

The Papers of John Marshall. Volume 1. 2:102-113 (1977).

A Private View of a Public Life. 2:102-113 (1977).

Privilege and Creative Destruction: the Charles River Bridge Case. 2:102-113 (1977).

Prophets with Honor: Great Dissents and Great Dissenters in the Supreme Court. 2:102-113 (1977).

Reconstruction and Reunion 1864-88. 2:102-113 (1977).

The Rise of Guardian Democracy: The Supreme Court's Role in Voting Rights Disputes, 1845-1969. 2:102-113 (1977).

The Role of the Supreme Court in American Government. 2:102-113 (1977).

Serving Justice; A Supreme Court Clerk's View. 2:102-113 (1977).

Simple Justice: The History of *Brown v. Board of Education* and Black America's Struggle for Equality. 2:102-113 (1977).

The Supreme Court and "Political Questions": A Study in Judicial Evasion. 2:102-113 (1977).

The Supreme Court and the Judicial Function. 2:102-113 (1977).

The Supreme Court and the Religion-Education Controversy: A Tightrope to Entanglement. 2:102-113 (1977).

The Supreme Court and Social Science. 2:102-113 (1977).

Supreme Court Decision Making. 2:102-113 (1977).

The Supreme Court in American Life. 2:102-113 (1977).

Supreme Court in the Political Process. 2:102-113 (1977).

The Supreme Court of the United States Nominations 1916-1972. 2:102-113 (1977).

The Supreme Court Review. 2:102-113 (1977).

The Taney Period 1836-64. 2:102-113 (1977).

United States Supreme Court and the Use of Social Science Data. 2:102-113 (1977).

The Vision and the Dream of Justice Hugo L. Black. 2:102-113 (1977).

Stephenson, D. Grier, Jr

The 168 Days. 24-2:314-324 (1999).

1983 The Supreme Court Review. 10:128-145 (1985).

Abe Fortas: A Biography. 17:109-135 (1992).

Advice and Consent: The Politics of Judicial Appointments. 32-1:96-112 (2006).

Advice & Dissent: The Struggle to Shape the Federal Judiciary. 35-2:177-192 (2010).

Affirmative Action on Trial: Sex Discrimination in *Johnson v. Santa Clara.* 24-1:138-152 (1999).

Aggressive Nationalism: *McCulloch v. Maryland* and the Foundation of Federal Authority in the Young Republic. 34-2:224-240 (2009).

All the Laws But One: Civil Liberties in Wartime. 24-3:333-347 (1999).

America's Court. 24-3:333-347 (1999).

The Amendments to the Constitution: A Commentary. 21-2:168-188 (1996).

The Antagonists: Hugo Black, Felix Frankfurter and Civil Liberties in Modern America. 15:152-177 (1990).

Antecedents and Beginnings to 1801. 2:102-113 (1977); 12:108-126 (1987).

Appointment of Judges: The Johnson Presidency. 13:98-117 (1988).

Armed with the Constitution: Jehovah's Witnesses in Alabama and the U. S. Supreme Court, 1939-1946. 21-2:168-188 (1996).

Arthur J. Goldberg: New Deal Liberal. 23-2:157-181 (1998).

The Ascent of Pragmatism: The Burger Court in Action. 16:105-131 (1991).

Contributors

Joel Fishman is Assistant Director for Lawyer Services at the Center for Legal Information at Duquesne University and a former law librarian at Allegheny County Law Library.

Mark R. Killenbeck is Wylie H. Davis Distinguished Professor at University of Arkansas School of Law.

John V. Orth is the William Rand Kenan Jr. Professor of Law at the University of North Carolina.

Barbara A. Perry is a senior fellow in the Presidential Oral History Program at the University of Virginia's Miller Center.

Donald Grier Stephenson, Jr., is Charles A. Dana Professor of Government at Franklin and Marshall College.

Illustrations

All illustrations are from the Library of Congress except as listed below:

Page 98, artist unknown, Collection of the Supreme Court of the United States

Page 97, Manuscript Division, Library of Congress, Papers of Thomas Jefferson

Page 111, Manuscript Division, Library of Congress, Papers of Thomas Jefferson

Page 145, Courtesy of The White House

Cover: First page of letter from William Johnson to Thomas Jefferson, dated December 10, 1822. Manuscript Division, Library of Congress, Papers of Thomas Jefferson. Oil portrait of William Johnson, artist unknown, Collection of the Supreme Court of the United States (left). Oil portrait of Thomas Jefferson by Rembrandt Peale, White House Historical Association.

Errata:

In volume 36, issue number 3, there were two errors that need correction:

On page 204, second column, first full paragraph, the sentence beginning "Only six years later . . . ." and the following sentence in the paragraph should be corrected to read as follows: "In *Muller v. Oregon*, the Court vindicated Holmes's reasoning by upholding an Oregon state law setting maximum work hours (Endnote: 208 U.S. 412 (1908)). The Court's decision in *Muller*, coupled with the overturning of other precedents in the early twentieth century, demonstrated the potential for dissents to be vindicated in subsequent decisions and helped establish the dissenting opinion as a legitimate means of contributing to the development of law."

On page 228, Justice Robert C. Grier is pictured at top left.

In volume 37, issue number 1, a photo of the Fuller Court was mistakenly substituted for the Waite Court. The Society regrets these errors.

LAW & POLICY

Edited by
FIONA HAINES,
NANCY REICHMAN, *and*
COLIN SCOTT

Published on behalf of The Baldy Center for Law and Social Policy, University at Buffalo Law School, State University of New York

International and interdisciplinary in scope, **Law & Policy** embraces varied research methodologies that interrogate law, governance, and public policy worldwide.

Law & Policy makes a vital contribution to the current dialogue on contemporary policy by publishing innovative, peer-reviewed articles on such critical topics, such as:

- government and self-regulation
- health
- environment
- family
- gender
- taxation and finance
- legal decision-making
- criminal justice
- human rights

WILEY-BLACKWELL

For more information and to subscribe online visit
wileyonlinelibrary.com/journal/lapo

Edited by
JONATHAN GOLDBERG-HILLER
and **DAVID JOHNSON**

*Published on behalf of The Law
and Society Association*

Founded in 1966, *Law & Society Review (LSR)* is regarded by
sociolegal scholars worldwide as a leading journal in the field. *LSR*
is a peer-reviewed publication for work bearing on the relationship
between society and the legal process, including:
- articles or notes of interest to the research community
  in general
- new theoretical developments
- results of empirical studies
- and reviews and comments on the field or its methods
  of inquiry

Broadly interdisciplinary, *Law & Society Review* welcomes work from
any tradition of scholarship concerned with the cultural, economic,
political, psychological, or social aspects of law and legal systems.

For more information and to subscribe online visit
wileyonlinelibrary.com/journal/lasr

Law & Social Inquiry

Editor
CHRISTOPHER TOMLINS
Review Section Editor
HOWARD S. ERLANGER

Published on behalf of the American Bar Foundation

Law & Social Inquiry (LSI) features both empirical and theoretical studies of law that make original contributions to the understanding of sociolegal processes. *LSI* content spans the social sciences disciplines, including:

- Anthropology
- Criminology
- Economics
- History
- Law
- Philosophy
- Political Science
- Sociology
- Social Psychology

Law & Social Inquiry offers readers a remarkable range of empirical analyses and theoretical studies on specific topics in law and society, including legal institutions, the legal profession, and legal history.

For more information and to subscribe online visit
wileyonlinelibrary.com/journal/lsi

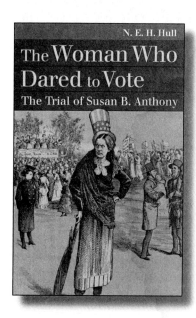
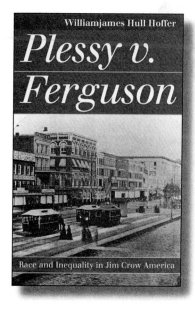

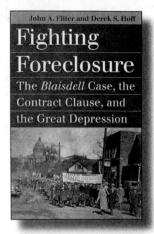
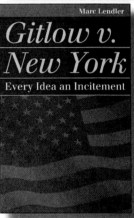
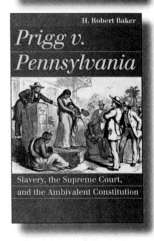